KINDERCULTURE

KINDERCULTURE

The Corporate Construction of Childhood

SECOND EDITION

Edited by

Shirley R. Steinberg

and

Joe L. Kincheloe

A Member of the Perseus Books Group

Copyright © 2004 by Westview Press, A Member of the Perseus Books Group

Westview Press books are available at special discounts for bulk purchases in the United States by corporations, institutions, and other organizations. For more information, please contact the Special Markets Department at the Perseus Books Group, 11 Cambridge Center, Cambridge MA 02142, or call (800) 255-1514 or (617) 252-5298, or e-mail special.markets@perseusbooks.com.

Published in the United States of America by Westview Press, 5500 Central Avenue, Boulder, Colorado 80301-2877 and in the United Kingdom by Westview Press, 12 Hid's Copse Road, Cumnor Hill, Oxford OX2 9JJ.

Find us on the World Wide Web at www.westviewpress.com

Library of Congress Cataloging-in-Publication data

Kinderculture : the corporate construction of childhood / edited by Shirley R. Steinberg and Joe L. Kincheloe.—2nd ed.
    p. cm.
    Includes bibliographical references and index.
    ISBN 0-8133-9154-7 (alk. paper)
    1. Early childhood education—Social aspects—United States.   2. Popular culture—United States.   3. Critical pedagogy—United States.   4. Curriculum planning—United States.   5. Child development—United States.   6. Educational anthropology—United States. I. Steinberg, Shirley R., 1952-   II. Kincheloe, Joe L.

LB1139.25.K55 2004
372.21--dc22

                                                        2004013608

10   9   8   7   6   5   4   3   2   1

to our brothers and sisters in psychedelic heaven...

there were all the "j's":
jimi, janice
jim, as lizard king
bonham, garcia, entwistle

and lennon.

keith's moon was shining as brian was jonesing

but freddie didn't fit as boy nor girl;

jerry wasn't ice cream;

so george left to be with john...

and

warren was our werewolf.

CONTENTS

INTRODUCTION

*Kinderculture, Information Saturation, and
the Socioeducational Positioning of Children*

Shirley R. Steinberg

Joe L. Kincheloe and

The theme of this book is very simple—new times have ushered in a new era of childhood. Evidence of this dramatic cultural change surrounds each of us, but many individuals have not yet noticed it. When we wrote the first edition of Kinderculture in 1997, many people who made their living studying or caring for children had not yet noticed this phenomenon. By the middle of the first decade of the twenty-first century more and more people are understanding this historic change, but we are still amazed by how many child professionals remain oblivious to these social and cultural alterations. In the domains of psychology, education, and to a lesser degree sociology few observers have seriously studied the ways that the information explosion so characteristic of our contemporary era has operated to undermine traditional notions of childhood. Those who have shaped, directed and used contemporary information technology have played an exaggerated role in the reformulation of childhood. Thus *Kinderculture* analyzes these changes in childhood, especially the role that information technology has played in this process. Of course, information technology alone has not produced a new era of childhood. Numerous social and political economic factors have operated to produce such changes. Our focus here is not to cover all of these factors but to question the ways media in particular has helped construct what we are calling the new childhood.

Childhood is a social and historical artifact—not simply a biological entity. Many argue that childhood is a natural phase of growing up, of becoming an adult. The cardinal concept here involves the format of this human phase that has been produced by social, cultural, political, and economic forces operating on it. Indeed, what is labeled as "traditional childhood" is only about 150 years old. In the Middle Ages, for example, children participated daily in the adult world, gaining knowledge of vocational and life skills as a part of such engagement. The concept of children as a particular classification of human beings demanding special treatment differing from adults had not yet developed in the Middle Ages.

CHILDHOOD AS A SOCIAL CONSTRUCTION

Childhood thus is a creation of society that is subject to change whenever major social transformations take place. The zenith of so-called traditional childhood lasted from about 1850 to 1950. Protected from the dangers of the adult world, children during this period were removed from factories and placed in schools. As the prototype of the modern family developed in the late nineteenth century, "proper" parental behavior toward children coalesced around notions of tenderness and adult accountability for children's welfare. By 1900 many believed that childhood was a birthright—a perspective that eventuated in a biological, not a cultural, definition of childhood. Emerging in this era of the protected child, modern child psychology was inadvertently constructed by the tacit assumptions of the period. The great child psychologists from Erik Erikson to Arnold Gesell to Jean Piaget viewed child development as shaped by biological forces.

Piaget's brilliance was constrained by his nonhistorical, socially decontextualized scientific approach. What he observed as the genetic expression of child behavior in the early twentieth century, he generalized to all cultures and historical eras—an error that holds serious consequences for those concerned with children. Considering biological stages of child development fixed and unchangeable, teachers, psychologists, parents, and welfare workers, as well as the community at large, view and judge children along a taxonomy of development that is fictional. Those children who don't "measure up" are relegated to the land of low and self-fulfilling expectations. Those children who "make the grade" find that their racial and economic privilege is confused with ability (Polakow 1992a; Postman 1994). Kinderculture joins the emerging body of literature that questions the biological assumptions of "classical" child psychology.

Living in a historical period of great change and social upheaval, critical observers are just beginning to notice changing social and cultural conditions in relation to this view of childhood. Categories of child development appropriated from modernist psychology may hold little relevance for raising and educating contemporary children. As childhood began to change in the 1950s, 80 percent of all children lived in homes where their two biological parents were married to each other (Lipsit 1994; Lipsky and Abrams 1994). No one has to be told that families have changed over the past fifty years. Volumes have been written specifying the scope and causes of the social transformation. Before the 1980s ended, children who lived with their two biological parents had fallen to merely 12 percent. Children of divorced parents— a group made up of more than half of the U.S. population—are almost three times as likely as children raised in two-parent homes to suffer emotional and behavioral difficulties—maybe more the result of parental conflict than the actual divorce (Mason and Steadman 1997). Despite such understandings, social institutions have been slow to recognize different, nontraditional family configurations and the special needs they encounter. Without support, the contemporary "postmodern" family, with its plethora of working and single mothers, is beset with problems emanating from the feminization of poverty and the vulnerable position of women in both the public and private spaces (Polakow 1992b).

PARADIGMS FOR STUDYING CHILDHOOD:
THE POSITIVIST VIEW OF CHILDREN

It is important to place *Kinderculture* in paradigmatic context, to understand what we're promoting in relation to other scholarship on childhood studies and childhood education. To begin with, we are directly challenging the positivist view of children promoted in mainstream articulations of psychology, sociology, education, and anthropology. Positivism is an epistemological position maintaining all knowledge of worth is produced by the traditional scientific method. All scientific knowledge constructed in this context is thus proclaimed neutral and objective. Critics of positivism (see Kincheloe 1993, 2001, 2003, 2004) argue that because of the narrow nature of what positivist research studies (or can study, given its rules of analysis), it often overlooks powerful normative and ideological assumptions built into its research design. In this naive realistic context it often seeks empirical proof of what are normative or political assertions—for example, adults always know better when it comes to issues involving children.

A key goal of critics of positivism involves bringing these normative and ideological assumptions to the surface so observers can gain a more textured perspective of what research involves and indicates. Indeed, critics of positivism insist that one dimension of research involves the researcher's analysis of his or her own assumptions, ideologies, and values and how they shape the knowledge produced. The editors and authors of *Kinderculture* in such a spirit openly admit their antipositivist orientations. Concurrently we admit our critical democratic values, our vision of race, class, gender, and sexual equality, and the necessity of exposing the effects of power in shaping individual identity and political/educational purpose. This is not an act of politicization of research; research has always been politicized. Instead, we are attempting to understand and act ethically in light of such politicization.

In the positivist perspective children are assumed to be subservient and dependent on adults as part of the order of the cosmos. In this context adults are seen as having a "natural" prerogative to hold power over children. Positivists turn to biology to justify such assumptions, contending that the physical biological immaturity of children is manifested in other domains as inferiority, an absence of development, incompleteness, and weakness. One does not have to probe deeply into these biological assumptions to discern similarities between the positivist hierarchy of adults and children and the one subordinating emotional women to rational men. In our challenge to the positivist view of children we focus on age and generation to depict children as different from adults but not inferior to them. Children are not merely entities on their way to adulthood; they are individuals intrinsically valuable for who they presently are. When positivists view children as lesser than adults, they consistently ignore the way power operates to oppress children around the axes of race, class, gender, sexuality, ability, and so on. The positivist construction of the "vulnerable" child in this context actually becomes more vulnerable as real and specific threats are overlooked because childhood is viewed as a naturally vulnerable state. The different threats of different social, economic, political, and cultural "childhoods" are erased (Mason and Steadman 1997; Seaton 2002).

The positivist view of childhood has been firmly grounded on developmental psychology's universal rules of child development. Regardless of historical or social context, these rules lay out the proper development of "normal" children. This mythos of the universal innocent and developing child transforms cultural dimensions of childhood into something produced by nature. By the second decade of the twentieth century this universal norm for the developing child had been established on the basis of "scientific authority" and was based almost exclusively on American white, middle-class norms and experiences. Schools fell into line, developing a white, middle-class, patriarchal curriculum that reflected the norms of proper development. Reformers blessed with the imprimatur of science used the principles of developmental psychology as the basis of their efforts to regulate play. Advocates of municipal playgrounds, the Boy Scouts, and the Girl Scouts worked to make sure that children made appropriate use of leisure time (Jenkins 1998; Spigel 1998).

The decontextualized aspect of the positivist view of childhood shapes numerous problems for those who don't fit into the dominant cultural bases of the proper development of normal children. In failing to understand the impact of race, class, gender, linguistics, national origin, and so on, positivism fails to understand the nature of and the reasons for differences between children. Too often, especially in twenty-first century education with its obsession with standards, standardization, and testing, such differences are viewed as deficiencies. Children from lower socioeconomic class, nonwhite, or immigrant backgrounds are in this positivist regime of truth relegated to the lower rungs of the developmental ladder. The idea that life experiences and contextual factors might affect development is not considered in the positivist paradigm because it does not account for such social and cultural dynamics (Mason and Steadman 1997).

As positivism came to delineate the scientific dimensions of child development, male psychologists replaced mothers as child-rearing experts. The psychologist in the early part of the twentieth century took on a socially important role; it was believed that if scientific principles were not followed, malleable children would be led en masse into immorality and weakness. A significant feature of these scientific principles involved exposing children to adult knowledge that was developmentally appropriate. The secret knowledge of adulthood, the positivist psychologists believed, should only be delivered to children at appropriate times in their development. With these ideas in mind one can better understand the impact TV made on a nation that bought into major dimensions of the positivist mythos. TV was the fly in the ointment, the window to adult knowledge that could undermine the nation's strength and moral fiber.

Thus the positivist view of childhood could only be maintained by constant social regulation and surveillance of the young. Since childhood is vulnerable and socially unstable, the control of knowledge becomes important in the maintenance of innocence. Indeed, in the positivist view childhood no longer exists if the young gain access to certain forms of adult knowledge. No wonder the last half of the twentieth century witnessed so many claims that after TV and other electronic media, childhood was dead. Many consider the positivist position elitist, as adults are deemed the trolls of the bridge of childhood. It is adults who decide what children should know and how they should be socialized. The idea that children should be participants in making decisions about their own lives is irrelevant here. Simply put, in the positivist paradigm children are passive entities who must submit to adult decisions about their lives (Spigel 1998).

A NEW PARADIGM FOR A NEW CHILDHOOD

With a plethora of socioeconomic changes, technological developments, globalization, and the perceived inadequacy of the old paradigm (which helps produce profoundly diverse actions and reactions), Western societies and increasingly other parts of the world have entered into a transitional phase of childhood. It has been accompanied by a paradigm shift in the way many scholars study childhood and situate it in social, cultural, political, and economic relations. This scholarly shift takes direct exception to the positivist view of childhood and its expression of a universal, uniformly developmentalist conception of the normal child. This positivist passive conception of children as receivers of adult input and socialization strategies has been replaced by a view of the child as an active agent capable of contributing to the construction of his or her own subjectivity. For those operating in the parameters of the new paradigm, the purpose of studying and working with children is not to remove the boundary between childhood and adulthood but to gain a thicker, more compelling picture of the complexity of the culture, politics, and psychology of childhood. With its penchant for decontextualization and its inability to account for contemporary social, cultural, political, economic, and epistemological changes, the positivist paradigm is not adequate for this task (Cannella 1997; Jenkins 1998; Hengst 2001; Cannella and Kincheloe 2002; Cannella 2002; Cook 2004).

The positivist view insisted that children existed outside of society and could only be brought in from the cold by adult socialization that led to development. Positivists constructed research and childhood professional practices that routinely excluded children's voices. Advocates of the new paradigm insist that such positivist silencing and general disempowerment is not in the best interests of children. In the name of child protection, they argue, children are often rendered powerless and vulnerable in their everyday lives. Constructing their view of children as active constructors of their own worlds, proponents of the new paradigm work hard to emphasize the personhood of children. The children of the new paradigm both construct their worlds and are constructed by their worlds. Thus in ethnographic and other forms of new paradigm childhood study, children, like adults, are positioned as coparticipants in research—not as mere objects to be observed and categorized. Advocates of the new paradigm operating in the domain of social, political, and educational policymaking for children contend that such activity must always take into account the perspectives of children to inform their understanding of particular situations (Mason and Steadman 1997; Seaton 2002; Cook 2004).

Thus, central to the new paradigm is the effort to make sure children are intimately involved in shaping their social, psychological, and educational lives. This new paradigmatic task, however, is the target of ridicule and dismissal by conservative child advocates in diverse social, political, cultural, and educational arenas. Such child-empowerment advocacy is represented by right-wing commentators as a permissive relinquishing of adult power over impudent and disrespectful children (Mason and Steadman 1997; Ottosen 2003). Undoubtedly, it will be a difficult struggle to reposition the child in twenty-first century social relationships. In this context Henry Jenkins (1998) argues as an advocate of the new paradigm that his work seeks to provide children with tools that facilitate children's efforts to achieve their own political goals and help them construct their own culture.

In rejecting the positivist paradigm of childhood passivity and innocence, advocates of the new empowerment paradigm are not contending that there is no time that children need adult protection—that would be a silly assertion. Children, like human beings in general, often find themselves victimized by abuse, neglect, racism, class bias, and sexism. The salient point is that instead of further infantilizing children and rendering them more passive, the new paradigm attempts to employ their perspectives in solving their problems (Mason and Steadman 1997; Jenkins 1998). In addition, such transformative researchers and child professionals work to help children develop a critical political consciousness as they protect their access to diverse knowledges and technologies. As is the nature of developing a critical consciousness in any context, we are arguing that children in social, cultural, psychological, and pedagogical contexts need help in developing the ability to analyze, critique, and change for the better their position in the world. This task is a central objective of *Kinderculture*.

Another dimension of the new paradigm of child study involves the explicit rejection of positivism's universalist conception of childhood and child development. When advocates of the new paradigm enter diverse class cultures and racial/ethnic cultures, they find childhoods that look quite different from the white, middle- and upper-middle-class, English-speaking one presented by positivism. In these particularistic childhoods researchers find great complexity and diversity within these specific categories. For example, the social, cultural, and political structures that shape these childhoods and the children who inhabit them are engaged in profoundly different ways by particular children in specific circumstances. Thus such structures never determine who children are no matter how much consistency in macrostructures may exist. The particular and the general, the micro and the macro, agency and structure always interact in unpredictable ways to shape the everyday life of children. A central theme of the new paradigm reemerges—children shape and are shaped by the world around them.

The editors and authors of *Kinderculture* maintain that the delicate, complex balance between these constructive forces must be carefully studied and maintained. If we move too far in our emphasis of structure over agency, we lapse into a structural determinism that undermines the prerogative of individual social actors. Thus there is nothing a child can do to escape the ravages of poverty. If we move too far in emphasizing agency, we often lose sight of the way dominant power operates to undermine children's role in shaping their own lives and constructing their own subjectivities. Indeed, the overemphasis of particularism and agency often obscures the powerlessness of specific children. To develop our thicker, more complex view of childhood, we must constantly work to integrate the micro and the macro, to discern new cultural and political economic contexts in which to view and make sense of child behavior (Garey and Arendell 1999; Ottosen 2003). In this context new paradigmatic researchers must not only nurture these macro (social, political, economic), meso (institutional; e.g., school, media, church, welfare agency), and micro (individuals) interactions but attend to the ways such levels connect to one another. For example, what is the proximity of the individual child to particular social and institutional structures?

As in any sociopolitical situation with the potential for hegemonic and ideological exploitation, children (or adults) can learn to be sensitive to the ways exploitation takes place while developing strategies for avoiding it. And as in any pedagogical situation, children (and adults) can both develop these strategies on their own or in a Vygotskian sense in cooperation with teachers who provide a new zone of proximal development that allows for a deeper understanding of the way power operates. This, of course, is the basis of *Kinderculture*'s critical media literacy for children. One scholar of childhood who dismisses the value of structuralist concerns with exploitation, David Buckingham (2003), argues that pedagogies of empowerment such as the one advocated here have "increasingly been seen to amount to little more than rhetoric."

By denying the possibility of a media literacy of power, Buckingham lapses into a pedagogy of nihilism that provides no raison d'être for scholarly activity in the area of children's culture. Power and exploitation are erased in Buckingham's articulation, as any effort to alert children to the ways the social, cultural, political, and economic domains operate to harm both them and other individuals is represented as a misguided form of "salvationism." Buckingham then equates this so-called salvationism with right-wing attempts to protect childhood innocence via forms of censorship and moralistic regulation. Most discussions between the agential and the structuralist positions in the new paradigm of child studies are not—nor should be—this contentious. It is important to specify the location of *Kinderculture* in this conceptual matrix.

Kinderculture represents the critical new paradigm in childhood studies and childhood education. The use of "critical" in this context signals the critical in critical theory (Kincheloe 2004) and its concern with power structures and their influence in everyday life. In the case of contemporary children the sociopolitical and economic structures shaped by corporate power buoyed by the logic of capital, as well as patriarchal structures with their oppressive positioning of women and children, are central concerns of the critical paradigm (Garey and Arendell 1999; Scott 2002). Using the production of pleasure as its ultimate weapon, the corporate children's consumer culture, which we label "kinderculture," commodifies cultural objects and turns them into things to purchase rather than objects to contemplate. Kinderculture thus is subversive but in a way that challenges authority in an effort to maintain rather than transform the status quo. It appeals to the agential child and agential child advocates as it offers children identities that Jane Kenway and Elizabeth Bullen (2001) label as autonomous, rational, and hedonistic. Thus kinderculture is produced by ingenious marketers who possess profound insights into the lives, desires, and cultural context of contemporary children. Such marketers know how to cultivate intense affect among children and use such emotion to elicit particular consumptive and in turn ideological reactions.

A key dimension of this consumptive-ideological dimension of kinderculture involves the marketers' understanding that children, especially middle-class children, are interested in TV, movies, Internet, toys, and even foods (see Kincheloe's chapter on McDonald's in this volume; and Kincheloe 2002) that transgress parental norms of "good taste," social status, and educational development. This ideology of opposition is central in many cases to what separates contemporary children from their parents and other adults. Such oppositionality operates to subvert the bourgeois educational project of modernity—rational child development based on the achievement of universal stages of reason reflecting adult behavior and ways of being. As it commodifies and lures children into this oppositional conspiracy, it meshes consumption, education, information, knowledge, cultural capital, emotional bonding, entertainment, and advertising (Kenway and Bullen 2001; Hengst 2001). Advocates of the critical new paradigm of childhood studies argue that kinderculture can no longer be ignored in the effort to understand the social, psychological, and educational dimensions of children. In the late twentieth and early twenty-first centuries corporate-produced children's culture has replaced schooling as the producer of the central curriculum of childhood.

IS CHILDHOOD IN CRISIS?
THE CHANGING SOCIAL ROLES OF CHILDREN

Changing economic realities coupled with children's access to information about the adult world have drastically changed childhood. The traditional childhood genie is out of the bottle and is unable to return. Recent writing about childhood in both the popular and scholarly presses speak of "childhood lost," "children growing up too fast," and "child terror in the isolation of the fragmented home and community." Images of mothers drowning children, baby-sitters torturing infants, kids pushing kids out of fourteenth-story windows, and trick or treat razor blades in apples saturate contemporary conversation about children. Popular culture provides haunting images of this crisis of childhood that terrify and engage our worst fears. The film *Halloween,* for example, at one level is a story of postmodern childhood—fear in isolation. This isolation involves separation from both absent parents and a nonexistent community. No one is there to help; even on the once festive Halloween night children are not present. Even in "safe" suburbia, the community has fragmented to the point that the safety of trick-or-treaters cannot be guaranteed (Ferguson 1994; Paul 1994). The crisis of contemporary childhood can be signified in many ways, all of which involve the horror of danger faced in solitude.

This crisis of childhood is part imagination, part reality. While children are vulnerable to social ills and to manipulation by unscrupulous adults and power wielders, there is a degree of moral panic and general hyperbole in the view that children are facing threats from predators unlike anything experienced in the historical past. While certainly not dismissing everyday threats to childhood in the twenty-first century, we should not let hysterics from diverse ideological perspectives paint a fear-driven portrait of the social landscape. A balanced view would demand that we position the crisis of childhood within the twenty-first century social, cultural, and economic context. Undoubtedly childhood in Western societies is affected by the decline of industrialized economic arrangements.

Labor was the most important force for social integration in industrialized societies. In a postindustrial condition people make life meaningful outside the boundaries of their work lives. The labor process in this new context plays a diminishing role in shaping identity and constructing life experiences. As industrial jobs that lasted a lifetime with pensions and social benefits decline, more women have entered the workforce. Buoyed by the women's movement, more and more mothers have sought work outside the home, subsequently placing more pressure on fathers to participate in child-rearing activities. In such contexts children learn to cope with busy, preoccupied parents and become more self-reliant than earlier generations of middle- and upper-middle-class children.

The changing role of women profoundly alters the role of children in contemporary Western societies. Even though more and more women work outside the home, this does not lead to an equal sharing of domestic work—women still do more than men (DuBois-Reymond, Suenker, and Kruger 2001). Increasing numbers of single poor women combine paid labor and child care without the help of a spouse or partner and with little assistance from the state. Without economic or social support, women and children in these categories have experienced harsher conditions and less and less hope for upward mobility. For middle- and upper-middle-class children these social, economic, and cultural trends have sometimes provided them more independence and influence in the family. In lower socioeconomic circumstances such trends exacerbate the effects of poverty and sometimes lead to more neglect and alienation.

In many homes, both middle and lower class, these larger socioeconomic trends operate to make children "more useful" than they were throughout much of the twentieth century. As women become more and more embedded in the workplace, traditional role expectations continue to erode. Children and youth from the ages of six to nineteen, in order to make up for these modified familial relationships, have taken on more responsibility, caring not only for themselves but for their parents as well. Studies (Hengst 2001) illustrate that children increasingly are the family members who buy the food. Indeed, the home appliance industry—understanding this trend—is directing more and more of its advertising budget toward magazines for children and youth. Industry demographics tell them that a key and growing segment of those who buy food, microwaves, and other kitchen appliances are from this six-to-nineteen age bracket (du Bois-Reymond, Suenker, and Kruger 2001). This represents a profound change in the way children are positioned in the social order.

This change in the social positioning of children holds dramatic implications for education. As age boundaries blur, as chronological age becomes less important in shaping human abilities and role expectations, the crisis of childhood becomes the crisis of education. Children emerging in the new social conditions no longer reflect the expectations for childhood embedded in the structures and organization of schools. "New children" who experience more adultlike roles in other phases of their lives may not react positively to being treated like "children" in the classroom. Teachers who infantilize their elementary students may be shocked by the resentment that independent children direct toward them. Indeed, such dynamics already occur as teachers voice complaints about "children who talk like adults and have little or no respect for their demands." What teachers sometimes perceive as impudence and a lack of respect may be as much a reflection of independent, self-sufficient children reacting to forms of regulation that they experience in no other aspect of their lives.

In this changing social context of childhood many scholars (Casas 1998; Hengst 2001) are arguing that children are far more cognitively capable than traditionally maintained by developmental psychology. The world of electronic media, along with these changing notions of the social role of the child, has expanded what Lev Vygotsky referred to as the ZPD (zone of proximal development)—the context that facilitates the learning process—of contemporary children. In the ZPD individuals learn to take part in social and cultural activities that catalyze their intellectual development. In the media-created electronic ZPD with its videos, TV, computers, video games, Internet, popular music, and virtual realities children learn to use the tools of culture, for example, language, mathematics, reasoning, and so on (Fu 2003). The skills learned may or may not be abilities valued by the school. They are valuable abilities nonetheless.

When sociologists, psychologists, and cultural scholars examine what children are able to construct employing the symbols and tools of mediated culture, they realize how sophisticated and intellectually advanced children's abilities can become in this new ZPD. This electronic kinderculture has quickly become a new culture of childhood learning. Indeed, the space in which many contemporary children play is the same domain in which their parents work. Children access these national and international information networks with the same tools their parents use. In this new domain of learning many children free themselves from the educational project of modern Western societies. Many children in Western societies are no longer learning a preplanned program of selected exposure to the adult world. Instead they are accessing previously considered "adult" information via electronic media. As this takes place, they are freed from parental norms and regulations common to bourgeois culture. A child cultural aesthetic develops that eschews cultural products provided for the purposes of education and refinement. Kinderculture thus emerges and is produced around the new childhood desire for independence and resistance to things adult. Traditional forms of school learning become less and less important and less applicable to the needs of these new children (Hengst 2001). Thus childhood is perceived in crisis because it resembles nothing most people have ever seen before.

NEW SITES OF LEARNING: CORPORATIONS AS EDUCATORS

The corporate production of popular kinderculture and its impact on children is a central concern of this book. Such an effort falls under the umbrella term "cultural pedagogy," which refers to the idea that education takes place in a variety of social sites including but not limited to schooling. Pedagogical sites are places where power is organized and deployed, including libraries, TV, movies, newspapers, magazines, toys, advertisements, video games, books, sports, and so on. Operating on the assumption that profound learning changes one's identity, we see the pedagogical process as one that engages our desire (our yearning for something beyond ourselves shaped by the social context in which we operate, our affective investment in that which surrounds us), captures our imagination, and constructs our consciousness. The emergence of cultural studies (Grossberg 1995) has facilitated our effort to examine the cultural practices through which individuals come to understand themselves and the world that surrounds them (McLaren 1995). Supported by the insights of cultural studies, we are better equipped to examine the effects of cultural pedagogy with its identity formation and production and legitimation of knowledge—the cultural curriculum (Kasturi 2002).

The organizations that create this cultural curriculum are not educational agencies, but rather commercial concerns that operate not for the social good but for individual gain. Cultural pedagogy is structured by commercial dynamics, forces that impose themselves into all aspects of our own and our children's private lives. Patterns of consumption shaped by corporate advertising empower commercial institutions as the teachers of the contemporary era. Corporate cultural pedagogy has "done its homework"—it has produced educational forms that are wildly successful when judged on the basis of their capitalist intent. Replacing traditional classroom lectures and seat work with dolls with a history, magic kingdoms, animated fantasies, interactive videos, virtual realities, kickboxing TV heroes, and an entire array of entertainment forms produced ostensibly for adults but eagerly consumed by children, corporate America has helped revolutionize childhood.

Such a revolution has not taken place with Lenin-esque corporate wizards checking off a list of institutions they have captured. Instead, the revolution (contrary to the 1960s idiom) has been televised, brought to you and your children in vivid Technicolor. Using fantasy and desire, corporate functionaries have created a perspective on the world that melds with business ideologies and free market values. The worldviews produced by corporate advertisers to some degree let children know that the most exciting things in life are produced by your friends in corporate America. The economics lesson is powerful when it is repeated hundreds of thousands of times.

One of the most profound events of the past century in world history as well as in the history of childhood involves the successful commodification of childhood by U.S. corporations. Corporate marketers opened a new market and helped generate a body of meanings, cultural practices, and ideological understandings that continue to shape our world and children everywhere (Cook 2004). By gaining access to children, advertisers early in the twentieth century induced children to buy more and nagged their parents to consume more (Spigel 1998). Though many argue to the contrary, it seems increasingly obvious that a large percentage of children and young people in the twenty-first century are enthusiastic participants in consumer society. In recent polls they express the belief that having more money would most improve their lives. Concurrently, they express great faith in the American economic system. Increasing numbers of children and young people own more than one credit card, and many own stocks. Corporate power wielders have worked hard to win such perspectives and orientations among the young. Indeed, consumer capitalism has succeeded in ways unimagined by previous advocates, as more and more children and young people come to hold the values and ideological dispositions that serve the best interests of corporate leaders (Spigel 1998; Allen 2003).

In an interesting and insidious way marketers and children enter into an unspoken alliance that helps children escape both the control and the educational-developmental agenda of middle- and upper-middle-class parents. Video games, Internet, instant messaging, TV, music CDs with earphones, and movie videos help create a personal, secluded domain for children free from direct parental regulation. Of course, many parents find such independence frightening and many understandably worry about children becoming targets for advertising and marketing. While many concerned individuals have expressed anxiety over what they thought was corporate advertising's violation of the social contract protecting the sanctity of childhood, others such as David Buckingham (2000) have argued that such fears are overblown. Children, Buckingham maintains, possess the ability to discern advertising strategies early in their lives and can thus protect themselves from corporate exploitation. Moreover, Buckingham posits, there is no evidence indicating that advertising makes children more materialistic than they would be otherwise. In an empirical research context Buckingham's assertion is a safe one. Since no one knows how children would have been otherwise, it is empirically impossible to prove such an assertion either true or false.

This volume maintains that it is our parental, civic, and professional responsibility to study the corporate curriculum and its social and political effects. Indeed, as parents, citizens, and teachers, we must hold corporations accountable for the pedagogical features of their activities, for the kinderculture they produce. We must intervene in this cozy relationship between popular culture and pedagogy that shapes our identities. In the interest of both our children and the larger society we must exercise our personal and collective power to transform the variety of ways corporate power gained via its access to media oppresses and dominates us. We must cultivate an awareness of the ways cultural pedagogy operates so that we can scold when appropriate and rewrite popular texts when the opportunity presents itself. Kinderculture is primarily a pedagogy of pleasure and, as such, cannot be countered merely by ostracizing ourselves and our children from it. Strategies of resistance must be formulated that understand the relationship between pedagogy, knowledge production, identity formation, and desire. This book attempts to open a public conversation about the effect of kinderculture as the central curriculum of contemporary childhood.

SITUATING KINDERCULTURE IN CULTURAL STUDIES

Questions concerning kinderculture and its relationship to cultural pedagogy can be clarified and discussed in the academic field of cultural studies. This book resides at the intersection of educational/childhood studies and cultural studies. Attempting to define cultural studies is a delicate operation, since the field has consciously operated in a manner that avoids traditional academic disciplinary definitions. Nevertheless, cultural studies has something to do with the effort to produce an interdisciplinary (or counterdisciplinary) way of studying, interpreting, and often evaluating cultural practices in historical, social, and theoretical contexts. Refusing to equate "culture" with high culture, cultural studies attempts to examine the diversity of a society's artistic, institutional, and communicative expressions and practices. Because it examines cultural expressions often ignored by the traditional social sciences, cultural studies is often equated with the study of popular culture. Such an equation is misleading; while popular culture is addressed by cultural studies, it is not its exclusive concern. Indeed, the interests of cultural studies are much broader, including the "rules" of academic study itself: the discursive practices (tacit regulations that define what can and cannot be said, who speaks and who must listen, and whose constructions of reality are valid and whose are unlearned and unimportant) that guide scholarly endeavor.

Thus cultural studies holds exciting possibilities for new ways of studying education, childhood education specifically, with its attention to the discursive dynamics of the field. How do children embody kinderculture? How do the power dynamics embedded in kinderculture produce pleasure and pain in the daily lives of children? How do critically grounded parents, teachers, child psychologists, and childhood professionals in general gain a view of children that accounts for the effect of popular culture in their self-images and worldviews? Such questions open new domains of analysis in childhood studies, as they seek out previously marginalized voices and the vantage points they bring to both scholarly and practitioner-based conversation (Grossberg 1995; Nelson, Treichler, and Grossberg 1992). While we are enthused by the benefits of cultural studies of childhood, we are simultaneously critical of expressions of elitism in the discourse of cultural studies—particularly its claim to the moral high ground of a politics of inclusivity. Unfortunately the study of children has traditionally been regarded as a low-status exercise in the culture of academia. So far, at least, the field of cultural studies has reproduced this power/status dynamic in its neglect of childhood study. Few students of cultural studies have targeted children as the subjects of their scholarship. *Kinderculture* attempts to address this absence and promote new literature in the area.

VALUE OF STUDYING POPULAR CULTURE

The study of traditional forms of kinderculture (e.g., fairy tales) has granted scholars insights into hard-to-reach domains of child consciousness. Moreover, the more disturbing and violent the fairy tale, some would argue, the more insight into the "primitive" feelings that arise and shape us in early childhood and, in turn, in adulthood. The connection between kinderculture and childhood desire/feeling blows the rational cultural fuse, thus connecting adults to the *Lebenswelt* (life world) of children and granting them better access to childhood perceptions (Paul 1994). The study of children's popular culture grants insights into childhood consciousness and provides new pictures of culture in general. Kinderculture, in this context, inadvertently reveals at a very basic level what is disturbing us in our everyday lives, what irritants reside at the level of our individual and collective subconsciousness.

POWER, PLEASURE, AND KINDERCULTURE

Our objective in this book is to promote understandings of kinderculture that lead to smart, democratic pedagogies for childhood at the cultural, familial, and school levels. Cultural studies connected to a democratic pedagogy for children involves investigations of how children's consciousness is produced around issues of cultural expectations for children, social justice, and egalitarian power relations. Thus our analyses focus on exposing the footprints of power left by the corporate producers of kinderculture and their effects on the psyches of our children. Appreciating the ambiguity and complexity of power, our democratic pedagogy for children is committed to challenging ideologically manipulative and racist, sexist, and class-biased entertainment for children. It is equally opposed to other manifestations of kinderculture that promote violence and social and psychological pathologies. Children's entertainment, like other social spheres, is a contested public space where different social, economic, and political interests compete for control. Unfortunately Americans are uncomfortable with overt discussions of power. Such unease allows power wielders to hide in the recesses of the cultural and political landscape while shaping cultural expression and public policy in their own interests—which may conflict with those of less powerful social groups such as children.

Americans have not been good students of power. All too often references to power are vague to the point of meaninglessness in the worst literature produced by critical scholars. For the purpose of clarification, when we refer to power wielders in America we are not merely referencing a social class or a category of human beings. Picking up on John Fiske's (1993) use of the term "power bloc," we are referring to particular social formations designated by race, class, gender, and ethnicity that hold special access to various resources (e.g., money, information, cultural capital, media, etc.) that can be used for economic or political gain. Power, as we use the term, involves a panoply of operations that work to maintain the status quo and keep it running with as little friction (social conflict) as possible. Therefore, it is beneficial to the individuals and groups who profit most from existing power relations to protect them from pests like us. When studying this power bloc, we employ Fiske's notion that it can be better understood by "what it does than what it is" (1993, 11). Importantly, our use of the concept of the power bloc in the production of kinderculture is not meant to imply a conspiracy of diabolical corporate and political kingpins churning out material to harm our children. Rather, our notion of the power bloc revolves around alliances of interests that may never involve individual relationships between representatives of the interests/organizations in question. Power bloc alliances, we believe, are often temporary, coming together around particular issues but falling apart when the issue is no longer pertinent.

Someone who perceives power as a complex issue will encounter little disagreement from us. Power and power bloc alliances are nothing if not complex and ambiguous. But because of the power bloc's contradictions and ephemeral nature, it is never able to dominate in some incontestable manner. Along the lines of its contradictions may exist points of contestation that open possibilities of democratic change. Larry Grossberg (1995) contends that since power never gets all it wants, there are always opportunities for challenging its authority. In this context we begin our study of the corporate production of kinderculture, analyzing the ways power represses the production of democratic artifacts and the way it produces pleasure for children. If power was always expressed by "just saying no" to children's desires, it would gain little authority in their eyes. The power of Disney, Mattel, Hasbro, Warner Bros., and McDonald's is never greater than when it produces pleasure among consumers. Recent cultural studies of consumption link it to the identity formation of the consumer (Warde 1994; Kincheloe 2002), meaning that to some degree we are what we consume. Personal status in a subculture, individual style, knowledge of cultural texts, role in the community of consumers, emulation of fictional characters, and internalization of values promoted by popular cultural expressions all contribute to our personal identities. Popular culture provides children with intense emotional experiences often unmatched in any other phase of their lives. It is not surprising that such energy and intensity exert powerful influences on self-definition and on the ways children choose to organize their lives.

Obviously power mixed with desire produces an explosive cocktail; the colonization of desire, however, is not the end of the story. Power enfolds into consciousness and the unconsciousness in a way that evokes not only desire but also guilt and anxiety. The intense guilt and anxiety a child may experience as a result of her brush with power is inseparable from the cultural context in which she lives. Desire in many cases may take a backseat to the repression of desire in the construction of child consciousness/unconsciousness and the production of identity (Donald 1993). The cocktail's effects may last longer than first assumed, as expression of the repression may reveal itself in bizarre and unpredictable ways. To make this observation about the relationship among power, desire, and repression of desire and the way it expresses itself at the psychological level is not a denial of human agency (self-direction). While the power bloc has successfully commodified kinderculture, both adults and children can successfully deflect its repressive elements. The role of the critical childhood professional involves helping children develop what John Fiske (1993) calls the affective moments of power evasion. Using their abilities to "reread" Disney films along fault lines of gender or to reencode Barbie and Ken in a satirical mode, children take their first steps toward self-assertion and power resistance. Such affective moments of power evasion certainly do not constitute the ultimate expression of resistance, but they do provide a space around which more significant forms of critical consciousness and civic action can be developed.

MEDIA/POPULAR CULTURAL LITERACY
NEEDED IN HYPERREALITY

The information explosion, the media saturation of contemporary Western societies with its access to private realms of human consciousness, has created a social vertigo. This social condition, often labeled hyperreality, exaggerates the importance of power wielders in all phases of human experience. Hyperreality's flood of signifiers in everything from megabytes to TV advertising diminishes our ability to either find meaning or engender passion for commitment. With so much power-generated information bombarding their senses, adults and children lose the faith that they can make sense of anything (see Kincheloe 1995 for an expansion of these themes). Thus the existence of hyperreality forces us to rethink our conversation about literacy. More than an add-on to a traditional curriculum, media literacy becomes a basic skill necessary to negotiating identity, values, and well-being in power-soaked hyperreality. In many schools such ideas have never even been considered. Media literacy, like power, is not viewed in mainstream circles as a topic for children (or even adults). The same educators who reject the study of media literacy or kinderculture are the ones who have to cope with its effects.

A critical understanding of media culture requires students to develop the ability to interpret media meanings as well as understand the ways they themselves consume and affectively invest in media. This encourages both critical thinking and self-analysis, as students begin to realize that everyday decisions are not necessarily made freely and rationally. Rather, they are encoded and inscribed by emotional and bodily commitments relating to the production of desire and mood, all of which leads, in Noam Chomsky's famous phrase, to the "manufacture of consent." These are complex pedagogical and ideological issues and they demand rigorous skills of questioning, analyzing, interpreting, and meaning making. Contrary to the decontextualized pronouncements of developmental psychology, relatively young children are capable of engaging in these cognitive activities (Nations 2001). Of course, in the contemporary right-wing, test-driven educational context such abilities are not emphasized, as memorization for standard tests becomes more and more the order of the school day.

The political dimension of our critical pedagogy of childhood requires developing and teaching this media literacy. Such a literacy respects children's intellectual ability to deal with the complexities of power, oppression, and exploitation, as it refuses to position them as innocent, passive, and helpless victims. As children instantaneously access diverse types of information, they need the ability to traverse this knowledge terrain in savvy and well-informed ways. A critical pedagogy of childhood finds this approach much more helpful than pietistic right-wing efforts to censor potentially offensive data from innocent childhood eyes. In their effort to perpetuate the discourse of childhood innocence, right-wing child advocates maintain a positivist developmentalist view that media literacy is irrelevant because children do not have the intellectual and emotional maturity to understand TV advertising and subtle marketing appeals (Cassell and Jenkins 2002). As much as the advocates of childhood innocence might wish for it, children in the twenty-first century are not going to return to the mythical secret garden of innocence. For better and worse, children now live in a wider, information-saturated adult world. The authors of *Kinderculture* believe that the best we can do in this circumstance is to prepare children to cope with it, make sense of it, and participate in it in ways that benefit everyone (Vieira 2001).

In this context our critical politics of kinderculture reemerges. Childhood has always been shaped by a potpourri of adult desires and childhood fantasies. The difference between childhood in hyperreality and in other places and times is that in the electronic, mediated world of the present era these desires and fantasies have been commodified and play themselves out in the corporate-produced children's culture central to this book. A critical politics of childhood recognizes these complex dimensions of kinderculture and in this understanding develops new and exciting ways for families, educators, and the society at large to care for and nurture children. Understanding that the positivist developmentalist paradigm always underestimated children's abilities, advocates of a critical politics of childhood help children develop the strategies and skills necessary for social reform and the pursuit of justice

(Jenkins 1998; Cannella and Viruru 2002). In this context educators, psychologists, sociologists, parents, and other citizens can reflect on children's activities represented by many as "misbehavior." Can we empathize with children who are positioned as self-directed agents in one social domain and incompetent adults in need of constant surveillance and punitive regulation in another? Can we understand the difficulty of dealing with such contradictions amid everyday pursuits? A critical politics of childhood urges us to take such questions seriously. Indeed, the authors and editors of *Kinderculture* maintain that a politics of childhood involves far more than just protecting children. As we reconsider the notion of competence, advocates of a critical politics of childhood work to ensure children can use their abilities in a way that improves their quality of life (Casas 1998).

DEVIL OR ANGEL? THE COMMERCIAL AND DEMOCRATIC IMPULSES OF TV

Commercial TV in America has always been structured by conflicting demands of commerce and democracy. A study of kinderculture finds these competing dynamics at various levels of the text. When analysts and consumers begin to understand the cultural authority mustered by children's TV and other entertainment forms, the bifurcated imperatives for the medium begin to take on unprecedented significance. The democratic moments of TV are profound but far too rare. The exposure of Joseph McCarthy's insanity, the evils of racial segregation, the perils of pollution, the most obvious abuses of patriarchy, the inhumane excesses of Vietnam, and the criminality of Watergate undoubtedly represented the zenith of TV's democratic impulse. The unfortunate consequence of such successes has been corporate constraint and governmental regulation of TV attempts to replicate such achievements. When such media management is combined with TV's tendency to fragment and decontextualize the issues it chooses to cover, events are often stripped of their meaning. Children (and adults) who depend heavily on TV for their entertainment and thus their worldview are cognitively impaired by this dynamic (Kellner 1990). Make no mistake, TV's curriculum for children is not crafted by media moguls' fidelity to the principles of democracy. Commercial concerns dictate media kinderculture—profit margins are too important to dicker around with concerns for the well-being of kids.

Society's most important teachers don't ply their trade in schools, just as the nation's "official" children's policy is not constructed by elected officials in Washington, D.C. America's corporate producers of kinderculture are the most influential pedagogues and children's policy-makers. There is nothing transparent about children's TV or movies—clear messages are being delivered to our children with the intent of eliciting particular beliefs and actions that are in the best interests of those who produce them. Bifurcated as TV's imperatives may be, democracy takes a backseat to the logic of capital. In comparison to the promotion of the multiple "products" of kinderculture, child advocates have limited access to the airways. Corporations that advertise children's consumer paraphernalia promote a "consumption theology" that in effect promises redemption and happiness via the consumptive act (ritual). Such advertising and pleasure production grant a direct line to the imaginative landscape of our children—a mindscape that children use to define their view of the society and self. Thus child professionals and parents must understand that humans are the historical product of the mechanisms of power—an appreciation often missed in the everyday world.

Kinderculture, like all social texts, speaks with an authorial voice that is either up front or covert about its ideological inscription (Lincoln 1995). Not surprisingly, corporate-produced kinderculture chooses Monty Hall's covert ideological curtain number 3. In this way kinderculture colonizes consciousness in a manner that represses conflict and differences. Thus the critical childhood professional understands ideology, and its refraction and its effect on consciousness construction, as the conceptual basis for his or her effort to expose kinderculture as a politically pristine, uncontested sphere of social activity. Just as classroom teaching and the school curriculum are never simply neutral, disinterested messengers/transmitters of data, corporate kinderculture harbors an agenda. Our recognition of, say, McDonald's family values-promoting ad campaigns of the early Reagan years and the company's financial ties to the right wing of the Republican Party is important to our understanding of the way politics works and the context in which kinderculture is conceived and displayed.

Such a recognition does not necessarily mean that we deprive our five-year-olds of their Happy Meals or their fascination with the Hamburglar. Our understanding of the patriarchal depiction of Kevin's (Macaulay Culkin) mother as failed caretaker of children in the *Home Alone* movies, while excusing his equally culpable father of blame for his part in the abandonment, grants insight into the way misogyny is transmitted across generations. It doesn't mean that we have to, as gender police, bar our eight-year-olds from renting the movie. Maybe an explanation of what is happening along gender lines and a mutual celebration of Kevin's self-sufficiency may turn *Home Alone* into a positive experience of (as our daughter puts it) "family bondation."

Although childhood professionals have not traditionally been students of power, given the power of kinderculture, they now have to be. As students of the power dynamics of children's popular culture, parents and professionals begin to understand the actions of children from a new perspective. Given their power to sink their kinderculture deep into the private lives of children, the corporate producers of kinderculture constantly destabilize children's identity. At the same time, however, new products—toys, movies, TV, video games, fashion clothing, texts—attempt to restabilize new identities through the consumptive act. The study of power vis-à-vis children and contemporary kinderculture provides a conceptual tool for criticizing social, economic, and political practices and explaining the ways young people's life choices are restricted. Artifacts of culture, whether toys or automobiles, have always helped us create ourselves and our social affiliations.

Our task as kinderculturalists is to expose these invisible yet influential forces, the micropractices that shape our children's lives. Our task is complicated, since the practices that are the most visible and unquestionable in commonsense observations of children at play are the ones most fully saturated by the humidity of power. The ability to appreciate these realities gives us the wisdom to distinguish between just and unjust kindertexts, manipulative and liberatory corporate activities. Thus empowered, we can begin to piece together the complex, often ambiguous way that corporate actions modify children's behavior, the way advertising and its promotion of childhood hedonism produce an ethic of pleasure and a redefinition of authority. Such issues reside at the core of who we are as a people and who we want to become (Kellner 1992; Wartenberg 1992; Seiter 1993; Ball 1992; Grossberg 1995; Abercrombie 1994).

CORPORATE POWER AND KINDERCULTURE

The study of power and kinderculture reveals insights into American politics that may at first glance seem only incidental to parents and child professionals—especially those of the positivist paradigm. Any exploration of child activist avenues immediately reveals the concentration of power in fewer and increasingly corporate hands. This reality cannot be ignored by child advocates and concerned parents, since the corporate-dominated power bloc is unafraid to retaliate against those who question the impact of its products. In light of the failure of oppositional institutions to challenge corporate hegemony, corporations to a large extent have free rein to produce almost any kinderculture that is profitable. Of the 7,000 interest organizations that are active in Washington, D.C., most are sponsored by businesses or corporations. Public interest organizations are typically outnumbered by ten to one in formal congressional proceedings on regulatory issues. The antidemocratic implications of the system with its corporate curriculum designed to adjust public opinion to support business agendas are chilling (Greider 1992).

This expansion of corporate power occurred over the past couple of decades. When pollsters in the 1970s uncovered a decline in public confidence in businesses and corporations, corporate leaders jumped into action. To counter public perceptions of them as greedy and uninterested in the public good, corporations dropped hundreds of millions of dollars into public relations advertising designed to promote corporate images and ideological dispositions. Designed to elicit consent, these legitimation ads focused on treasured common experiences in our lives—family, childhood, and parental events in particular. Among many others, the Ethan Allen furniture company latched on to the family, childhood, and parental triad, attaching its corporate identity to a right-wing notion of traditional family values. The Ethan Allen legitimation ads talked about the rise of juvenile delinquency and its threat to those of "us" who care about "our" children. Our treasured ways of raising our children, the ads asserted, are under threat by an unidentified group of people who don't care about traditional family values and the sanctity of old-fashioned ideals.

Corporations and the free enterprise system that protects their right to operate in the best way they see fit make possible these warm, familial moments of our lives. Maybe "we" should protect them from meddlers who want to regulate them and interfere with all the good they do. Of course, the truth is obviously irrelevant in these legitimation ads. General Motors was audacious enough in the early 1980s to run a multimillion dollar ad campaign demonstrating the extraordinary amount of input line workers had in the automobile production decisionmaking process.

Indeed, the decline of particular forms of traditional family life and the safe climate for children is a casualty of corporate development (Goldman 1992). After the end of World War II corporate America pursued a variety of policies jeopardizing traditional family arrangements, including demands on employees, the promotion of hedonistic and individualized life courses, and opposition to government aid to families fragmented by economic need, as well as the promotion of childhood consumption designed to pit children against parents and parents against children in a battle for consumer satisfaction. Nevertheless, the legitimation ads have worked well enough to protect companies from calls for authentic forms of social responsibility.

CHANGING CHILDHOOD VIA KINDERCULTURE/POPULAR CULTURE

Clearly childhood has changed, often as a result of its contact with kinderculture and more adult manifestations of media culture. While all audiences of popular culture play an important role in making their own meanings of its texts, kinderculture and adult popular culture exert specific affective influences, creating maps that emerge in the social contexts in which children encounter it. Since parents are no longer in control of their children's cultural experiences, they have lost the role that parents once played in shaping their children's values and world-views. In the 1920s, for example, with the protected childhood firmly established, middle- and upper-middle-class children had few experiences that fell outside of parental supervision or child-produced activities shared with other children. Since the 1950s more and more of our children's experiences are produced by corporations—not parents or even children themselves. TV shows, movies (now on pay/cable TV), Internet, video games, and music (with earphones that allow seclusion from adults) are now the private domain of children. The key theme of this book rests here: Traditional conceptions of childhood as a time of innocence and adult dependency have been undermined in part by children's access to popular culture.

Children no longer live in the secret garden of childhood. This is disturbing to the elements of the culture that constructed the mythology of such a garden. In this new social space children possess an open door to the adult world. Through this door they see images and hear messages constantly delivered about a variety of topics (Vieira 2001; Hengst 2001). While some scholars argue that such mediated access is not real access, such observations imply a positivist epistemological notion that there is only one true understanding of the adult world. David Allen (2003) writes:

> I have often observed that the fascination children experience in watching TV is connected to the promise that many of the mysteries of adult life are bound to be revealed by simply watching more. But just how many? The contrived stories on television that children see so often take back with one hand what they offer with the other. Kids may enjoy the feeling they have access but in reality they don't.

When children participate in "real-life" adult activities, do they have access to the adult world? Are their constructions of such events the "correct" ones? What exactly counts as a real revelation of adult life? The most profound experiences human beings encounter are all "mediated" in some manner. Of course, actual media experiences involving TV, computers, videos, video games, and so on continue to increase in number and show no sign of abating in the future (Spigel 1998). These media affect all people's access to the world, not just children's. Instead of denying the reality of such experiences, it is better to understand how they filter and construct our view of the world and ourselves and whose interests they serve. Unfortunately, this is not a form of literacy deemed important by U.S. political and educational leaders in the contemporary era.

THE DILEMMA OF THE POSTMODERN CHILDHOOD

The new reality presents adults (parents and teachers in particular) with a complex problem that might be called the "dilemma of the postmodern childhood." Contemporary children's access to commercial kinderculture and popular culture not only motivates them to become hedonistic consumers but also changes the nature of their relationship to adults. Advocates of traditional family values and severe discipline for children understand that something has changed; for some reason their authority has broken down. Such advocates often attribute the breakdown of authority to feminism and its encouragement of mothers to pursue careers outside of the home and to permissive liberals who oppose corporal punishment and other harsh forms of child control— but they are wrong. In fact adult authority over children has broken down but not because of feminist mothers or wimpy liberals. Children's access to the adult world via the electronic media of hyperreality has subverted contemporary children's consciousness of themselves as incompetent and dependent entities. Such a self-perception does not mix well with the traditional family or the authoritarian school, institutions both grounded on a view of children as incapable of making decisions for themselves.

The change in children's access to adult knowledge about the world and the changes in the nature of childhood that it produces have undermined the conceptual/curricular/managerial bases on which schooling has been organized. We do not believe it hyperbolic to argue that in light of these cultural changes schools must be reconceived from the bottom up. Presently the school curriculum is organized as a continuum of experience developmentally sequenced as if children learned about the world in school in progressive increments. Right-wing efforts to protect outmoded school organizations and the traditional notions of childhood that come with them are ultimately doomed to failure. The No Child Left Behind reforms of the first decade of the twenty-first century, with their standardized and fragmented knowledge and promotion of low-level cognition, attempt to protect an innocent, disempowered childhood with a positivistic vengeance.

We cannot protect our children from knowledge of the world hyperreality has made available to them. Such a task would demand a form of sequestration tantamount to incarceration. The task that faces us is intimidating but essential. Advocates of a critical politics of childhood must develop education, parenting skills, and social institutions that will address this cultural revolution in a way that teaches our children to make sense of the chaos of information in hyperreality. In this context school becomes less an institution of information delivery and more a hermeneutical site—a place where meaning is made, understanding and interpretation are engendered. The task is difficult, but road maps to negotiate it are already being produced (see Kincheloe 1995, 2001, 2003 for a detailed picture of what this meaning-making education might look like).

Children are at the center of an information revolution—they understand it better than anyone else, they are connected to one another by it, and their self-images and view of their social role are altered by it. Educators, psychologists, sociologists, parents, and citizens in general must come to terms with these realities. Presently many political and educational leaders are fighting such changes, resisting them at every opportunity. Of course, advocates of a critical politics of childhood must be careful not to overstate the impact of technology on the nature of childhood. Technology, like any other structural force, does not determine everyday life. Instead, it interacts with a variety of social and cultural contexts and diverse individual agents to produce an interactive social process. We can see this interactive process in twenty-first-century kinderculture with the diverse and idiosyncratic responses to children's interaction with technology. Nevertheless, this interaction of children and technology has produced profound—but not uniform—social changes. It is the responsibility of those concerned with the welfare of children to understand the impact of these changes and what it means for young people to construct social spaces (cyber and other knowledge locales) outside of traditional forms of adult control (Jenkins 1998; Vieira 2001).

In a recent marketing report entitled *Power to the Children* advertising experts argue that children have never had more social, political, and economic power than in the present. Because of their computer and Internet skills, many children are obtaining power from their parents who are still uncomfortable with cyber technologies. Because of these realities, the advertisers contend, marketing strategies to both adults and children must change immediately—children must be viewed and approached in a more empowered, adultlike manner (Veira 2001). Hyperreality has helped construct this new childhood. Operating in addition to TV, radio, video, and CDs as yet another site of knowledge and social access, the Internet creates the possibility for children to move farther outside the orbit of adult regulation. Children using the Internet can not only access even more adult secrets but also produce secrets of their own as they create virtual children's cultures via Web sites and Web spaces inaccessible to technologically challenged adults.

Here in cyberspace we find the ultimate contemporary expression of the dilemma of the postmodern childhood. Cyberspace offers unlimited possibilities for changing children's relationship with adults. By way of Internet usage (e.g., in chat rooms) children can impersonate adults (and adults can impersonate children), creating an often disconcerting type of child–adult interaction. Thus in this social space children can assume adult powers in economic transactions and other situations as well as chatrooms. While a playful dimension of Internet usage promotes the blurring of age distinctions between adults and children by promoting "juvenation," the "adultification" dimension of children's Internet activity is certainly important (Vieira 2001; Kasturi 2002; Cannella 2002). Whatever process dominates an Internet interaction, it certainly creates a new relationship between children and adults and new dilemmas in the postmodern childhood. Whatever direction these social dynamics ultimately take, a new day for childhood has arrived.

THE BACKLASH: HATING THE WORLDLY CHILD

An important theme in the recent history of childhood thus emerges: parents starting to fear the latent monster in all children, a parental fear of what their children may become. The middle-class and positivist concern with order and equilibrium is reasserted in light of these repressed parental fears. The precocious child must be rendered obedient; the body must be regulated in the it's-for-your-own-good discourse of justification. Parental fears find legal expression in new laws defining new classes of juvenile crime, making public juvenile records, establishing boot camps for young criminals, outlawing the sale of spray paint to curb graffiti, and eliminating age guidelines in treatment of youth offenders (Vogel 1994). Recently published children's books attempt to frighten precocious children who become "too big for their britches" into obedience and then a new form of dependency. Written to counteract too much child identification with Macaulay Culkin's precocious, independent, and successful Kevin character in *Home Alone*, Francine Pascal, Molly Mia Stewart, and Ying-Hua Hu's *Ellen Is Home Alone* (1993) paints a gruesome picture for children who want to stay home alone. Her message is simple and straightforward: Staying home alone is scary; as a child you are incompetent; if you try to act like an adult you will be severely punished; if you resist parental control, you may *die*. The infantiphobia of Pascal, Stewart, and Hu, as well as the "hellfire pedagogy" they use to enforce discipline, is not unlike Jonathan Edwards's imagery of children in the hands of an angry God or the conclusion of *The Bad Seed*, as the precocious Rhoda is killed by a lightning bolt.

FAMILY VALUES: CODE WORDS FOR CHILD NEGLECT

The doublespeak of the right-wing call for family values is in actuality a misleading code for an antifamily and children agenda. It is an expression of fear of the empowered, agential child and the new childhood discussed here. The antifamily reality of family values establishes discouraging obstacles for working-class families—working single mothers in particular—and great suffering in the everyday lives of their children. In the Reagan-Bush revolution of the 1980s, the Gingrich-Dole insurrection of the mid-1990s, and the W. Bush right-wing agenda of the first decade of the twenty-first century, family values were used as a cover for greed and excess and mean-spirited punishment of the poor. As a smoke screen for more malevolent goals, the discourse of family values has served the right-wing agenda gloriously. Providing the facade of concern, conservatives are able to convince millions of Americans that new moneys for education, antipoverty programs, and child care are pointless when the real problem is the absence of family values. A central but often unasked question involves how many families struggling in poverty would be saved if they embraced traditional family values. The answer: very few. To understand the economic problems that plague an alarming proportion of America's children, one must explore a panoply of structural changes in the global economy in the 1970s, 1980s, and 1990s, and the first decade of the twenty-first century. Traditional family values and structures characterized by working fathers and homemaking, child-rearing mothers are inconsistent with changed economic realities.

The family, Norman Denzin (1987) reminds us, has been a locale of political and ideological struggle since the late eighteenth century. Such struggles worked in the second half of the twentieth century to reveal to many observers that the all-American nuclear family is no longer the social norm. Such a structure is not now and may never have been the familial model experienced by most Americans. In the present era the nuclear family is a site of submerged hostilities as precocious, empowered children wrestle with their parents for adult privileges and material goods. The *Home Alone* and *Spy Kids* movies, for example, work diligently to cover up the familial fault lines introduced by the plots. As a result, screenplay writers and directors must walk a political tightrope over a canyon of family and child-related issues. The seismic waves emanating from these family battles—from the fear of precocious, empowered children—are clearly reflected by the right-wing family values rhetoric. Precocious behavioral problems, the conservative argument goes, are the direct product of liberal permissiveness. Such problems of undisciplined youth, the right maintains, are especially prevalent among the poor and the nonwhite, and the only way to deal with these "sociopaths" is to get tough (Griffin 1993). With the help of feminists in particular, the story continues, family values and traditional family structures continue to erode, and jailing youth is the only alternative to utter chaos. Thus a juveniphobia is deployed for political capital. In this context the rhetoric of family values does not connote a loving, supportive approach to child advocacy.

The political climate for children is indeed hostile with Gingrich's Boys Towns and W. Bush Republican social service cuts in the name of "tough love," as justified by Dr. Phil. Incarceration for criminal children is virtually antithetical to crime prevention, rehabilitation, or the reduction of repeat offenses. Juveniles in adult institutions are five times more likely to be sexually assaulted, twice as likely to be battered by institutional staff, and 50 percent more likely to be beaten with a weapon than young people in juvenile facilities. Repeat offenses by juveniles in adult institutions is significantly higher (Vogel 1994). Equally depressing is the discourse of many liberal child advocacy groups premised on a positivist instrumental view of children that demands public investments in children must eventuate in quantitative cost-benefit outcomes. In this context childhood intervention programs are invaded by unending tests for academic progress, social appropriateness, crime reduction, and decreased welfare dependency. Such a positivist mind-set is often indifferent to the need for a quality child care system in a nation where over half of children under six have working mothers. Funds for such a service are withheld on the family values belief that mothers, not child care workers (or husbands), should care for their children at home. Thus right-wing pro-family policies that cause children to suffer unnecessarily continue to throw up obstacles for working families, single mothers in particular. (Polakow 1992; Books 2002).

KINDERCULTURE AND QUESTIONS OF JUSTICE

Any analysis of childhood in the middle of the first decade of the twenty-first century must attend to questions of race, class, and gender-related injustice that plague segments of kinderculture's child audiences and shape the format of the media, print, and interactive dimensions of kinderculture. From the perspective of many poor and minority children, the world they have been encouraged to trust no longer works. Poor American children have seen their dreams stolen from them, replaced by a hopelessness that narrows their choices and undermines their sense that their actions can make a difference. Youth suicide was not even a category before 1960; by the 1980s it was second to "accidents" as the leading cause of death among young people. By the 1990s suicide among kids was described as an epidemic. What kind of hopelessness must a child feel to take his or her own life? By the time many children enter middle school, they are world weary, drained of a sense of possibility. Many have heard it all, the charlatans with their manipulative pseudo-hope grounded on everything from televangelism to drugs to schooling (Ferguson 1994; Gaines 1990; West 1993). Kinderculture must often provide a welcomed escape from such harsh realities—no wonder TV viewing time is so high among poor and dispossessed children.

These sobering descriptions of marginalized children's experiences in America are not found in corporate-produced kinderculture. Too often kinderculture refuses to challenge patriarchal power structures or provide alternative vantage points on the world. The "good guys" of kinderculture are too often white males who fight the good fight for neoimperialist causes. The advertising of children's consumer products that supports TV programming for kids is uncritical of the gross economic inequalities that characterize it (Seiter 1993). In the name of a common culture kinderculture ignores experiences of economic inequality and lived understandings of oppression endured by too many American children. Here questions of children's differences in opportunity and privilege are erased. An important distinction involves the fact that cultural racial differences may be represented by TV, movie, or print producers, but they are dehistoricized and stripped of any depiction of the power differences that cause suffering among marginalized children and their parents.

The TV heroes of kinderculture are typically inscribed with dominant and mainstream cultural values. As white, male, classless (read: middle-class) protagonists, they carry WASP values to violent villains who remarkably often are nonwhite or non-American. White heroes frequently are provided with a nonwhite or female sidekick to overtly signify the value of diversity—a strategy that covertly registers the need for white male control of a diverse society (Fiske 1993). Thus the presence of difference can be noted in kinderculture; indeed, advertisers and marketers have enthusiastically embraced difference from exoticized Jamaican Barbies to ethnic snack foods. A post-Fordist niche marketing strategy uses diversity to reach beyond standardized mass production's economies of scale. It is, however, a safe, common-culture type of diversity that sanitizes and depoliticizes any challenge to the harmony of the status quo.

RACIALIZED KINDERCULTURE

Analysis of commercials on cable TV for children and Saturday morning network programs reveals advertising set in a WASP-oriented middle-class reality. The homes that serve as backdrops for toys are spacious with kid-dominated play areas—suburban utopias. Casts for the ads are reported by talent agents to be chosen around the "all-American" standard of appearance (read: white). When nonwhites are cast, they are frequently placed in the periphery (the left third of the TV screen) of the action, leaving leading and instigating roles to white boys. Black characters in children's commercials often dance and play basketball and often display vivacious and loose characteristics—they are not the scholars, the kids with a secure vocational future. McDonald's, more than most children's corporations, employs African American children in its ads. Often nonwhite children in McDonald's commercials are shown on the edges of the TV picture slightly out of focus. Outside the conscious realization of their viewers, children's commercials that use nonwhite actors reproduce racial hierarchies that privilege whites. In one McDonald's ad connecting the corporation to traditional family values the lyrics "families like . . ." of the "song-over" are visually accompanied by a picture of an early immigrant family arriving in America. By the time the song's lyrics get to ". . . yours" the visual scene has shifted to a WASP upper-middle-class family. While referencing the great American melting pot, the commercial covertly labels "your" family, the normalized all-American family, as white and upper middle class (Seiter 1993; Goldman 1992; Steinberg 2001).

GENDERED KINDERCULTURE

It is amazing, with all the gender analysis and reconceptualization that has taken place over the past several decades, that kinderculture can remain as gender differentiated as it has. While the gender analysis of popular culture advances and grants important insights into media constructions of gender, kinderculture continues to promote delineated gender roles. Advertising for girls' toys has changed little since the 1950s—missing are the allusions to how well the toy stoves provide training for home economics and the demands of motherhood. Similarly, toy ads for boys have witnessed only minor alterations in the past forty years. The adult male voice-over is gone, but close-ups of the toys and boys' voices making engine and weapon sounds continue uninterrupted. Boys still become one with their toys, while girls take care of theirs—ever the adoring spectators of their dolls in girl commercials. In Disney animated films, for example, girls and women are depicted in constrictive gender roles.

At work in films and other manifestations of kinderculture is a hegemonic masculinity. Such a patriarchal form obviously holds serious implications for women, but it distorts male development as well. Boys are encouraged by various forms of the kinderculture curriculum to assume patriarchal roles that allegedly entitle them by birthright to define reality and enjoy the rewards of privilege through their domination of subordinates. Such an identity, unfortunately, is often formed through the young boy's denial of his connections with other people. Conservative-oriented American patriarchal culture defines manhood in terms of separation and self-sufficiency—the Clint Eastwood loner character comes to mind in his man-with-no-name *High Plains Drifter* movies. Setting the standard for male disconnection, Eastwood's characters in this genre repressed their hurt feelings and learned to hide and disguise them from the world. Indeed, in hegemonic masculinity the only approved techniques for dealing with emotions involve evasiveness, bravado, boasting, bluster, lying, and various forms of aggression—the "how long" and "how many" motif. In an attempt to master such techniques, young boys in our culture begin to cultivate a "cool and detached male pose" around the time they enter the fifth or sixth grade. In its fullest manifestations such a pose negates public emotional display—obviously crying is forbidden and even smiling and displays of enthusiasm are restricted (Nightingale 1993).

The emotional repression and lack of interpersonal connection that this hegemonic masculinity breeds among boys creates severe social dysfunctionality. Boys who are unable to deal with emotional conflict and the interpersonal dynamics of family and peer relationships grow up to be men who have difficulty loving. They may leave and/or abuse their wives and families—a growing trend in the last third of the twentieth and the first part of the twenty-first centuries. Such social psychological issues push the kinderculture gender curriculum to the front burner. A home or school curriculum that takes kinderculture seriously involves children in the recognition and analysis of such gender issues and their effects on the pedagogical formation of their own and other individuals' self-concepts.

WHAT DO WE DO? LEARNING TO UNDERSTAND KINDERCULTURE

What often inhibits understanding of the pedagogical power of popular culture in general and kinderculture in particular involves this society's failure to recognize that dominant power plays an exaggerated role in shaping personal experiences. This relationship is so apparent that it is often lost in its obviousness (Grossberg 1995). Power produces images of the world and the people who inhabit it that help make meaning for those who receive the images. The films, books, video games, and TV shows of kinderculture shape the way white children, for example, understand the poor and racially marginalized—and in turn how they as white people come to recognize and act on their own privilege. Language patterns connect with this production of images to reinforce power's influence, its ability to provide the context in which children encounter the world. The advent of electronic hyperreality has revolutionized the ways knowledge is produced in this culture and the ways children come to learn about the world. Parents and educators need to appreciate the nature of this revolution, children's relationship to it, and its role in identity formation. Simple condemnation of kinderculture by Republican politicians, together with calls for censorship, is insufficient; equally ineffective is a policy of benign neglect. Concerned individuals should begin with an attempt to understand these dynamics in all their complexity and ambiguity, followed by an effort to involve themselves in the public conversation about them. In this context adults may come to appreciate the fact that postmodern children's confusion and identity disorientation may be a reasonable reaction to the incongruity between kinderculture's and schooling's positioning of children.

WHAT DO WE DO? RETHINKING CHILDHOOD EDUCATION

As we begin to understand these issues, the need for a reconceptualization of childhood education presents itself. At the foundation of this rethinking is the rejection of a child psychology predicated on the adjustment of children to the existing social order. Valerie Polakow (1992) argues that this adjustment psychology demands an "order ideology of schooling" that is structured around the removal of the child from any experience of conflict. Inherent in this psychological model is an infantilization impulse that denies children the autonomy to make decisions about issues that affect their lives and to negotiate their relationships to conflicting imperatives. Rejection of the order ideology does not mean that we embrace anarchy; instead, we understand and learn to appreciate desire, the libidinal impulse that begins to bubble in childhood and reaches full expression in adolescence.

Kinderculture in this context does not incite rebellion or violence; it pokes and irritates the beast of desire—an affective force that is present in romantic love, the bond between parent and child, advertising, fast food, Internet chat rooms, movies, TV shows, and video games (Ventura 1994). A critical pedagogy of childhood is aware and unafraid of childhood desire, often connecting it to children's efforts to understand the world and themselves. As Paulo Freire maintained years ago, a critical childhood education is interested in the knowledge and intuitions children bring to school. In hyperreality such a pedagogical principle means that educators are obligated to study kinderculture, its effect on its consumers, and its relationship to desire. If we are interested in knowing our children, such a pedagogy provides us a direct line into their consciousness as well as their perceptions of themselves, the world, and even us (adults). What happens when children nurtured by kinderculture encounter the certified knowledge of the school? The answer to such a question leads us to new forms of learning, new insights into the construction of contemporary childhood around which we can restructure schools and rethink the role of parenting in hyperreality.

Jane Kenway and Elizabeth Bullen (2001) convincingly maintain that education systems have not been very concerned with the new paradigm of childhood studies, especially its analysis of the impact of globalized hegemonic culture on the formation of children's identity. Schools have ignored the implications of this and other dimensions of the new childhood for thinking about the purpose of schools in the first decade of the twenty-first century. Instead, Kenway and Bullen conclude that many school systems around the world have moved in an opposite direction, retreating to a form of hyperpositivism that abstracts children from the world in the name of teaching to high standards and basic knowledge. In this process they accomplish neither the former nor the latter. It is important to reiterate that contemporary schooling, especially in the United States, has sought to use the classroom as the bulwark of the old positivist order. In this configuration the child is positioned as an incompetent, dependent, and passive entity who is regulated and socialized as she passes through determined developmental stages.

Although parenting styles have evolved in relation to the agential child (duBois-Reymond, Suenker, and Kruger 2001), education in its mainstream articulation has resisted such changes. Thus the gulf between childhood schooling and children's lives out of school grows wider in hyperreality. As more and more of their learning takes place in leisure activities out of school, particularly in edutainment, schools are increasingly perceived by children as anachronistic and quaint. Schools and too many educational experts seem all too disinterested in the ways children use technology for recreation, communication, relationship, and community building. Educational and political leaders often seem more threatened than amazed by children's accomplishments in computer technology and forms of technoliteracy and knowledge production. Traditional conceptions of intergenerational divisions of intellectual labor in this context have been shaken like a monkey on a fuzzy tree. Indeed, a central tenet of kinderculture and its critical pedagogy of childhood involves the reassessment of the everyday activities, cognitive processes, social and cultural experiences, and political positioning of contemporary children. Additionally, such a pedagogy demands the serious analysis of the relationship between these dynamics and the assumptions of childhood education.

Kinderculture's critical pedagogy of childhood is not reticent about providing its "take" on this relationship. Our pedagogy for the new childhood moves away from the unproblematized transmission of dominant cultural norms and knowledges toward the development of cognitive skills and abilities that empower students to

- teach themselves to become rigorous scholars
- make sense of the mass of information with which they are confronted in hyperreality
- understand regardless of their social location questions of power and justice
- gain social mobility from marginalized and disempowered locales
- become good citizens, agents of democracy in an antidemocratic era
- make sense of complex real-life situations from which advocates of childhood innocence might try to protect them
- and communicate their insights as children unabashedly to a variety of audiences

Kinderculture's depiction of these disjunctions between the policy drift of school pedagogy vis-à-vis learning outside of school raises questions about the efficacy of schooling and the benefits of deschooling. The critical pedagogy of childhood is dedicated to the notion of universal public schooling that is intimately connected to informal, out-of-school learning. While we are harshly critical of the contemporary right-wing cooptation of public schooling, we have not given up on the possibilities offered by public education. Most teachers care deeply about what is best for children but are pushed and pulled by myriad forces working for disparate goals and political agendas. Central to any reasonable reform of schooling is the understanding of the social, cultural, and psychological dimensions of the new childhood and the ways right-wing reforms attempt to "recover" an older notion of childhood. In this context the issues raised by *Kinderculture* are central, not only to the state of childhood in the first decade of the twenty-first century but also to the future of public education itself.

REFERENCES

Abercrombie, N. 1994. "Authority and Consumer Society." In R. Keat, N. Whiteley, and N. Abercrombie, eds., *The Authority of the Consumer.* New York: Routledge.

Allen, D. 2003. "Is Childhood Disappearing?" www.sussex.ac.uk/units/spt/journal/archive/pdf/issue6–1.pdf.

Ball, T. 1992. *New Faces of Power.* In T. Wartenberg, ed., *Rethinking Power.* Albany: State University of New York Press.

Books, S. 2002. *Making Poverty Pay: Children and the 1996 Welfare Law.* In G. Cannella and J. Kincheloe, eds., *Kidworld: Childhood Studies, Global Perspectives, and Education.* New York: Peter Lang.

Cannella, G. 1997. *Deconstructing Early Childhood Education: Social Justice and Revolution.* New York: Peter Lang.

———. 2002. "Global Perspectives, Cultural Studies, and the Construction of a Postmodern Childhood Studies." In G. Cannella and J. Kincheloe, eds., *Kidworld: Childhood Studies, Global Perspectives, and Education.* New York: Peter Lang.

Cannella, G., and J. Kincheloe, eds. 2002. *Kidworld: Childhood Studies, Global Perspectives, and Education.* New York: Peter Lang.

Cannella, G., and R. Viruru. 2002. "Euro-American Constructions of Education of Children and Adults Around the World: A Postcolonial Critique." In G. Cannella and J. Kincheloe, eds., *Kidworld: Childhood Studies, Global Perspectives, and Education.* New York: Peter Lang.

Casas, F. 1998. "Children, Media, and the Relational Planet: Some Reflections from the European Context." www.childresearch.net/cybrary/mabm/cmrp/comments.htm.

Cassell, J., and H. Jenkins. 2002. "Proper Playthings: The Politics of Play in Children." www.web.media.mit.edu/~andrew_s/andrew_sempere_2002_politics_of _play.pdf.

Cook, D. 2004. *The Commodification of Childhood: The Children's Clothing Industry and the Rise of the Child-Consumer.* Durham, N.C.: Duke University Press.

Denzin, N. 1987. "Postmodern Children." *Caring for Children/Society,* March-April, 22–25.

Donald, J. 1993. "The Natural Man and the Virtuous Woman: Reproducing Citizens." In C. Jenks, ed., *Cultural Reproduction.* New York: Routledge.

Dorfman, A. 1971. *How to Read Donald Duck: Imperialist Ideology in the Disney Comic.* Paris: International General.

DuBois-Reymond, M., H. Sunker, and H. Kruger, eds. 2001. *Childhood in Europe.* New York: Peter Lang.

Ferguson, S. 1994. "The Comfort of Being Sad." *Utne Reader,* July-August, 60–61.

Fiske, J. 1993. *Power Plays, Power Works.* New York: Verso.

Fu, V. 2003. "Multiculturalism in Early Childhood Programs: Culture, Schooling, and Education in a Democracy." ericeece.org/pubs/books/multicul/fu.html.

Garey, A., and T. Arendell. 1999. *Children, Work, and Family: Some Thoughts on Mother Blame.* Working Paper no. 4. workingfamilies.berkeley.edu/papers/4.pdf.

Goldman, R. 1992. *Reading Ads Socially.* New York: Routledge.

Grieder, W. 1992. *Who Will Tell the People? The Betrayal of American Democracy.* New York: Touchstone.

Griffin, C. 1993. *Representations of Youth: The Study of Youth and Adolescence in Britain and America.* Cambridge, Mass.: Polity.

Grossberg, L. 1995. "What's in a Name One More Time." *Taboo: The Journal of Culture and Education,* Fall, 11–37.

Hengst, H. 2001. "Rethinking the Liquidation of Childhood." In M. du Bois-Reymond, H. Sunker, and H. Kruger 2001. *Childhood in Europe.* New York: Peter Lang.

Kasturi, S. 2002. "Constructing Childhood in a Corporate World: Cultural Studies, Childhood, and Disney." In G. Cannella and J. Kincheloe, eds., *Kidworld: Childhood Studies, Global Perspectives and Education.* New York: Peter Lang.

Kellner, D. 1990. *Television and the Crisis of Democracy.* Boulder: Westview.

———. 1992. "Popular Culture and the Construction of Postmodern Identities." In S. Lash and J. Friedman, eds., *Modernity and Identity.* Cambridge, Mass.: Blackwell.

Kenway, J., and E. Bullen 2001. *Consuming Children: Entertainment, Advertising, and Education.* Philadelphia: Open University Press.

Kincheloe, J. 1993. *Toward a Critical Politics of Teacher Thinking: Mapping the Postmodern.* Westport, Conn.: Bergin & Garvey.

_____. 1995. *Toil and Trouble: Good Work, Smart Workers, and the Integration of Academic and Vocational Education.* New York: Peter Lang.

_____. 2001. *Getting Beyond the Facts: Teaching Social Studies/Social Sciences in the Twenty-First Century.* New York: Peter Lang.

_____. 2002. *The Sign of the Burger: McDonald's and the Culture of Power.* Philadelphia: Temple University Press.

_____. 2003. *Teachers as Researchers: Qualitative Paths to Empowerment.* 2d ed. London: Falmer.

_____. 2004. *Critical Pedagogy.* New York: Peter Lang.

Kunzle, D. 1992. "Dispossession by Ducks: The Imperialist Treasure Hunt in the Barks-Disney Comics." Unpublished paper.

Lincoln, Y. 1995. "If I Am Not Just One Person, but Many, Why Should I Write Just One Text?" Paper presented to the American Educational Research Association, San Francisco, April 13.

Lipsky, D., and A. Abrams. 1994. *Late Bloomers.* New York: Times Books.

McLaren, P. 1994. *Critical Pedagogy and Predatory Culture.* New York: Routledge.

McLaren, P., R. Hammer, D. Sholle, and S. Reilly 1995. *Rethinking Media Literacy: A Critical Pedagogy of Representation.* New York: Peter Lang.

Mason, J., and B. Steadman 1997. "The Significance of the Conceptualisation of Childhood for Child Protection Policy." *Family Matters,* 31–36. www.aifs.org.au/institute/pubs/fm/fm46jm.pdf.

Mumby, D. 1989. "Ideology and the Social Construction of Meaning: A Communication Perspective." *Communication Quarterly* 37, no. 4: 291–304.

Nations, C. 2001. "How Long Do Our Children Have to Wait? Understanding the Children of the Twenty-first Century." pt3.nmsu.edu/edu621/cynthia2001.html.

Nelson, C., P. Treichler, and L. Grossberg. 1992. "Cultural Studies: An Introduction." In C. Nelson, P. Treichler, and L. Grossberg, eds., *Cultural Studies.* New York: Routledge.

Nightingale, C. 1993. *On the Edge: A History of Poor Black Children and their American Dreams.* New York: Basic.

Ottosen, M. 2003. "Children as Social Actors: A Critical Comment." Paper presented at the Danish Sociology Conference, Aalborg, Denmark. www.sociologi.dk/db/03papers/72.doc.

Pascal, F., M. Stewart, and Y. Hu. 1993. *Ellen Is Home Alone.* New York: Bantam.

Paul, W. 1994. *Laughing and Screaming: Modern Hollywood Horror and Comedy.* New York: Columbia University Press.

Polakow, V. 1992. *The Erosion of Childhood.* Chicago: University of Chicago Press.

Postman, N. 1994. *The Disappearance of Childhood.* New York: Vintage.

Scott, D. 2002. "What Are Beanie Babies Teaching Our Children?" In G. Cannella and J. Kincheloe, eds., *Kidworld: Childhood Studies, Global Perspectives, and Education.* New York: Peter Lang.

Seiter, E. 1993. *Sold Separately: Parents and Children in Consumer Culture.* New Brunswick, N.J.: Rutgers University Press.

Spigel, L. 1998. "Seducing the Innocent: Childhood and Television in Postwar America." In H. Jenkins, ed., *The Children's Culture Reader.* New York: NYU Press.

Steinberg, S. 2001. *Multi/Intercultural Conversations.* New York: Peter Lang.

Thiele, L. 1986. "Foucault's Triple Murder and the Development of Power." *Canadian Journal of Political Science,* June, 243–260.

Ventura, M. 1994. "The Age of Endarkenment." *Utne Reader,* July-August, 63–66.

Vieira, C. 2001. "Alt.cyberkid: Contingencies of the Technological Child." www.cf.ac.uk/jomec/vieira/altcyberkidpap.htm.

Vogel, J. 1994. "Throw Away the Key." *Utne Reader,* July-August, 56–60.

Warde, A. 1994. "Consumers, Identity, and Belonging: Reflections on Some Theses of Zygmunt Bauman." In R. Keat, N. Whiteley, and N. Abercrombie, eds., *The Authority of the Consumer.* New York: Routledge.

Wartenberg, T. 1992. "Situated Social Power." In *Rethinking Power.* Albany, New York: State University of New York Press.

Chapter 1

BUFFY THE VAMPIRE SLAYER AS SPECTACULAR ALLEGORY: A DIAGNOSTIC CRITIQUE

Douglas Kellner

SINCE THE APPEARANCE OF THE 1992 FILM *Buffy the Vampire Slayer* (hereafter *BtVS*) and the popular 1997–2003 TV series based on it, Buffy has become a cult figure of global media culture with a panorama of Web sites, copious media and scholarly dissection, academic conferences, and a fandom that continues to devour reruns and DVDs of the 144 episodes. The series caught its moment and its audience, popularizing Buffyspeak, the Buffyverse (the textual universe of the show), and Buffypeople. They dedicated themselves to promoting and explicating the phenomenon and exemplified the British cultural studies ideal of the active audience, able to both quote and interpret, while citing episode and season. Enjoying global popularity by the time the series reached its apocalyptic conclusion in summer 2003, it was widely recognized as one of the most striking cult TV shows of the epoch.

In this chapter, I argue that *BtVS* functions as an allegorical spectacle about contemporary life. I then provide a diagnostic critique concerning some of what the series tells us about life in the United States today and the situation of contemporary youth. Popular television articulates in allegorical forms the fears, fantasies, and dreams of a given society at a particular point in time. Reading popular TV like *The X-Files* and *BtVS* provides access to social problems and issues and hopes and anxieties that are often not articulated in more "realist" cultural forms. The richness of symbolic allegorical structure and content in these shows allows the production of meanings and identities beyond that of more conventional TV and provides a wealth of different readings and appropriations.

THREE LEVELS OF READING *BUFFY THE VAMPIRE SLAYER*

Encompassing realist, mythological, and allegorical levels, *BtVS* provides a polysemic, complex hermeneutical challenge to contemporary criticism to depict how the series works and how it presents a startling diversity and intensity of themes. The series combines genres of horror and fantasy, gothic romance, teen dramas, soap operas, and epic adventure tales. It pastiches the perennial figures of the vampire, werewolf, witch, and a panorama of traditional monsters, while adding new ones. Mixing comedy and drama, *BtVS* offers social satire and profound insight embodied in a wide array of compelling characters, engaging narratives, and clever commentary on contemporary culture.

On the *realist level,* the show presents down-to-earth, revealing relations between teenagers, and between young people and parents, teachers and mentors, and a diverse range of authority figures. *BtVS* engagingly deals with social relationships, love, rejection, loss, and all the complexities of family, school, work, constructing identity, and finding oneself, growing and evolving, or failing and regressing as a human being.

It is particularly realistic and boundary breaking in its depiction of sexual relations with a considerable amount of gay and lesbian sexuality and quite frank and explicit depictions of an extensive variety of sexualities. The series abounds with steamy sex and mutating relations where hate turns to love and violence to erotic entanglement. Playing with S&M and taboo-breaking eroticism to a degree hitherto unseen on U.S. television, *BtVS* sizzles and titillates with throbbing music, yearning looks, passionate kisses, and more.

On the realist level, the series depicts typical relationships and problems, such as teen and young adult angst, desires for love, acceptance, identity, and community, as well as a panorama of teen desires and fears. It engages painful problems like rejection and loneliness; drugs and addiction; violence, gangs, rape, destructive behavior, death, and a range of other issues that concern young people and adults. It often does this, as I argue below, in the mode of allegory, rather than movie-of-the-week style realism. It deals with the hell of high school with its group conformity, hierarchies, and ostracism, anti-intellectualism and oppressive authority figures, and meaningless rules and regulations. Moreover, *BtVS* deals with existential crises like coping with divorce, creating a relationship and life with one's single mother, and dealing with the death of a parent or loved one.

Families are presented as essentially dysfunctional in Buffy's world. Mothers depicted are largely ineffectual or perhaps destructive, while fathers are mostly absent; divorce appears to be a norm. Depicting ways to cope with the problems of contemporary life, the series shows how teenagers and young people often have to forge alternative families and in effect create friendships and communities as traditional families disintegrate. Clearly Buffy's group (eventually referred to as the "Scooby gang") offers its members a substitute family that they can count on in times of trouble, as well as a cadre of friends and lovers to share the agonies and ecstasies of growing up and becoming initiated into life's pleasures and disappointments.

One of the most distinctive themes in the series concerns how individuals with exceptional powers and abilities can develop these capacities and find and cultivate love, friendship, affirmation of difference, and identity. Grappling with difference, otherness, and marginality is a major theme of the show and puts on display its affinity with postmodern theory. On one hand, it affirms certain types of difference and otherness, as it shows the main positive characters as outsiders who refuse to conform to the dominant teen subculture and cultivate their individual powers and abilities, while relating to others in respectable ways. The series also shows how certain types of otherness, embodied in the program's monsters, threaten school, community, and everyday life and must be stood up to and dealt with. The dialectic of otherness is complicated further, as I will note, by showing slippages between "good" and "bad" otherness, as, for example, when the vampires Angel and Spike exhibit abilities to do both significant good and evil and are forced to make important moral choices.

Buffy can also be read on the more traditional and realis• narrative level as a female *Bildungsroman* (i.e., a coming of age and growing up story focused on a young woman). It provides a fantasy of an empowered woman who controls her environment and holds off and defeats forces of evil. While the *Bildungsroman* is associated with Goethe, Thomas Mann, and novels about young men coming of age, Buffy breaks ground in having a female protagonist. Indeed, the series exhibited the most fully developed female *Bildungsroman* narrative in the history of popular television and earned a cult following and incredibly dedicated audience.

The theme of how to cultivate exceptional abilities and deal with monstrosity takes us to the level of the series mythology as Buffy is a vampire slayer and her antagonists are often demons and monsters of a certain pop cult genre type. I'm using "mythology" as Chris Carter did in relation to *The X-Files* and Joss Whedon does with Buffy as the particular mythical universe and narrative of the series, rather than in the traditional sense of mythology. I'll argue that it takes us more to the allegorical level. The series mythology comprises the particular supernatural powers that the characters possess, the demons they fight, and the conflicts they face in particular story arcs and narrative sequences.

The specific *BtVS* mythology was introduced by series creator Joss Whedon in the 1992 film *Buffy the Vampire Slayer* on which Whedon is credited as writer and Fran Rubel Kuzui is credited as director (she served as longtime producer on the TV series). The film opens with the portentious narrative frame: "Since the dawn of man the vampires have walked among us, killing, feeding. The only one with the strength or skill to stop the heinous evil is the Slayer. . . . Trained by the Watcher, one Slayer dies and another is chosen." A caption appears "Europe: The Dark Ages" showing the vampire slayer emerging, and then after the titles, the picture cuts to a title "Southern California: The Lite Ages." Buffy and her friends are introduced as Valley Girls who are into cheerleading, shopping, boys, and the prom. But the Chosen One, Buffy

(Christy Swanson), has dreams of dark events in the past involving vampires, and her Watcher Merrick (Donald Sutherland) tells her of her "birthright" and initiates her into the art of vampire slaying. First resisting her calling, as the vampires invade the student prom, Buffy displays her mythical powers and slays the Evil Ones.

The film sets up the Buffy mythology and displays its blend of humor, horror, and social satire, but the TV series that appeared on the fledging Warner Bros. WB channel in 1997 went much further into developing a complex mythology, characters, and plotlines that generated a genuine pop culture sensation. The WB channel was looking for programming that would appeal to a youth market and was willing to gamble on offbeat, idiosyncratic programming that would give the fledging network buzz, publicity, and ratings in the competitive world of network television. Although *BtVS* was never a major ratings hit, as was *The X-Files* for some years, it picked up enough viewers that a smaller network like WB would be inclined to promote and renew it.

Series creator Joss Whedon called his company Mutant Enemy, and the corporate logo that appeared at the end of the show featured a squiggly animated character tearing across the screen and screeching "Grrrr . . . Arrgh!" The logo codes the series as subversive and offbeat, and at its best the show has dissident and oppositional features, although it also, as I will show, reproduces dominant ideology and has its flaws and blemishes.

On the series mythology level, *BtVS* creates stories about vampires and the vampire slayer, monsters, various forms of evil and their defeat; the mythology follows story arcs, as does the realist narrative level of the series. From our retrospective position at the end of the series, we can see that the first three seasons dealt with high school and introduced the mythology, season four dealt with college life, and seasons five through seven dealt with work and college and postcollege life and initiation into adulthood.

The two-part 1997 opening episodes, "Welcome to the Hellmouth" and "The Harvest," introduce viewers to Buffy Summers (played by Sarah Michelle Gellar), a sixteen-year-old high school student who has just transferred to the small town of Sunnydale from Los Angeles, where she got into trouble with school authorities for her erratic behavior (we learn that she was fighting vampires). Buffy's parents are divorced, and she and her mother attempt to begin life anew, a theme of renewal and change that becomes central in the unfolding episodes.

In the series mythology, Sunnydale high school is located on the Hellmouth, a portal to nether regions where demonic forces enter to threaten everyday life and wreak havoc, portending apocalypse. The opening episode introduces a hideous Master who plans to open the Hellmouth to legions of monsters that will unleash their demonic fury. Buffy learns that she is the Chosen One with the powers to fight evil monsters and bonds with the bookish Willow (Alyson Hannigan) and awkward but loyal Xander (Nicholas Brendon). They are tutored by the English librarian Giles (Anthony Stewart Head), who possesses a vast collection of books that identify the various monsters that emerge in Sunnydale. Giles serves as Buffy's "Watcher," providing guidance and mentorship to help her deal with her occult powers and portraying a rare TV image of a nurturing mentor able to relate to and work with youth.

Season 1 displayed a series of salient fears of contemporary youth and won a devoted audience by providing characters, situations, and narratives that embodied contemporary worries and anxieties. The series resisted the assaults on youth and demonization of the young that is a major theme of many films, media representations, academic studies, and political discourse. Instead *BtVS* presented images of youth who are intelligent, resourceful, virtuous, and able to choose between good and evil and positively transform themselves, while also capable of dealing with their anxieties and grappling with the problems of everyday life.

In season 1, episode 3 ("Witch") dealt with fears of an overbearing, overpowering mother wreaking havoc on her daughter. Episode 4 ("Teacher's Pet") showed Xander falling in love with a beautiful substitute teacher who was actually a she-mantis, displaying fears of being overpowered by a seductive and destructive sexuality. Several episodes dealt with fears of dating (e.g., "Never Kill a Boy on the First Date"), and episode 7 introduced the mysterious Angel, with whom Buffy falls in love and who reveals himself to be a vampire, exhibiting fear of falling for someone bizarre and potentially destructive.

"The Pack," episode 6, portrayed fears of group conformity leading to teen brutality and violence, while episodes 9 ("The Puppet Show") and 11 ("Out of Sight, out of Mind") portrayed alienated teens turning viciously on their schoolmates, as happened in Columbine and other well-publicized episodes of high school violence. Episode 8 ("I Robot . . . You Jane") exhibited fears of computers and the Internet while ultimately valorizing the technology as a powerful instrument for research and knowledge. Episode 10 ("Nightmares") exhibited fears of one's worst anxieties materializing, while episode 12 ("Prophecy Girl") unleashed a coterie of monsters wreaking havoc in the community, articulating fears of uncontrolled gang violence.

Although I'll return to some of the specific mythologies of the series, now I want to argue that Buffy has an *allegorical level* that makes it more interesting than a self-contained vampire-slayer narrative and Slayer mythology or conventional story of growing up teen in the United States. The allegorical level builds on the levels already mentioned and has its own complexities.

In general, a complex, multidimensional allegory like *BtVS* has a theological and religious dimension that copes with life and death; sin, guilt, and redemption; the choice between good and evil; and how to understand and deal with life and an afterlife. There are also moral and philosophical allegories that present ethical lessons ranging from children's stories to philosophical treatises like Kant, Hegel, and Marx that convey specific ethical, social, and political ideals or lessons, as when the Brothers Grimm terrify their young audiences into accepting conservative German values or the Disney factory indoctrinates its audiences into proper white, middle-class American morality. More sublime philosophical allegories include Kant's presenting the Enlightenment as a mode of salvation or Marx positing the proletariat and socialism as solutions to the evils of the present. As critics ranging from Georg Lukács to Frederic Jameson tell us, literature can also be read as allegory about life in specific milieus in particular historical periods that conveys concrete sociohistorical truths. Finally, popular culture can be allegorical in a sociopolitical mode—it can tell stories about contemporary life in a symbolic and narrative structure, providing specific life lessons, as well as commentary and critique of contemporary life and specific events, institutions, and types of persons.

Although popular culture allegory can provide a vehicle for ideology, reproducing the values and prejudices of the dominant class, race, and gender, it can also resist and subvert the dominant ideology, valorizing outsiders and resistance to hegemonic norms, and can present alternative ways of relating, living, and being, as I'll argue in the succeeding analysis. Thus reading complex texts like *BtVS* includes a critique of its ideologies and politics of representation, as well as a presentation of its critical and subversive moments.

I developed this notion of the use of allegory for interpreting media culture from Frederic Jameson, "Class and Allegory in Contemporary Mass Culture: *Dog Day Afternoon* as a Political Film" (2000), which presents the film from the 1970s as an allegory about class, sexuality, the media, the police, the city, and other central aspects of contemporary American life. Unlike social realism, allegory uses symbolic representation to comment on, interpret, and provide a vision of a historical moment without the pretenses of realism, which purports a one-on-one representation of the real. Allegory has multiple dimensions of meaning and makes no claim to capture the real in a clear, straightforward way, although allegory may better capture, Jameson suggests, the complexities and ambiguities of a contemporary situation than realism does.

I applied this model of allegory in "Fear and Trembling in the Age of Reagan: Notes on *Poltergeist*" (1983), where I argued that the *Poltergeist* films, as well as *The Amityville Horror* and other horror/fantasy films of the era, depicted fears of losing one's home, downward economic mobility, family breakdown, and other fears of the era. These horrifying problems were too distressing and traumatizing for a realist aesthetic depiction. But horror and fantasy could represent these themes in ways that allowed audiences to face these fears and dangers. Horror and fantasy films could also allegorize themes such as the corruption of capitalism or opposition to patriarchy more accessibly and less threateningly than realist films.

BtVS can be read the same way, as an allegory about contemporary life with its monsters as metaphors for societal difference and threats, and the special powers of Buffy and her friends can be read as metaphors for how knowledge, skill, and courage can help solve problems and dispatch evil. Classically, monsters like vampires symbolize predatory sexuality; werewolves connote bodily energies and growths exploding out of control; witches signify traditional female powers, including sexuality, which threaten the rational patriarchal order; and a wide range of demons signify various sorts of deviance and threats to contemporary order and security. In the current situation, for instance, many of the demons on *BtVS* signify dangers of drug addiction, and the gangs of monsters signify dangers of gang violence. Obviously many of the monsters are figures for alienated teens who strike back at their classmates with violence and often murder.

Yet, as Gregory Erikson suggests (2002), vampires have a historical specificity as well as more universal connotations. Early vampires in European folklore were peasants who emerged from the grave to avenge grievances. By the time of Bram Stoker's *Dracula*, aristocrats embodied vampiric evil and could only be destroyed through elaborate rituals. In the representation of vampires in German expressionist horror films of the 1920s (e.g., *Nosferatu*) the vampire was disturbingly similar to representations of Jews (as in, e.g., the anti-Semitic film *Jud Süß*). In contemporary U.S. culture, vampires have been largely represented as anarchic individuals who can emerge from any class, age, or social grouping.

The allegory of *BtVS* is that all of these teen monstrosities create a conflictual, dangerous situation for youth today that must be dealt with skillfully and successfully to defeat the monstrosities and evils of the contemporary era. Buffy's method of dispatching vampires is dusting the creatures with a stake or sharp weapon, turning them into dust and avoiding the blood associated with more traditional vampire slaying. The series provides positive characters and models who embody a creative otherness and difference and are able to overcome and destroy the monstrous threats to community and security.

The term "allegorical" is in some ways honorific and suggests that Buffy is more than both a realist narrative about teen angst and growing up and a vampire slayer mythology that constructs its own world and system of meanings. Although it does both of these things, I argue that the series is interesting and important because it also produces an allegorical system of meaning that connects it with traditional religion, philosophy, mythology, literature, and popular culture. Allegory, more than metaphor, points to a complex structure and depth of meaning and interpretation. It is allegory, then, that provides the structure and levels of meaning for the series as a whole, as well as holding together the various story arcs and narrative sequences. Yet the allegory of *BtVS* does not produce a seamless whole or convey a unified system of messages, as did Christian allegory, but rather provides a more fragmented and contradictory postmodern set of meanings.

As we will see, the characters and plot situations of *BtVS* are highly unstable and transformative, as seemingly bad characters show themselves to be good, good characters turn bad, and many flip from good to bad in a specific episode and thus display themselves to be highly ambiguous and mutable. Although traditional allegory had stable, fixed meanings and provided a consistent, unified allegorical tale and system (e.g., concerning the Christian salvation narrative in Dante or Milton), the postmodern allegory of *BtVS* is highly fragmented, insecure, complex, and subject to constant change and transformation. The characters of the series thus exhibit flexible and transformative postmodern selves valorized in a contemporary postmodern theory as opposed to the fixed, unified, and stable selves valorized in some forms of traditional culture.

Hence the concept of allegory works to call attention to what *BtVS* does as a series and how it relates to the whole world of culture and contemporary society. I want to illustrate this notion of *BtVS* as allegory through a reading of season 4, which deals with Buffy and her friends leaving high school and entering college. I suggest that it provides an allegory of the trials and tribulations of college life, as well as a broad range of other issues.

BUFFY GOES TO COLLEGE

In season 4, Buffy leaves her suburban home and high school to go to the local University of California, Sunnydale, and live in the college dorm. The Buffy in college allegory encompasses social realist commentary on contemporary college life and the story arc advances and complexifies the mythology of the series. But it also uses allegory to drama-tize certain problems or challenges of youth and provides a more gen-eral articulation of the trials and tribulations of growing up and surviving the rigors and challenges of college life. Moreover, à la *The X-Files*, the season's story arc articulates fears of biotechnology and genetic engineering, the military and the government, technoscience, and vari-ous monstrosities of the present moment.

The first two episodes of season 4 ("The Freshman" and "Living Conditions") depict, among other things, the roommate from hell, who does everything to get on Buffy's nerves from labeling all the food in the refrigerator to loudly clipping her toenails. Not surprisingly, it turns out she's a monster, setting up the thematic that college, like high school, is hell.

"The Freshman" presents Buffy as lonely and insecure among all the new students. The show begins with Buffy and Willow deciding what courses to take. Willow takes a literature course, recommending to Buffy a popular culture course that turns out to be traumatic for Buffy, who is late to the first class and berated by the nasty professor, shown as a superior-type intellectual who patronizingly dissects popular culture (and also turns out to be a monster). Both Buffy and Willow take a psychology course that provides the matrix for the story arc of the season concerning the mysterious Initiative, one that is similar to *X-Files* in the depiction of government conspiracies, genetic engineer-ing, and biotechnology.

On the whole, Buffy is confused and overwhelmed by the demands of college life. She waited too late to choose her courses, she has the roommate from hell, she's thrown out of her first class, and she must re-connect with old friends while making new ones and attempting to ad-just to college life. A subplot of "The Freshman" suggests that college is too much for some, presenting a student who seems overwhelmed by college and disappears, leaving a suicide note, although it turns out that he was waylaid by monsters. The young student Eddie, who disappears after Buffy meets him, has been vampirized, and college vampires ap-pear more vicious and predatory than high school ones. The tale pro-vides a cautionary warning not to get in with the wrong crowd; there are deadly monsters in college who can seduce and destroy you.

The episode points to a general philosophical vision that runs through *BtVS*, providing an allegory of radical finitude. Destructive events happen frequently in the series, characters and actions are fraught with ambiguity and contingency, and the universe as a whole is highly insecure. Shit frequently happens in Buffy's world, death happens, relations break up and turn ugly, and happiness can dissolve rapidly. There is heavy ambiguity in the Buffyverse. The characters and the viewers cannot always tell who is good and bad, and Buffy and her friends often do not know what to do or if their actions will have negative consequences.

Probably no show in the history of television has so consistently articulated chance and contingency in life and confronted finitude: that relations end, that stages of life (i.e., youth) end, and that life can end anytime and in any place. Probably no popular TV show has so exemplified this existential ontology, expressed by thinkers such as Nietzsche, Heidegger, and Sartre, that provides a philosophical bite and vision rare in American television.

Further, otherness and monstrosity are major allegorical tropes of *BtVS* as a series that provides allegories about evil, violence, death, and how to deal with the major challenges and negativities of life. As suggested, the monsters in Buffy can be read as symbols of various forms of contemporary evil and monstrosity. The vampires can be read as figures of predatory sexuality, which is the traditional form of vampire; demons can be interpreted as forms of contemporary monsters ranging from criminal gangs to drug addicts to rapists to whatever demonic form you might imagine. One character, Oz, is a werewolf—an allegorical figure of losing control over one's aggressive and bodily desires. More mysterious forms of evil and monsters include the First and a panorama of various monsters that cumulatively symbolize the presence and prevalence of evil in the world, in all places and at all times, and particularly in the contemporary era.

In season 4 of Buffy, the demons were more advanced and threatening, just as, for the most part, they are in the spin-off series *Angel*, which ran from 1999 through May 2004. Season 4 also dealt intensely with Buffy and her friends trying to establish new relationships and with the difficulty and fragility of sexual relations. The series dealt in various seasons with the major characters' traumatic loss of virginity (or not losing it). Willow's relationship with the werewolf Oz ended, and Willow explored alternative sexualities in her college year (to the great delight of lesbian audiences). Buffy's fateful relationship with the vampire Angel, who left for Los Angeles and his own series, was on hiatus, and she was ready for a new relationship. In "The Harsh Light of Day," season 4, episode 3, Buffy has a sexual encounter with a sleazy, insincere seducer Parker Abrams, who beds Buffy and then unceremoniously dumps her. Her second relationship is with a teaching assistant in her psychology class, Riley Finn, who appears to be Middle West Joe Normal but turns out to be not at all what he seems.

Indeed, in the mythology of season 4, there was a new story arc with new demons to battle and a new government conspiracy with overtones of *The X-Files*. Riley is involved with the Initiative, a secretive government project devising ways to better eliminate demons but also involved with creating superkillers. Riley and others in his group are being genetically engineered and are taking part in a project to create supersoldiers. Curiously, this theme was a motif of both *The X-Files* and *Dark Angel*, at roughly the same period. All three shows dealt with genetic engineering and biotech experiments for the military to create supersoldiers. Obviously there was a generally unarticulated fear of militarism among some segments of U.S. society, as well as fears of genetic engineering and posthumanism, fears that came out in the debate, intense at the time, over stem cell research and human cloning.

A subplot of the theme of biotechnology also dealt with the creation of a superhuman being, appropriately named Adam, who would constitute a new posthuman being. Of course, Buffy and her friends had to defeat these threats to life as it was and, simultaneously, all of the monsters of everyday life and college. How, then, does *BtVS* do its allegorical work and what are the series contributions and limitations in engaging the situation of contemporary youth?

THE BUFFY ALLEGORY MACHINE

BtVS does its allegorical work through the mechanics of a TV spectacle that combines witty commentary, fully developed characters and social relations, complex mythology and narrative arcs, metacommentary on the series as a whole, and extravagant action adventure sequences. The virtues of the series include the highly impressive mise-en-scène, with original design and production values, a strong sound track, and tightly edited narrative structures. Rarely has a relatively low-budget TV series had such cool sets and design, such excellent cinematography, sound, and editing conveyed in witty dialogue, an amazing array of characters, and over-the-top plots combining an aesthetic of excess and polysemic complexity with camp and social satire.

BtVS contains knowing commentary on popular culture and astute social commentary and critique. Yet, given my allegorical emphasis on its more serious themes, I should stress that much of the pleasure of viewing *BtVS* flows from its highly satirical, tongue-in-cheek camping and vamping; hence, the Initiative arc in season 4, for instance, obviously goes into *X-Files* territory and could be read as satirical commentary on the hyperbolic, intense government conspiracies, existential psychodramas, and hyperbolic anxieties about mushrooming technologies of the *The X-Files* (see Kellner 2003). Yet the spectacular allegory of *BtVS* is that it goes both ways; it provides serious commentary and drama and comic satire and humor at the same time.

Moreover, *BtVS* contains an incredible amount of metacommentary on the series itself. One of the treats to Buffy fandom are the metacommentary remarks as previous characters and events are referred to or brought back (even from the dead). There is also a lot of intercultural metacommentary on literature, mythology, philosophy, and art, as well as references to previous television and film programs and other, sometimes arcane, cultural references.

In addition, the images and spectacle in the series display transmutation of characters from monsters to humans, sometimes reverting back from one to the other, as well as metamorphoses from animals to humans or vice versa. The "Halloween" episode, season 2, episode 6, shows the characters becoming their costume figure (i.e., fantasy) when a magic spell is cast on Sunnydale during the all-hallowed night. Children become the monsters they are dressed as, while Xander becomes a macho soldier, Willow a ghost, and Buffy an eighteenth-century ultra-feminine belle, unable to fight monsters.

The sudden switch in identities exemplifies postmodern identity construction, which in the age of makeover calls for major reinventions and representations of the self. The most spectacular metamorphosis in the series, of course, involved the dramatic transformation of Angel into Angelus. Angel is introduced as the vampire with the soul that Buffy falls deeply in love with. A gypsy curse hundreds of years ago gave him a soul so he could contemplate the suffering and evil he brought forth. But if he ever found a moment of perfect happiness in love, he would lose his soul and become a completely predatory vampire.

Angel is presented as a brooding, Byronic romantic figure, yet he becomes a version of the vampire self when angered or threatened. His eyes narrow, his forehead furrows, and fangs appear on a monster visage as he assumes his superhuman vampire powers. The metamorphoses arguably provide allegories of the radical transformation of identities. Willow does this on a sexual level, transforming herself into a lesbian, and then as a violent avenger when her lover Tara is killed. Angel and Spike do it on the level of the series mythology in transforming themselves from evil to good vampires (with much backsliding and intense conflict between their opposed selves). The frequent metamorphosis and existential transformations show the potential in changing oneself from bad to good, or backsliding, as so often happens on Buffy, and the possibility of dramatically changing one's identity and creating new and better selves.

This thematic emphasizes the possibility and importance of radical self-transformation but warns of the perpetual possibility of regression and backsliding. At the same time, the series provides allegories about reconstituting relationships and friendships in changed existential conditions, highlighting the theme of the fragility of identity and friendships. Identity is presented in *BtVS* as mutable, unstable, and always subject to transformation, sometimes dramatic. One striking episode in season 4, "Fear Itself," deals with loss of personal identity. The title refers to FDR's slogan that "the only thing we have to fear is . . . fear itself." The episode probes specific fears and phobias that the characters must overcome: Buffy's fear of being rejected and of losing her authority as slayer; Oz's fear of losing bodily control and collapsing into his animal self, thus being deprived of human identity; Willow's fear of losing her magical powers and thus potency; and Xander's fear of rejection and failing to become a respected, responsible person.

One of the dominant narrative mechanisms of *BtVS* includes spectacles and allegories of violence in which evil is dispatched. One of the major iconic images of Buffy as vampire slayer and empowered woman, spectacularized in the opening credits and montage of character images punctuated by the theme song, is that of Buffy killing vampires and fighting and defeating monsters of various sorts. These representations provide a kinetic rush accompanied by pulsating music and establish the basis of Buffy as woman warrior and empowered woman.

The hyperbolic, excessive violence increased as the series went on. This is partly because television, film, and societal violence were increasing, because the mythology and aesthetic of the show demanded it, and audiences seemed to merrily consume it. Yet the extreme violence on the series between men and women, as well as women and women, had the potential to promote violence or privilege violence as the solution to conflict. Rhonda Wilcox (2002) points out some of the ways *BtVS* breaks with the patterns of patriachical allegories of violence, such as Buffy's vulnerability (which would never be included in male vehicles of patriarchal violence), her immersion in community opposed to the loner hero, her involvement in sexuality and relationships, and the questioning of violence and her own slayer role. Yet Wilcox concedes (and I think this is a good cautionary warning) that "nonetheless, the constant quick killing can be seen as desensitizing." Since I argue the violence intensified as the series proceeded, I think that this concern is valid.

The growing violence in *BtVS*, I believe, can be correlated between shifts in attitudes toward violence and militarism from the Clinton to the Bush years. Buffy's period (1997–2003) was one of unparalleled cynicism, skepticism, and irony in the late Clinton years and then unmatched political trauma, horror, and violent conflict in the Bush years. Early Buffy in the Clinton years tended to be light, satirical, and ironical, catching the wave of an intense postmodern moment circulating through U.S. and global culture. It was a time for apolitical cynicism, skepticism toward U.S. political culture, escapism, and hedonism.

BtVS fit this moment. It made fun of patriarchy and militarism, and its monsters were by and large figures of threats to everyday life and societal normality.

But as the world became more dangerous, violent, and insecure after the September 11, 2001, terrorist attacks and the ultramilitarism in the Bush administration's largely unilateral interventions in Afghanistan and Iraq, Buffy took a darker, more violent, pessimistic turn. Willow's transformation into a cruel avenger after the death of her lover Tara in season 5 presaged the violent, aggressive vengeance that informed the Bush administration response to 9/11; the escalating violence between Buffy and Spike, as well as the increasingly dark, apocalyptic ethos that informed the series, replicated the violent response of the Bush administration to terrorism and imagined threats from the "axis of evil," a phrase that would fit well into the *BtVS* universe.

Yet the constant undermining of distinctions between good and evil and refusal of Manicheanism in *BtVS* put the series at odds with a dominant ideology of the Bush administration (see Kellner 2003b). Ultimately the *BtVS* boundary subversion—showing that good and evil are often mixed and can slide from one pole to the other—and its showing that violence often is not a productive solution to problems put it at odds with the crusading Manicheanism and simplistic national chauvinism of the Bush administration.

However, *BtVS* potentially promoted violence or privileged violence as empowerment and problem solving, and exaggerated the ease of radical self-transformation. While it is useful for a TV series to show that moral choice, existential authenticity, and radical self-transformation are possible and sometimes necessary, it is not useful to show radical change happening as quickly and easily as *BtVS* usually does (although Willow's transformations are often a result of long study, practice, commitment, and hard work).

Buffy Summers as a role model or heroine is obviously a strong female figure of empowerment. But I'm bothered that Buffy is often presented as exemplifying the woman warrior and is frequently anti-intellectual and demeans school and academic endeavor. Buffy at best has an ambiguous relation to intellectuality: She is more visceral and action oriented than intellectual; she is distanced and alienated from high school and drops out of college; she is a warrior who generally uses violence to solve problems rather than intellect, empathy, or social skills.

Nonetheless, *BtVS* is one of the most intellectually friendly shows on TV in terms of ideas and positive valorization of the intellectual. I have mentioned the mentoring role of Giles, the valorization of books, libraries, the Internet, research, and importance of knowledge in the story arcs and specific narratives. There are copious references to literature, religion, philosophy, and other cultural phenomena; part of the fun of viewership is catching the sometimes esoteric cultural references. Furthermore, Willow is arguably the most fully articulated, positive representation of an intellectual in TV history. She is usually celebrated as a positive lesbian figure since she makes a turn on the series from heterosexuality to lesbianism. But from the beginning to the end of the series, Willow was a highly developed intellectual who was interested in science, technology, research, problem solving, conscious self-transformation, and translating ideas into practice.

But Buffy herself was often anti-intellectual, and in the beginning of season 4 the producers made Giles something of a buffoon, showing him unemployed, having a midlife crisis, and not knowing what to do with himself; however, he is quickly redeemed and there are some poignant Giles episodes as he copes with growing old and redefining his relations with young people. Yet teachers in high school and professors in college are generally presented negatively. In the opening episode of season 4 a pop culture prof is revealed as a monster who torments Buffy while Maggie Walsh, the psychology professor, who also runs the Initiative, is very sinister; there are no positive representations of college teachers.

The series missed the chance to interrogate college experience as thoroughly, originally, and critically as it did high school. Although exploration of the hellish aspects of college life began promisingly, the program turned away from academics to focus on the romantic relationships of the key characters and the battle with monsters. Allegory allows popular television creators to deal with heavy existential themes and do critical social commentary that they probably couldn't get away with in more realist forms. In terms of the politics of the Buffy monster-killing spectacle, there is a problem that the allegory distracts from social causes and origins of evil and puts a supernatural aura on contemporary life. The same problem exists with *The X-Files,* which is a contradictory matrix of rational social critique, concern with government conspiracy and misdeeds, and irrationalist projection of evil onto aliens and occult forces (Kellner 2003).

Allegory also provides a front for ideology and frequently serves to reproduce conventional notions. As I have suggested, the rather dark and critical vision of Buffy is for the most part counterideological and subversive of many dominant ideologies. Reflecting on the series politics of representation raises some of the show's limitations and problems.

BUFFY AND THE POLITICS OF REPRESENTATION

A critical cultural studies interrogates the politics of representation, as well as the allegorical meanings and cultural resonances and effects of a media culture phenomenon (Kellner 1995, 2003). Most of the ideological focus on *BtVS* has been on its representations of gender and sexuality, in which its powerful images of strong women and alternative sexualities have been positively valorized. Indeed, the series provides a systematic critique of patriarchy, showing how its structures permeate schooling, politics, the military, and other social institutions. Curiously, patriarchy in the family on the series is glossed over, as fathers are usually extremely weak or in most cases absent, although the opening mythology of the Master and his minions arguably contains a satirical critique of patriarchy. The minor demons treat the Master with obsequious obedience and a young child, the Anointed One, arguably constitutes a parody of patriarchical succession, an ideological trope subverted on the series by having a female slayer.

Patriarchal conservativism is shown as ascendant and is negatively portrayed in the representations of high school principles Flutie and Snyder (the latter being presented as an authoritarian conservative, not really concerned with students or learning, while the former is merely ineffectual and quickly dispatched with). Buffy and Giles rebel against the patriarchal structure of the Watcher Council, while the presentation of the mayor and his political associates as monsters in season 3 constitutes a tongue-in-cheek attack on patriarchy in the sociopolitical system, as does the assault on the patriarchal military in season 4 (discussed above).

Although *BtVS* gender politics are progressive in many ways, the ideal women are invariably thin and beautiful. The images of high school and college women depicted in the series are largely white, middle-class, and conventional. More punkish or countercultural types of women are usually associated with monsters in the series, and working-class women are shown as largely unattractive. As noted, mothers are usually ineffectual, absent, or malicious. Hence, while the images of Buffy, Willow, and some of the other women are unusually strong and women's relations and solidarities are at the heart of *BtVS*, the series is at best Feminism Lite, soft-pedaling feminist ideas in images and narratives rather than discourses or more progressive representations and narratives.

Hence, traditionally feminine ideals of beauty and desirability are upheld, although patriarchy is under assault. Likewise, *BtVS* representations of class are problematic. The main characters are identifiably white and middle-class, and many monsters appear to be rough, threatening working-class types and people of color. Faith is the most identifiably working-class character of the major figures in the series. She is introduced and often presented as an unruly, undisciplined, amoral, and potentially destructive person, although eventually she is more or less integrated into the community, a figure of working-class mobility and assimilation. At the start of season 3, Buffy is presented as a waitress while in season 4, she is shown working in a burger joint and Xander is presented in a series of menial working-class jobs, all portrayed as dead-end loser scenes, to be overcome and transcended by proper(ly middle-class) individuals.

The series is extremely limited and seriously problematic in its representation of race. In the first seasons, there were few black characters and they were often killed or were vampires. There was little interaction between the in-group and people of color. Although the final season displayed a variety of young women from varied ethnicities as potential slayers, few exhibited any individuality and the attempt at multiculturalism was largely cosmetic and visual, displaying a diversity of rainbow-colored bodies rather than racially interactive groups and social relations.

Throughout the series, threats to the middle-class community come from outside, not only from hell but from non-Western cultures. "Inca Mummy Girl," season 4, episode 4, features a vampirish Inca princess from an ancient Peruvian culture who comes to life and causes Xander much pain as he falls in love with her and then discovers her monstrosity. The subtext of the story is a foreign exchange program, and the representatives of other cultures are shown as potentially destructive or, in the case of a Swedish male student, boring and uninteresting. "Halfbreeds" and "nonhumans" also come from Egypt, Pakistan, the Middle East, or other countries once labeled Third World, so the cultural ethos is rather parochially Southern California white and middle-class.

Although *BtVS* is sometimes presented as critical of religion, it privileges Christianity in iconographies of the cross, holy water, and other images, as well as themes such as salvation and redemption. Willow is "kinda Jewish," but Judaism and other world religions do not appear centrally in the series. Despite the privileging of Western Christianity, the demonology undermines strict Christian ideology, and some episodes depict monstrous demonic rites taking place before Christian iconography (as in the episode "Innocence" [4014]), thus presenting contradictory relations to Christianity and bringing fundamentalist Christian flack on the series.

On the level of the politics of representation, *BtVS*, like most television programs, reproduces much dominant ideology. A popular medium that must attract mass audiences and does not want to catch flack from conservatives or traditionalists of various sorts must be subtle and sly in its subversion. The Mutant Enemy production team of *BtVS* has in many ways, as I've argued in this chapter, provided significant satire and subversion of many dominant societal and social codes, and consistently attacked patriarchy. Moreover, it treated the situation of contemporary youth with engaged critical awareness, often brilliant social satire and commentary, and narrative arcs that together constitute one of the classics of contemporary television and an important artifact of youth culture that deserves serious critical attention.

REFERENCES

Benjamin, Walter. 1977. *The Origins of German Tragic Drama*. London: New Left Books.

Best, Steven, and Douglas Kellner. 1991. *Postmodern Theory: Critical Interrogations*. London: Macmillan; New York: Guilford.

_____. 1997. *The Postmodern Turn*. London: Routledge; New York: Guilford.

_____. 2001. *The Postmodern Adventure*. London: Routledge; New York: Guilford.

_____. 2003. "Contemporary Youth and the Postmodern Adventure." *Review of Education/Pedagogy/Cultural Studies*, April-June, 75–93.

Erickson, Gregory. "Sometimes You Need a Story: American Christianity, Vampires, and *Buffy*." In David Lavery and Rhonda Wilcox, eds., *Fighting the Forces: What's at Stake in* Buffy the Vampire Slayer. Lanham, Md.: Rowman & Littlefield, 2002.

Giroux, Henry. 1996. *Fugitive Cultures: Race, Violence, and Youth*. New York: Routledge.

_____. 2000. *Stealing Innocence: Youth, Corporate Power, and the Politics of Culture*. New York: St. Martin's.

_____. 2003a. "Neoliberalism's War Against Youth: Where Are Children in the Debate About Politics?"

_____. 2003b. *The Abandoned Generation: Democracy Beyond the Culture of Fear*. New York: Palgrave Macmillan.

Jameson, Frederic. [1977] 2000. "Class and Allegory in Mass Culture: *Dog Day Afternoon* as Political Film." In Michael Hardt and Kathi Weeks, eds., *The Jameson Reader*, 288–307. London: Blackwell.

Kellner, Douglas. 1983. "Fear and Trembling in the Age of Reagan: Notes on *Poltergeist*." *Socialist Review* 54: 121–134.

_____. 1984. *Herbert Marcuse and the Crisis of Marxism*. Berkeley: University of California Press.

_____. 1995. *Media Culture*. London: Routledge.

_____. 2000. "New Technologies/New Literacies: Reconstructing Education for the New Millennium." *Teaching Education* 11, no. 3: 245–265.

_____. 2003a. *Media Spectacle*. London: Routledge.

_____. 2003b. *From September 11 to Terror War: The Dangers of the Bush Legacy*. Lanham, Md.: Rowman & Littlefield.

Lavery, David. 2002. "*Slayage* Six." www.slayage.tv.

Lavery, David, and Rhonda Wilcox, eds. *Fighting the Forces: What's at Stake in* Buffy the Vampire Slayer. Lanham, Md.: Rowman & Littlefield, 2002.

Males, Mike. 1996. *The Scapegoat Generation*. Boston: Common Courage.

Marcuse, Herbert. [1922] 1978. *Der deutsche Kunstlerroman*. Frankfurt: Suhrkamp.

Turnball, Sue, and Vyvyan Stranieri. 2003. *Bite Me*. Victoria: Australian Centre for the Moving Images.

Wilcox, Rhonda W. 2002. "'Who Died and Made Her the Boss?': Patterns of Morality in *Buffy the Vampire Slayer*. In David Lavery and Rhonda Wilcox, eds., *Fighting the Forces: What's at Stake in* Buffy the Vampire Slayer. Lanham, Md.: Rowman & Littlefield, 2002.

Chapter 2

READING NICKELODEON: SLIMED BY THE CONTRADICTIONS AND POTENTIALS OF TELEVISION

John Weaver

IN THEIR EDITED BOOK *Kidworld* (2002), Gaile Cannella and Joe Kincheloe map out two dominant themes in the construction of childhood: child as innocent and child as consumer. Teachers, parents, and, most effectively and disingenuously, corporations have cultivated these constructions to manipulate and control young people. The child-as-innocent mind-set treats young people simultaneously as naive and as potential victims of a "pedophile" world. The child is unaware of the dangers of the world—that there is an adult ready to corrupt the child lurking on every street corner, in every television program, and at every sporting event. Therefore young people must be protected. Clearly the world is a dangerous place; however, Cannella and Kincheloe point out that when adults attempt to protect kids from the realities of the world, they smother and manipulate them. Bills are introduced in state and federal legislatures in the name of children but rarely are children consulted in regard to this legislation. When adults dictate public policy, cultural tastes, and political beliefs to young people, the message is clear that adults view young people as incapable of making rational and intellectually mature decisions (they are too innocent to know what is best for them). They also send a clear message that young people are not yet human.

As smothering as child as innocent may be, the child as consumer is more lethal to the intellectual and civic development of young people. Until the 1980s corporations rarely if ever marketed products directly to the child. Today it is common practice to market directly to the young person. This approach works from the assumption that young people are able to think and act on their own. However, it also works from the assumption that children as young as two can be manipulated into becoming a lifelong customer. Direct advertising reduces young people to consumers and redefines the role of young people in democracy as being a shopper. The consequences of this shift to directly targeting young people are numerous. Kincheloe (2002) points out that corporations are now the most prominent source of our cultural curriculum. No longer are schools, churches, and families dominant in the education of young people; corporations are. As a result, concerns for fostering and continuing a democracy, fostering certain ethics in young people, and reminding young people that a nation-state is a community based in and on the well-being of others are shuttled to the periphery while the social needs of corporations are ushered to the forefront and projected as vital goals for young people to promote. The relationship between young people and the world becomes one of which neoclassical economists would be proud: Young people act as conduits through which the values of corporations flow into the world, and in exchange young Western people can get their Happy Meals, PlayStation 2 games, and Mickey Mouse autograph books at a low, Chinese slave-labor price. In the "free" market United States shouldn't this make every parent proud? Their children at a young age have assimilated into the consumer society, enabling adults to continue to live in a stable world of cell phones, SUVs, and vacation homes, unthreatened by young people who question the values of their parents.

In this chapter I suggest that just as popular culture has been the site of child as innocent and child as consumer, it is also the site for young people to contest these adult configurations. The best place to see young people making sense of the world and reacting to events in the world from consumerism to war is the first network for children:

Nickelodeon. Among Nickelodeon's most memorable features was the sliming of anyone who replied "I don't know" on the syndicated Canadian show *You Can't Do That on Television!* The green goo has become synonymous with Nick TV. It is no longer the lone channel that offers programming specifically geared toward kids. Discovery Kids presents sophisticated programming for children, and Noggin is geared toward preschoolers. Nickelodeon, however, is the only channel that spans the life cycle of young people from a historical perspective. After 9:00 P.M., when the children are supposedly asleep, adults can watch Nickelodeon for many of the programs that they enjoyed when they were young. Nickelodeon offers an array of programming that spans the life cycle. In the mornings and early afternoons, programming is geared toward preschoolers; after 2:00 P.M., when the elementary school children are getting home, the programming shifts to them; and later in the evening programming moves toward teenagers with *The Amanda Show*, *The Brothers Garcia*, *All That*, and *Kenan and Kel*. With the possible exception of the programming for preschoolers, the program directors and creators do not work from the assumption of childhood innocence, and the idea of child as consumer is at least challenged.[1] The viewers of Nickelodeon are treated as possessing the intellectual abilities to grasp serious problems facing young people while at the same time "loose" enough to let themselves be freely entertained by the silly humor of many of the Nickelodeon programs. In the next section I want to explain why it is important for critical pedagogues and curriculum theorists to explore the myriad dimensions of television and then explain my theoretical approaches to understanding television and its potential impact on young people.

TELEVISION: A FORGOTTEN MEDIUM

Television, for all its power and potential, is virtually ignored by critical pedagogues and curriculum theorists. There are a few exceptions, such as Peter Appelbaum's (1995, 1999) groundbreaking work on mathematics education, game shows, and Saturday morning cartoons; Mary

Reeves's (1999) work on *The Simpsons*; and David Buckingham's (1996, 2002) work on children and television.[2] There is little doubt that the primary focus has been film. The work of Henry Giroux (2002), William Reynolds (2002, 2003, forthcoming), Joe Kincheloe (1997), Shirley Steinberg (2000, 2002), Penny Smith (1999), and Debra Freedman (1999) demonstrate the rich textual, political, and cultural meanings found in film. Yet television holds just as much promise and insight into pedagogical and cultural issues. In what follows I outline some of the theoretical issues that the study of television can present as we seek to understand the impact of popular culture on young people.

Marshall McLuhan was one of the first cultural critics to embrace the impact of television on people. For McLuhan, all forms of media offer an intense sensory and neurological experience that engulfs mind and body; television is one of the more intense sensory and neurological media, especially for children. McLuhan opens his thoughts on television with these words:

> Perhaps the most familiar and pathetic effect of the TV image is the posture of children in the early grades. Since TV, children—regardless of eye condition—average about six and half inches from the printed page. Our children are striving to carry over to the printed page the all-involving sensory mandate of the TV image. . . . They pore, they probe, they slow down and involve themselves in depth. (1997, 308)

McLuhan describes the sensory dominance of the television image and how the print medium cannot provide the same depth of experience as the television image because the relationship between human and medium is too close. The eyes of the reader cannot take in the entire environment, while the television viewer watching from a distance can experience in an image that rivals full sensory virtual reality; the outside world is blocked out. The user of virtual reality experiences only what appears through the full-immersion goggles and glove. As a result of this full mind and body experience with the television image, the viewer is not passive but active in the construction of meaning. Interestingly, McLuhan views the filmgoer as a "passive consumer of actions" while the television viewer "participates in the shaping and processing of a community" (1997, 320).

In her introduction to Raymond Williams's book *Television: Technology and Cultural Form*, Lynn Spigel suggests that Williams challenges McLuhan's technological determinism. McLuhan's work is "apparently sophisticated technological determinism . . . for if the medium—whether print or television—is the cause, all other causes, all that men ordinarily see as history, are at once reduced to effects" (Spigel 1992, xiv). Williams believed that McLuhan reduced technology to the only active force in history while humans were passive watchers of history rather than active shapers. For Williams, the television image was not a neutral projection but rather a historical and cultural creation; therefore, it was important to consider the creators of television images. The power to create meaning from television was not as universal and equal as McLuhan assumed. Rather, meaning making from television varied according to the power one had in the production, distribution, and consumption of images.

While those who controlled television possessed more power than those who viewed it, television watchers did not lack an active ability to create meaning. Television, for Williams, offered a resolution to the contradictions of modern social life. As Spigel (1992, xxi) notes, television resolved the tensions between geographical mobility and privatization. Both of these phenomena of modern society uprooted humans from their communities and created a heightened sense of alienation among industrialized, urban dwellers. Television changed this because it "brought a picture of the outside world into the private home." As a result the television image acted simultaneously as a defense against alienation from the world and against unnecessary intrusions of the outside world into one's home.

The literary and cultural critic Samuel Weber builds on Williams's ideas on television as a screen to the outside world. For Weber (1996, 123), the word "screen" to describe television is most revealing. First, screen "allows distant vision to be watched." Television literally means to view from a distance. The image brings into the home the outside world, which still remains at a distance. "Second it screens, in the sense of selecting and filtering, the vision that is watched." The power of the television image to serve as a filter does not render the viewer into a passive conduit through which images flow. Weber's idea of a filter suggests that those who transmit and produce the images maintain a level of power that dictates what will be watched, but the viewers also have the power to filter what images they take in and what those images mean. The third, and final, meaning of the word "screen" is its ability to stand "between the viewer and the viewed." The television is a technological medium that creates a relationship between the viewer and the image. The television in this sense acts as a reminder that we see the world only through some form of mediation, whether our own eyes or the television screen, and this medium influences how we see the other. Weber is clear that the viewers, like the viewers constructed in McLuhan's and Williams's theories, are active in their relationship with a television and the outside world.

Television scholar Lynn Spigel adopts a similar view in her study of the medium, challenging Adorno and Horkheimer's view that the culture industry controlled and forced television on American people. Spigel takes issue with those who suggest that

> television's rise as a cultural form was brought about solely by big business and its promotional campaign. While it is true that television was in the hands of large corporations, it would be a logical leap to assume that the sales effort determined the public's fascination with television. Instead, this fascination was rooted in modern American culture and its long-standing obsession with communication technologies. (1992, 7)

Television rose to prominence as a technological artifact in the households of the United States on a twentieth-century continuum connecting meaning and progress to technology. Television, just like radio and the automobile before it and the personal computer after it, represented the active attempt of many Americans to define their lives according to the technology that they used.

Lawrence Grossberg offers yet another take on the impact of television on our lives. In Grossberg's work viewers are not constructed as passive recipients of images. They are interpreted as having a more spontaneous, haphazard, multitasking relationship with television. "Viewers rarely make plans to watch TV—although it is on occasion a social event to be shared with friends," Grossberg suggests (1997, 34). "Moreover, television is rarely intently gazed at, with the viewer absorbed into the work, but rather distractedly glanced at or accommodated within the viewer's own momentary mood or position, or treated merely as a framework of another reality." Television has become such an ingrained part of our existence that it has escaped to our subconscious, where it is assimilated into our everyday imagery. It has become a part of our neurological landscape; therefore, we no longer purposively seek it out even though we find ourselves spending a great deal of our time in front of the small screen. As a result, "its taken-for-grantedness makes it appear trivial. . . . Yet its power to restructure the temporal and spatial aspects of our lives remains unquestionable" (Grossberg 1987, 34–35). Television is powerful because it has become a part of us in shaping how and what we see. Television has reshaped us into posthumans and consequently is an active ingredient in our construction of reality, both as it is represented in our minds and externally from other perspectives.

THE COMPLEX RELATIONSHIP BETWEEN NICKELODEON AND CHILDREN

Preschool programming is by far the most problematic, especially in regard to recent changes. When Nickelodeon initially developed its programming for preschoolers, the shows were geared toward social consciousness. Many of the shows introduced preschoolers to a community or public ethos which demonstrated that the world was much bigger than they were and that people were dependent on one another to create a sustainable environment. Social consciousness as a theme is found in many of the programs Nickelodeon purchased from Great Britain and Canada. This flow from the creative minds of British and Canadian animators, writers, producers, and creators to American viewers offers an interesting shift away from critics, such as David

Buckingham, who suggest that Nickelodeon, through its British subsidiary, Nickelodeon UK, has "Americanized" British preschoolers. If
anything, the programming found on Nickelodeon from the early to
late 1990s suggests that a new wave of British culture has made a dramatic impact on American soil, in the form of animation.

From *Rupert* to *Richard Scarry's Busy Town* and from *Little Bear* to
Kipper, British and Canadian animators offered preschoolers entertaining cartoons with a clear social message. By far the most socially conscious program was *Rupert*. In every episode Rupert faces a new
dilemma in which he depends on the help of others, his own imagination, and the timely assistance of magic to solve problems. Rupert and
his many friends are animals. When Rupert faces a nemesis, it is usually
a human, usually represented as a member of the leisure class or upper
class. Rupert's most persistent nemesis is an animal poacher who is financially well off but fosters greed and destruction as an ethic. Rupert
and his friends take it on themselves to thwart this human interloper in
order to maintain the well-being of their town and environment. Children who watched this program had the opportunity to create a stark
alternative to the hypercompetitiveness that exists among friends and
family and the shrinking public sphere in which the community plays a
diminishing role in their lives.

The other programs take a slightly different approach to social consciousness. *Richard Scarry's Busy Town* offers a functional perspective of
community life to preschoolers, as everyone in the town has a designated
job and no one ever complains about his or her role in society. There are
itinerant characters (Bamboons) of Busy Town, but they are always fishing and never raise a concern with the more "established" members of
the community. In Richard Scarry's world everyone is doing something
constructive, even if it is not paid work. In spite of this perfect utopic
world, Scarry's message includes a social reminder that people depend
on one another to accomplish their goals and to survive in society. This
message prevails as well in *Little Bear*, *Kipper*, and *Maisy*. Everyone has a
place to maintain in society, but each character is expected to respect
others and the environment in which they live.

In each of these shows, the theme of child as innocent is prominent. The programming, writing, and producing never go beyond basic

issues such as trust, dishonesty, and certainty. The pace of these shows is telling. Never frantic or rushed, every moment is savored and enjoyed as an opportunity to play or just take in the scenery. On one hand, such a pace is to be expected for a program whose primary viewing audience is preschoolers; but on the other, underwriting the pace of these shows often is the idea that children live in a hostile, threatening world and they by no means are capable of dealing with this adult world. As a result, the assumption continues, it is paramount that we, as adults, create an alternative world that is an escape for children from this world of uncertainly and violence. It can also be argued that in each episode, with the exception of *Little Bear*, who is quite dependent on his parents and grandparents, the young characters in these shows solve problems on their own. As a result, we see the construction of a very healthy social consciousness which suggests to young people that they are active participants in their world and they need to act in the world in order to create a sustainable community.

Many of these characteristics continue to be a part of the current programming for preschoolers on Nickelodeon. However, the primary focus is not the construction of a social consciousness in young people but on the idea that preschool television should be first and foremost "educational." Of the current programs on Nick Jr., only one, *Bob the Builder*, is created and produced outside of the United States; yet it is *Bob the Builder*, along with *Dora the Explorer* and *Blue's Clues*, that makes a concerted effort, either before or during each show, to highlight the "educational" material that is introduced to the child. Instead of the child as innocent, it is the child as learning objective that prevails in this type of programming. In the United States, standardized tests dominate educational discourse and yuppie parents want their children to learn to read before they are four. Nick Jr. tries to put these overly anxious parents at ease by introducing lesson plans for their children. It is not uncommon for Steve or Joe to appear on the television screen to remind us that "today we will learn about different shapes or basic numbers." Unfortunately such a message does nothing to encourage young people to interact in their world and create alternatives to a world seemingly dominated by individualism, competition, and anxiety. Instead, young people are encouraged to view even their leisure time as an opportunity to get that edge over their neighbors so that when they enter the adult world they can have that same edge over their "competitors."

At the same time that the child is being turned into an anxiety-ridden miniature of their parents, one can still see ways in which these newer programs on Nick Jr. are more than cleverly disguised educational manipulatives. If *Blue's Clues* and *Dora the Explorer* are two of the more overt "educational" programs, they are also by far the most interactive. In the section dealing with television as the forgotten medium I tried to show that many theorists view the medium as an active mechanism for viewers to create meaning. If these theorists are correct, then *Blue's Clues* and *Dora the Explorer* serve as the most obvious examples. It is always a staple of these shows for the characters to stop what they are doing and interact with their viewers. Embedded in each episode of *Blue's Clues* is mail time. The mailbox delivers a letter sent to Steve or Joe from real children who perform an activity on screen for Steve, Joe, Blue, and other viewers to enjoy. This interactive approach to preschool television reminds viewers that they are not expected to be passive conduits to receive messages from this box that is sitting in their living room or playroom. It also reminds us that we live in a computer age in which entertainment needs to be interactive if it is to capture the imaginations and hearts of its viewers.

By 2:00 P.M. the programming shifts from preschool to elementary and middle school young people as the primary focus. In the sophisticated programming for this age-group, the child as innocent disappears almost completely and the young person as sophisticated individual and the child as consumer appear more prominently. However, even when the child as consumer is presented on afternoon and early evening programming it is still challenged in interesting ways.

The most interesting, sophisticated programs in the afternoon time slots are the *Wild Thornberrys*, *Rugrats*, and *Hey Arnold*. Each program constructs its child characters as precocious, inquisitive explorers of the world. Elisa Thornberry is forever interested in interacting with the environment, educating herself on the ways of nature and other cultures while helping animals and other people overcome their local problems such as poachers, modernization, and pollution. An interesting dimension of the *Wild Thornberrys* is that when Elisa gets involved in a cause, especially dealing with animals, she usually makes things worse. The message here is that people make environmental problems worse when they think nature needs help. There is a fine line here because the creators of the *Wild Thornberrys* can be accused of suggesting that there is nothing we can or should do as humans to deal with environmental problems. However, what the creators demonstrate on the *Wild Thornberrys* is that we can be most helpful to animals and the environment if we try to see the world through their eyes. When we suggest solutions to environmental problems from our lens, the problems usually get worse. However, when Elisa begins to interact with the animals, she discovers that there are different ways to see the world and therefore to deal with a problem.

By far the most intriguing program for young people in the afternoon is *Hey Arnold*. Arnold is a city boy who is expected to be a responsible and wise young man. His friends are from all walks of life and include a country redneck transplant, an entrepreneurial African American friend named Gerald, and a bewildered secret admirer named Helga. In each episode Arnold confronts a new problem. The problems range from meeting his many responsibilities to helping his grandparents (who own a boarding house) to encouraging a baseball hero (Mickey Kaline, who is a cross between Mickey Mantle and Al Kaline) to retire gracefully. Whatever the problem he is faced with, Arnold finds a way to deal with it. This does not mean he solves every problem, since some of them are beyond his strength (e.g., when he moves to block city plans to tear down and develop a part of Arnold's neighborhood). Whatever the magnitude of the problem, the characters on *Hey Arnold* are encouraged to take an active public stance on issues that concern their well-being. Young people are presented neither as innocent nor solely as consumers who should accept their plight in a world controlled by adults. In this sense *Hey Arnold* continues Nickelodeon's tradition of creating socially conscientious programming that began with such programs as *Rupert*.

Another common thread that runs through these afternoon programs is the representation of parents. At best the parents in these shows are eccentric and at worse borderline abusers. In the *Wild Thorn-*

berrys the parental figures are more interested in their exotic travels then taking responsibility for their children. In *Hey Arnold*, Arnold is forced to be responsible because his grandmother rarely knows where she is and never knows who she is while the grandfather has the tendency to go off on tangents that have little bearing on Arnold's needs. On *Rugrats*, all the parents are professionals who in real life would have had their children taken from them years ago, making it impossible to create a highly successful animated program. The parents are constantly losing or "misplacing" their children. Fortunately for them and their viewers, the children, even though only infants, are able to find their way home or back into the arms of their bewildered but loving parents. The interesting dimension of this topic of inept parents is the creative issue of whether an animated program can be created that projects entertaining and challenging experiences for children while avoiding the approach of the parent as negligent. To this point in time only one show has been successful in creating such a story line, *As Told By Ginger*. Short of this program, animators have gone with the mantra that in order for a kids show to be successful the parents have to be constructed as inept.

As I mentioned above, the child as consumer appears more often during the afternoon and early evening programming. This is not to suggest that the child-as-consumer construct is not prevalent during Nick Jr. It is. This should come as no surprise, since scholars of young people's popular culture have pointed out how prevalent consumerism has become in their lives. What is interesting is how Nickelodeon deals with this menace of consumerism.

Just how prevalent and dominant consumerism is for young people depends on who is cited. Joe Kincheloe (2002, 98) suggests that children spend $9–$11 billion a year on goods while they influence another $160 billion. Dominic Scott (2002, 60) reports that children spend $8 billion directly and influence another $130 billion. Clearly young people control more money than they ever have in American history, and for the first time advertisers are going straight to young people rather than through the parents to persuade them to spend their money on specific products. Besides magazines and films, television, especially those programs geared toward young people, is the primary mode to influence young people's spending. Nickelodeon, of course, is a primary site for such activity. From 6:00 A.M. to 9:00 P.M. Nickelodeon is peppered with commercials for children's toys, educational games, and clothing. In my household, my children constantly ask if they can have the latest toy on television for their birthday or Christmas. The effects of this inundation of consumerism are obvious. Children learn that to have an identity in the United States one must spend. Children are reduced to consumer objects to be manipulated, and parents are shrunk into wallets with unlimited credit cards.

Cultural critics have demonstrated that there are long-term consequences in targeting advertising campaigns at young people. Joe Kincheloe (2002) and Eric Schlosser (2002) both demonstrate that reconfiguring the relationship between parents and young people directly underpins advertising geared toward youth. Children have accumulated a new form of knowledge that relates to things such as video games, television programming, and fashion that parents are hardly aware of. As a result, Kincheloe points out, this knowledge "surpasses almost every adult. How can they respect those individuals (most adults) who have so little knowledge about such an important dimension of life?" (2002, 96). Schlosser adds that besides chipping away the respect young people have for adults, advertisers teach them that manipulation is an acceptable and necessary part of life. "The aim of most children's advertising," Schlosser suggests, "is straightforward: get kids to nag their parents and nag them well" (2002, 43).

Many public schools, especially those that face severe budget crises because of reduced revenues, have conceded that advertising is a great way to increase revenue. However, the impact on the intellectual and social development of young people is tragic. Jane Kenway and Elizabeth Bullen purport that "the schools are used by producers to sell products to consumers, school students have become commodities to be sold by schools and systems to producers" (2001, 91). Schools have become not sites of education but sites for propaganda as advertisers are advised to get into schools early because "research indicates that even 6 month-old babies are already forming mental images of corporate logos and mascots. . . . [and] 'school is the perfect time to communicate to young people directly . . . the ideal time to influence attitudes, build

long-term loyalties, introduce new products, test market, . . . to generate immediate sales'" (Kenway and Bullen 2001, 97).

There can be little doubt that schooling has become more and
more about manipulation and propaganda, and advertisers have become the new gods of disinformation and illusion making. When it
comes to targeting young people as they are being targeted in schools,
Nickelodeon is no different, to a point. Where scholars such as Alex
Molnar (2002) and Jane Kenway and Elizabeth Bullen (2002) demonstrate how schools have been under siege from advertisers and the corporations they represent, Nickelodeon offers a strategy to combat this
brazen, amoral approach to young people. Placed among the regular
commercials on Nickelodeon are commercials that are farcical.[3] For instance, Nickelodeon purports to sell a product called "scream-in-a-
box." It is geared specifically to young people who wish to give up
sleeping in order to avoid missing any important television show or
peer event. This farcical approach to advertising, right under the noses
of advertisers, subtly questions the whole concept of selling to young
people. Hierarchical power relations are turned upside down and the
status of those in power is questioned. These farcical commercials offer
young people the opportunity to question how advertisers and corporations are trying to manipulate them, and at a minimum remind young
people that the reality commercials try to construct consists of constructions and embellishments that rarely if ever reflect reality. It is during these moments of critical analysis that Nickelodeon is at its best.

This critical analysis is also demonstrated when Linda Ellerbee con-
ducts her *Nick News* segments. These are half-hour programs that speak
directly with, not at, young people. In the past Ellerbee has conducted
discussions with young people on AIDS, marital arrangements (including same-sex marriages), and war. Ellerbee works from the assumption
that young people have concerns and questions about the very issues
that concern adults but most adults feel are "above the heads" of young
people. By working from the premise that young people can tackle serious issues, *Nick News* demonstrates that there are alternative ways of
communicating with young people other than assuming the more traditional and damaging positions of the child as innocent and the child
as consumer. When adults assume that the child is the embodiment of

innocence the tendency is to avoid controversial and uncertain topics, but the result is to let the concerns of young people go unnoticed and therefore unaddressed. When children are viewed as consumers, then their opinions (unless solicited in a consumer survey) are unimportant. Both of these approaches create unhealthy worlds for young people, and *Nick News* offers an alternative that provides young people a healthier and intellectually challenging way to grow up in the United States, even if their parents don't want them to.

Nick News often airs during the early evening hours of Nickelodeon's programming schedule, when Nickelodeon also targets teenagers. During this time *Jimmy Neutron*, *As Told by Ginger*, and *Chalk Zone* appear regularly, as well as *Sponge Bob Square Pants* (which is also a book) and *Rugrats*. During this time Nickelodeon also showcases its live action programming, including *The Amanda Show*, *The Brothers Garcia*, and *Kenan and Kel*. Both the animated and live action programs speak to the needs of young people. *As Told by Ginger* is perhaps the most realistic television show in the history of animation. The issues that Ginger and her friends go through are what a typical teenager experiences, and her relationship with her mother rivals the realistic tension found only in *Roseanne*. *As Told by* Ginger does not have the same dark comedic undertones, of course. Then there is *Jimmy Neutron*, which focuses on the overarching issue of teenagers struggling to fit into a superficial world obsessed with fashion and acceptance while being labeled a geek, nerd, or loser.

The live action shows offer a different look at Nickelodeon because animation dominates Nick programming. What is most interesting about these live action shows is that young people play a major role in producing and creating them. These shows have launched the careers of Amanda Bynes, Nick Cannon, Kenan Thompson, and Kel Mitchell. These shows have continued the careers of child stars from the 1980s who wish to experiment with other dimensions of television and film, Brian Robbins being the most prolific. In the 1980s he starred as the geeky heartthrob in *Head of the Class*. After his time on this show he created and produced *All That*, along with his *Head of the Class* costar Dan Schneider. In the past Kim Fields and Malcolm-Jamal Warner have directed episodes of *Kenan and Kel*. These child stars of the 1980s understand what it is like to grow up in front of the cameras and lights, so they act as important influences on the next generation of young stars. This relationship between different generations of young stars demonstrates another way in which Nickelodeon offers an alternative to the child as innocent and child as consumer mentality that dominates the discussion of young people.

NICKELODEON AND THE CREATION OF A CRITICAL TELEVISION PEDAGOGY

If we are interested in talking with young people in a manner that moves beyond the dominant modes of thinking (i.e., child as innocent and child as consumer), I believe Nickelodeon offers an alternative. Whether it is through *Blue's Clues*, *Dora the Explorer*, *Nick News*, or *All That*, Nickelodeon treats young people with a certain sophistication. Through its interactive approach to learning and entertainment, Nickelodeon has made a commitment to engage young people, no matter if the program pertains to silly antics or serious geopolitical issues. Unfortunately, most educational institutions have refused to engage young people in a constructive manner. As Julie Webber (2003) has pointed out, most schools are responding to the needs of young people through a strategy of containment that rivals the U.S. strategy in dealing with the Soviet Union during the Cold War. Instead of engaging students about issues that concern them, school officials are enforcing zero-sum policies that have turned schools into preparatory prisons in which students get a taste of what the future holds for them as they are locked down, frisked for weapons, herded through metal detectors, and encouraged to spy on their fellow classmates. Nickelodeon offers an alternative pedagogy that makes a commitment to the needs and concerns of young people. What does Nickelodeon's direction in dealing with young people, when compared with the prison model of most schools, tell us about the state of public education? What does it say about the intellectual vitality of our universities when a children's network provides a more constructive curriculum for young people than most educational institutions?

I do not want to give the impression that Nickelodeon is a pedagogically radical network that shuns the negative trends of consumerism and predatory capitalism. Nickelodeon embraces consumer capitalism in order to compete in the television marketplace. However, I have tried to show that Nickelodeon is shot through with meaning, able to be iterated in many different ways, and adopted for numerous articulated purposes. One of these pedagogical possibilities is to read Nickelodeon as a critique of the effects of predatory capitalism on young people through its parodies and general approach to communicating with young people. Nickelodeon offers a starting point for critical theorists and curriculum studies scholars to construct a pedagogy that is based in popular culture and the lives of young people. Such a pedagogy recognizes that these modes of communication are active agents in creating identities and meanings for young people. It is my contention that as soon as we accept television as an active agent in the lives of students, and not some passive agent feeding even more passive receptors called young people, we can begin the process of rebuilding public schools in a way that permits young people an opportunity to make sense of the world they have inherited and actively change it into a more democratic world. Nickelodeon has begun this process; now we have to wait and see if educators are up to the challenge.

References

Appelbaum, P. 1995. *Popular Culture, Educational Discourse, and Mathematics.* Albany: State University of New York Press.

_____. 1999. "Cyborg Selves: Saturday Morning Magic and Magical Morality." In T. Daspit and J. Weaver, eds., *Popular Culture and Critical Pedagogy,* 83–115. New York: Routledge Falmer.

Bakhtin, M. 1994. *The Dialogic Imagination: Four Essays by M. M. Bakhtin.* Edited by M. Holquist. Austin: University of Texas Press.

Buckingham, D. 1996. *Moving Images: Understanding Children's Emotional Responses to Television.* Manchester, U.K.: Manchester University Press.

Buckingham, D., ed. 2002. *Small Screens: Television for Children.* London: Leicester University Press.

Cannella, G., and J. Kincheloe, eds. 2002. *Kidworld: Childhood Studies, Global Perspectives, and Education.* New York: Peter Lang.

Derrida, J. 1988. *Limited Inc.* Chicago: Northwestern University Press.

Freedman, D. 1999. "Images of the Teacher in Popular Culture: Preservice Teachers' Interpretations of *Dangerous Minds.*" *Journal of Curriculum Theorizing* 15, no. 2: 71–84.

Giroux, H. 2002. *Breaking into the Movies: Films and the Culture of Politics.* London: Blackwell.

Grossberg, L. 1987. "The In-Difference of Television." *Screen* 28, no. 2: 28–45.

_____. 1996. "On Postmodernism and Articulation: An Interview with Stuart Hall." In D. Morley and K.-H. Chen, eds., *Stuart Hall: Critical Dialogues in Cultural Studies,* 131–150. New York: Routledge.

Jenkins, H. 1992. *Textual Poachers: Television, Fans, and Participatory Culture.* New York: Routledge.

Kenway, J., and E. Bullen. 2002. *Consuming Children: Education-Entertainment-Advertising.* Philadelphia: Open University Press.

Kincheloe, J. 2002. "The Complex Politics of McDonald's and the New Childhood: Colonizing Kidworld." In Gaile Cannella and Joe Kincheloe, eds., *Kidworld,* 75–121. New York: Peter Lang.

McLuhan, M. 1997. *Understanding Media: The Extensions of Man.* Cambridge, Mass.: MIT.

Molnar, A. 2002. "Commercial Transformation of America's Schools." In W. Doll and N. Gough, eds., *Curriculum Visions,* 201–212. New York: Peter Lang.

Reeves, M. 1999. "School Is Hell: Learning with and from *The Simpsons.*" In T. Daspit and J. Weaver, eds., *Popular Culture and Critical Pedagogy,* 55–82, New York: Routledge Falmer.

Reynolds, W. M. 2002. "Shooting Arrows into the Air: Deleuze and Vampires." *Journal of Curriculum Theorizing* 18, no. 3: 41–52.

_____. 2003. *Curriculum: A River Runs Through It.* New York: Peter Lang.

_____. Forthcoming. *Deleuze and Cultural Curriculum Studies.* New York: Routledge.

Schlosser, E. 2002. *Fast Food Nation.* New York: Harper Perennial.

Scott, D. 2002. "What Are Beanie Babies Teaching Our Children?" In G. Cannella and J. Kincheloe, eds., *Kidworld: Childhood Studies, Global Perspectives, and Education,* 59–74. New York: Peter Lang.

Smith, P. 1999. "Rethinking Joe: Exploring the Borders of *Lean on Me.*" In T. Daspit and J. Weaver, eds., *Popular Culture and Critical Pedagogy,* 3–32. New York: Routledge Falmer.

Spigel, L. 1992. *Make Room for TV: Television and the Family Ideal in Postwar America.* Chicago: Chicago University Press.

Steinberg, S. 2002. "French Fries, Fezzes, and Minstrels: The Hollywoodization of Islam." *Cultural Studies, Critical Methodologies,* May.

_____. 2000. "From the Closet to the Corral: Neo-stereotyping in *In & Out.*" In S. Talburt and S. Steinberg, eds., *Thinking Queer: Sexuality, Culture, and Education.* New York: Peter Lang.

Webber, J. 2003. *Failure to Hold: The Politics of School Violence.* Boulder: Rowman & Littlefield.

Weber, S. 1996. *Mass Mediauras: Forms, Technics, Media.* Stanford: Stanford University Press.

Williams, R. 1992. *Television: Technology and Cultural Form.* Hanover, N.H.: University Press of New England.

Chapter 3

KIDS AND THE NEWS

Carl Bybee

W HEN SCHOOL BEGAN IN THE FALL, my fifth grade daughter brought home in her backpack a copy of *Scholastic News* for September 1, 2003.[1] This was the "senior" edition of the Scholastic weekly newsmagazine that proclaims itself "America's Leading News Source for Kids." On the cover of the eight-page magazine was a close-up of a prairie dog and the headline "Problem Pets." The subhead read, "A health scare linked to prairie dogs turns the nation's attention to exotic pets." In the lower left-hand corner was a smaller headline that read, "Prairie dogs can make cute pets. But are they worth the risk?"

In the upper right-hand corner of the front page was a small inset photograph. In the foreground a woman with a scarf tied around her head was walking to the left. In the background was a soldier, hands on a mounted machine gun, sitting atop an armored assault vehicle, facing to the right. The caption below the picture read "Rebuilding Iraq, page 2." In the lower right-hand corner was a Web site address, www.scholastic.com/news.

At this time daily casualties of U.S. soldiers killed or wounded were being reported, as the latest Iraq war, declared officially over, continued. A debate was raging over the quality and sources of the military intelligence the Bush administration had used to justify launching the U.S. attack on Iraq. Still no weapons of mass destruction, offered by the

Bush administration as the primary justification for the immediate need to invade Iraq, had been found. The Bush administration was drafting a resolution to take to the United Nations to ask for help in managing the deteriorating situation in Iraq. Nearly four months had passed since President Bush had landed in the copilot's seat of a Navy S-3B Viking on the deck of the USS *Lincoln* to declare, in regard to the Iraq war, "Mission accomplished." U.S. news media were reporting polls indicating that more than two-thirds of U.S. citizens believed that Saddam Hussein had been personally involved in planning the attacks of September 11, 2001, on the United States. Given the absence of any evidence of such a link and given President Bush's repeated representations that such a connection existed, the president, in the interest of preserving his credibility, was forced to make a national statement the following week that there was no evidence of such a link. The second anniversary of September 11, 2001, was a few days away.

I looked at the picture of the prairie dog on the cover of *Scholastic News* and the woman and the armored assault vehicle, and I thought about the civics lessons my daughter had received two years ago, as an eight-year-old, on September 11. The lessons she had learned from the events of that day and the days afterward, from her teachers, from watching and listening to her parents, and from the media. Even though she was my own daughter, it was hard to imagine what sense she pulled from that day and the two years and two unfinished wars that followed. Now she constantly heard the word "terrorist," a word that had not existed in her vocabulary until the September 11 attack.

So I opened up the magazine and went directly to the Iraq story, headlined on the second page as "Rebuilding a Nation." I read the 250-word story, noting that one of the words in the last sentence was in boldface. My eye then traveled to the bottom of the page, where I noticed a small feature that was repeated on each page of the magazine. It was a small box with the heading "What's that word?" One word from each page of the magazine was selected to be highlighted and defined.

I looked back at the last sentence of the "Rebuilding a Nation" story. It read, "Street vendors are *hawking* their wares, and people are beginning to go about their normal lives." For that week, in *Scholastic*

News, the continuing war in Iraq had been reduced to "Rebuilding a Nation." And "Rebuilding a Nation" had been reduced to a word quiz featuring the single word "hawking." No other "fact" from the story made it into the multiple choice news quiz on the last page of the magazine. The "democratic" liberation of Iraq proceeded. The first Scholastic Book Club order form had already been sent home filled with not just books published by Scholastic Press, but toys and video games with name brand tie-ins. The first Scholastic book fair of the year had been scheduled for the end of the month by teachers and administrators desperate for the additional funds it would generate to supplement slashed school budgets.

NEWS FOR KIDS

No matter what educators and civic leaders say about how important the news (they tend to call it "current events") is for kids, everyone knows, adults included, that news is the piece of cold, overcooked, rubbery broccoli on the plate of media culture. At best. At worst it is an ongoing reminder that whatever peace and safety children may feel in their homes or with their families is under constant threat by a world seemingly out of control. And these feelings are increasingly shared by adults, who continue to tune out of the news in ever increasing numbers. This may be why in early 2003, Citytv, a Toronto television station, launched its evening *Naked News* program. During the program female newscasters strip while they read the news. The executive producer said, "The news right now is somber and morbid; there is a lot of stress and tension in the world and this makes the news a little more carefree."

This chapter is not about *Naked News* or about the naked "truth" about news. It is not about sex and news, at least until later. It is about the cold, rubbery broccoli called news, the fearful anxiety it calls up, and particularly news produced for kids. It focuses on where "news for kids" comes from and how it is sold to children and how the attention of the children who watch it is sold to corporations who want to sell them or their parents something. It is also about what all this selling of news and of kids offers young people as ways to think about democracy and citizenship.

The concept of kinderculture asks that we take these seemingly innocuous moments in the everyday construction of childhood and carefully "read" them to understand the brave new meanings of childhood that our society is, intentionally or inadvertently, creating. And to ask, Is this what we want for our children? For ourselves? Is this the people, the society, we choose to be?

As Shirley Steinberg and Joe Kincheloe argue in the introduction, one of the defining hallmarks of the current crisis of childhood is that the corporation has emerged over the past several decades as one of the primary sources of learning for youth and adults alike. This has meant a radical displacement of the educating roles of parents, families, teachers, schools, and traditional communities. At the same time it has meant that as corporations move into the production of kinderculture, their driving aim is first and foremost economic gain and not the social good. With youth having greater and greater disposable income at their command and greater and greater influence over family purchasing decisions, they have become key marketing targets to achieve immediate profits and to establish brand loyalties that will guarantee future corporate revenue.

The corporatization of children's culture has also created marketing challenges—from how to reach an audience increasingly fragmented by the wide array of privatizing media technology, to marketing to a "marketed-to-death" audience, to finding the pitch that will ingratiate corporations to young people increasingly resistant to adult authority.

This has forced corporations to seek increasingly sophisticated marketing strategies and technologies to reach kids, strategies and technologies that are increasingly invisible to parents, educators, and civic leaders. This chapter follows the insight of cultural pedagogy that the aggressive movement of "corporate-think" into producing children's culture requires that we begin the job of mapping out and making visible the dimensions of this invasion, and begin raising questions concerning power and responsibility in producing a democratic culture that promotes raising democratic citizens.[2]

This chapter takes up Steinberg and Kincheloe's challenge of "exposing the footprints of power" in the production of children's consciousness "of social justice and egalitarian power relations." It focuses on one of those critical, yet nearly invisible sites where the new corporate-produced kinderculture struggles daily with our society's commitment to democratic culture: news for kids.[3]

Recently a growing chorus of political, social, and educational leaders told us that we are facing a "crisis of citizenship." This is a crisis so grave, we are told, that our democratic way of life is threatened by our society's inability to instill in our young people a respect for and willingness to be engaged in the work of democracy. This threat within, we are told, is as dangerous (if not more dangerous) as the various threats our nation faces from without. And this threat emanates primarily from the wave of political apathy and cynicism that affected our children and young adults for decades. The answer, we are told, is to launch a great new movement, based primarily in our schools, to inform our children of our democratic principles and history, of their democratic responsibilities, and to inspire them to take the role of active citizens, informing themselves on the issues of the day and preparing to involve themselves in the formal and informal duties of the political process.

With declining interest in politics, with stunningly low voter participation rates, and with the growth of political cynicism among our young people, this is a powerful story and a powerful call to action. In the wake of September 11, 2001, and the "war on terrorism" declared by President George W. Bush and described by Attorney General John Ashcroft as a "long, hard slog," this "crisis" of citizenship appears even more compelling in its need to be addressed.[4]

At the same time the story leaves out at least two crucial, related questions. First, is there a crisis of citizenship and, if so, what kind of citizenship are we talking about? Political leaders, think tank directors, and political scientists bemoan the growing lack of knowledge about current events and democratic principles and institutions, as well as the lack of interest or participation in the formal political process. At the same time they are forced to admit that there are many indications of a growing willingness among youth to get involved in helping their communities through volunteerism, as long as they steer clear of the formal political system. And there is mostly silence on what to make of the growing participation of U.S. youth in the antiglobalization movement ignited in the 1999 Seattle protests against the World Trade Organization that has moved back and forth across the nation and around the world. While this movement appeared to recede after September 11, by late 2003 from Cancun, Mexico, to Miami, Florida, it was again gaining strength. This movement has been joined by protests against the strategic policy decisions of the Bush administration as it pushes forward with its domestic and international "war on terrorism." Again there is mostly silence on the meaning of this activism and its relationship to the so-called epidemic of youth political apathy. With the U.S. infrastructure for children and families in tatters, a reasonable person might ask, Could this be the "real" crisis of citizenship?

The second crucial question is, Why does this "official" story of the "crisis of citizenship" focus so heavily on the public schools, both as a cause and as a solution to civic reengagement? In the portrait of this crisis and the action to be taken to address it, where is the sustained consideration of the educational institution that easily rivals the power of schools—the media, or, more accurately, the corporate media, since nearly 99 percent of all media culture produced for and consumed by children and youth is a corporate product. This absence seems even more surprising, given that most parents and teachers understand the profound imbalance between the amount of time children spend in classrooms as contrasted with the time they spend surrounded by media culture. Even if they haven't thought through these connections in a critical fashion, they certainly experience the disproportionate amount of money spent on the seductions of media for children as compared with school funding.

Putting these two questions together, the focus of this chapter is straightforward: When we look at the growing presence of corporate media culture in our children's everyday life, what effect is this likely to have on their civic health? Can corporate media help parents and educators raise healthy democratic citizens? And more specifically, what vision of citizenship and democracy is encouraged by corporate-produced "news for kids," which young people are most likely to see in their schools? To answer these questions, the cultural pedagogy approach directs us to look not only at selected examples of the world of news produced for kids but also the corporate media world from which kids piece together their understanding of power, politics, democracy, and citizenship.

WHICH CRISIS OF CITIZENSHIP?

Early in the fall of 2002, President George W. Bush, standing in the White House Rose Garden, said, "Ignorance of American history and civics weakens our sense of citizenship."[5] Citing "disturbing gaps" in students' knowledge of history, from a fifth of high school seniors believing Germany was an ally of the United States in World War II to nearly a third of eighth graders not knowing why the Civil War was fought, the president said this is more than an "academic failure. . . . To be an American," he said, "is not just a matter of blood or birth; we are bound by ideals, and our children must know those ideals."

To follow through on this call to reignite a sense of civic engagement in our schools, the president announced three initiatives: a small program to provide seminars and lectures for teachers and an essay contest focused on the principles and ideals of America; the convening of a White House forum on American history, civics, and service; and the Our Documents project created to make key historical documents available on the Internet, along with lesson plans, competitions, and discussions.

Even as the president spoke, a "Declaration of Independence road trip" had been under way since summer, bringing an original copy of the declaration to museums across the country for viewing by citizens. The cochairs of the nonprofit project were former Presidents Jimmy Carter and Gerald Ford. The primary corporate sponsor was the antilabor building supply chain Home Depot.[6]

While some might find these actions weak, underfunded, and conflicted in terms of inspiring a new sense of civic awareness, commitment, and action, the president's words gave added weight to the growing sense of unease among those concerned with increasing political apathy and cynicism among young people. While these concerns were expressed with growing frequency for more than a decade, September 11 added urgency to their message.

In November 2001, in the immediate aftermath of 9/11, the report *From Inspiration to Participation: A Review of Perspectives on Youth Civic Engagement* was released by a consortium of foundations concerned with community and national service.[7] The Center for Information and Research on Civic Learning and Engagement (CIRCLE) released its most recent report, *The Civic and Political Health of the Nation: A Generational Portrait,* in September 2002.[8] In October 2002, the Kaiser Family Foundation released its report, *A Generational Look at the Public: Politics and Policy.*[9] The Carnegie Corporation joined with CIRCLE in early 2003 to release *The Civic Mission of Schools.*[10] In September 2003, the *Education for Democracy* report was released by the Albert Shanker Institute, linking the report to the second anniversary of 9/11 and raising concerns about "what are America's students learning about our democratic values and institutions, our struggles to overcome inequality, our remarkable capacity for self-correction?"[11] These reports and surveys joined similar reports such as *A Nation of Spectators: How Civic Disengagement Weakens America and What We Can Do About It,* produced by the National Commission on Civic Renewal formed in 1998.[12] In September 2003 the first annual Congressional Conference on Civic Education was held Washington, D.C.[13]

If there isn't a crisis of citizenship, there seems to be an enormous outpouring of national concern for no reason. These various groups and their various surveys and reports identify a series of concerns about civic engagement and the quality and quantity of civic education our children are receiving in schools. And some of them offer up a set of what they claim are surefire, empirically tested methods to reinvigorate a sense of engaged citizenship among our young people that will follow them into adulthood.

But in these often bipartisan accounts of failures and solutions concerning the crisis of citizenship, what tends to be left out is the recognition that the meaning of democracy has undergone a startling transformation—under way since the end of World War II but deeply intensifying since the beginning of the 1980s. Since then there has been a significant unleashing of the powers of corporations, not only to do business but under the banner of the "free market" to do the work of democracy as well.

The corporate model emerged as the dominant metaphor to be applied to almost every aspect of U.S. culture, from government to schools, from child care to health care. The market was cast as the truest form of democratic action, where individual choice was rapidly translated into social, political, and economic outcomes. This represented a major transition from the post–World War II pluralistic vision of democracy, which viewed government as the people's referee, seeing that conflicts over social, political, and economic resources were fought in a just and equitable manner. In the new vision of democracy, substantially influenced and underwritten by neoliberal philosophy and power, the job of government is to get out of the way so that entrepreneurs are free to maximize their desires as they see fit.[14]

Looking at this transformation of the meaning of democracy from pluralism to neoliberalism, particularly over the past twenty-five years, we can find another way to characterize the "crisis of citizenship." Here the problem is less growing political apathy, cynicism, and distrust and more the growing disenfranchisement of increasing numbers of citizens from the wealth and resources produced by the work of the nation and their marginalization from the political process. There are at least two leading indicators relevant to this second view of the "crisis of citizenship," what might be called the "crisis of disempowerment," a crisis many would say was graphically illustrated in the spectacle of the 2000 presidential election.[15] These are the declining fortunes of children and families, which include the commercial invasion of public schools and public space, and the growing conflict in the corporate media between commercial success and democratic responsibility.

The period in which this crisis of disempowerment among our youth has been growing most rapidly, roughly since the "Reagan revolution" of 1980, is also the time when the social support network for children and families in the United States has increasingly been stripped away; the gap between the rich and poor has grown at a historically unprecedented rate. Reagan viewed "big government" as responsible for most of society's ills, even viewing programs such as Medicare as, in the words of biographer Robert Dallek, "the advance wave of socialism which would invade every area of freedom in this country."[16]

Actually corporatism has turned out to be the expanding, invading force. Sylvia Hewlett and Cornel West have called this attack an undeclared "war against parents."[17] Henry Giroux, surveying many of the same trends, has called our current generation of young people the "abandoned generation."[18] Ezra Suleiman has called the attack "dismantling democratic states."[19] Hewlett and West, writing in 1998, and Giroux and Suleiman in 2003 detailed the extent and nature of this decades-long "war."

These attacks have come from government, with its movement away from programs committed to social justice and equity in favor of an economic and social playing field deregulated, or as media scholar Robert McChesney has put it, "reregulated" in favor of wealth and corporate power. The attacks have come from the corporate sector itself, valuing short-term gain over social or community responsibility, undermining wages and benefits, and increasing job insecurity. And they have come from a corporate media that tends to celebrate the neoliberal economics and politics of the enduring "Reagan revolution" from which they have benefited enormously or celebrate the amnesia of fantasies of escape from and violent revenge against simplistic images of power, authority, and evil—from which they have also benefited enormously.

Surprisingly, these on-the-ground accounts of social, political, and economic attacks on youth and families failed to be addressed or incorporated into the outcries of the citizenship crisis papers and reports mentioned above.

Many of the problems of civic disengagement detailed in the crisis of citizenship movement tend to ignore this transformed democratic landscape, neglecting the connection between the outcome of the new vision of neoliberal democracy inaugurated under Reagan and carried to nearly frenzied fruition under the George W. Bush administration. Instead they have tended to focus on factors such as decontextualized aspects of educational policy and vague calls to civic responsibility. And yet none of these reports issue a call to name this new model of democracy nor, for the most part, question its basic premises as to whether or not this is the model of democracy the majority of citizens want to work to carry forward.

In certain reports, such as *The Civic Mission of the Schools,* the criteria of citizenship they advocate includes what many consider the building blocks of a more participatory model of democracy. Competent and responsible citizens, the report states:

1. [Are] informed and thoughtful; have a grasp and appreciation of history and the fundamental processes of American democracy; have an understanding and awareness of public and community issues; and have the ability to obtain information, think critically and enter into dialog among others with different perspectives
2. Participate in their communities through membership in or contributions to organizations working to address an array of cultural, social, political, and religious interests and beliefs
3. Act politically by having the skills, knowledge, and commitment needed to accomplish pubic purposes, such as group problem solving, public speaking, petitioning and protesting, and voting
4. Have moral and civic virtues such as concern for the rights and welfare of others, social responsibility, tolerance and respect, and the belief in the capacity to make a difference[20]

These criteria recognize or at least give a nod to the deep interdependence of citizens, the need for a critically informed and active citizenry, the need for equity, and the need for economic as well as social justice. However, the National Standards for Civics and Government (NSCG), adopted in 1994 by the Center for Civic Education and held by many mainstream civic education organizations as the benchmarks for national civic education initiatives, have been harshly criticized.[21] For instance, political scientist Richard Merelman reviewed the CIVITAS curriculum, which was produced by the Center for Civic Education in an effort to put the NSCG into practice. What Merelman found are national civics standards that "emphasize shared political values over political participation; oversimplify the relationships between

American political values; assert a highly contestable function (cohesion) for shared values; and rely mainly upon elite statements to identify these political values." Merelman labels this the symbolic model of civic education, attuned to reassuring political elites that "something is being done" to meet the "crisis of citizenship" without actually encouraging any fundamental change.[22]

And while the debate goes on over the crisis of citizenship, and initiatives are proposed and underfunded (like the No Child Left Behind Act of 2001) or not funded at all, the neoliberal assault on government has worked its way down to the state level, leaving state governments reeling from lost federal revenue and lost state taxes from corporations and higher-income taxpayers.[23] The spring of 2003 was a fiscal disaster for nearly every state in the union, a disaster years in the making but dramatically intensified by the collapse of the stock market in 2000–2002. Defunded school systems continued to be forced into "partnerships" with businesses and corporations, the same groups who successfully lobbied to decrease their support of state and federal government, continuing and intensifying the invasion of public schools by commercial interests.[24]

When we turn to the second indicator of the "crisis of disempowerment" driven by the neoliberal turn in U.S. democracy—the growing conflict in the corporate media between commercial success and democratic responsibility—we find another neglected, yet critical context for the consideration of the "crisis of citizenship."

In the entertainment media industry there never was much of a conflict in the first place. After all, the chores of public service, always viewed as money losers, were largely carried by the broadcasting networks' news divisions and taxpayers through the government-funded public broadcasting system. They were the ones expected to carry the major burden of democratic responsibility for the media industry.

But then in 1976 CBS network's weekly newsmagazine *60 Minutes* showed up in the top ten television ratings. The idea that news programs could make money instead of losing money launched a wave of corporate media activism that continues up to the present. News divisions were expected to operate with the same profit projections as the entertainment side of the media industry. The result was the rapid closure or downsizing of unprofitable news ventures, such as foreign news bureaus and investigative reporting, and the rise of copycat cheap news production such as the wild proliferation of the news magazine format in the 1980s, which morphed into the reality shows of the 1980s and 1990s. Celebrity journalism was in. Sensational journalism was in. Government bashing, in line with the neoliberal politics of the period, was in. Corporate watchdogging was out.[25]

In 1984, with the neoliberal philosophy of democracy firmly entrenched in Washington, D.C., the media industry joined other corporate sectors in having its wish list satisfied. Mark Fowler, the Reagan-appointed chair of the Federal Communications Commission (FCC), led the charge to deregulate broadcasting. By the end of 1984 the FCC had (1) increased the number of radio and television stations that a company could own nationally from seven to twelve of each; (2) exempted radio and television stations from government-imposed limitations on the number and extent of commercials during a given hour; (3) eliminated the requirement that broadcasters carry a certain amount of public service broadcasting and provide a minimum amount of educational material for children; (4) extended license renewal periods from three to five years while eliminating requirements to keep program logs and financial records for public inspection or FCC ascertainment for license renewal, which would presumably be automatic in the future; (5) exempted broadcasters from the requirement that they own a television station three years before selling it, thus triggering mergers and takeovers among television stations; and (6) promoted the deregulation of cable. The FCC later eliminated the Fairness Doctrine, which mandated that television networks present a diversity of controversial issues of public importance. Also eliminated was the equal-time rule, which stipulated that opposing sides would be fairly treated; that is, representatives of different positions would be allowed to express their opinions, and qualified candidates for public office be permitted to answer opponents.[26]

In November, Reagan signed the Cable Television Act of 1984, advocated by the FCC and passed by Congress, which virtually deregulated the cable industry.

While various provisions and aspects of these actions were fought or challenged, almost all of them were upheld and then further radicalized, particularly with the Telecommunications Act of 1996 and the FCC Ownership Rules issued in mid-2003 to further weaken ownership regulations pertaining to the communications industry. Consequently citizens of the United States were left, by the end of 2003, with seven media giants, from Time Warner to the News Corporation to Disney, controlling most of what they heard, saw, or read, and with almost no public interest mandate.

Children's advocates have fought these legislative and administrative changes to media policy in the balance between corporate profitability and democratic responsibility for decades, but with little success. The 1980s, in particular, were a disaster for children's media rights. Early in Fowler's tenure as chairman, the FCC withdrew regulations requiring broadcast stations to air educational and informational programming.[27] By the end of the decade the average number of hours of network educational programming for children had dropped from more than eleven to less than two hours per week. Limits on the number of commercials and program tie-ins to products were eliminated or minimized. As James Steyer, founder of the child advocacy group Children Now, wrote, "In a mind-boggling decision, the FCC ruled in 1985 that these toy-based TV programs were now by definition in 'the public interest' on the basis of their phenomenal sales success."[28] In 1990 Congress introduced the Children's Television Act in an effort to reimpose some minimal social responsibility on the media industry. The act, as watered-down (calling for the media to provide *some* children's programming) as it was, had to be passed over a veto from President George H. W. Bush.

So grave were the assaults on the democratic mandates of the media that in the late 1980s and early 1990s a movement, sometimes called the public journalism or civic journalism movement, came into being. This group, which organized throughout the 1990s, was composed of professional journalists and academics who argued that the transformations taking place in the media industries and the news rooms were undermining the capacity of the news media to serve democracy.[29] One group representative of this movement, the Committee of Concerned

Journalists, drafted a statement of concern in 1997, now signed by thousands of journalists from the United States and around the world. The statement begins with:

> This is a critical moment for journalism in America. While the craft in many respects has never been better consider the supply of information or the skill of reporters—there is a paradox to our communications age. Revolutionary changes in technology, in our economic structure and in our relationship with the public, are pulling journalism from its traditional moorings. As audiences fragment and our companies diversify, there is a growing debate within news organizations about our responsibilities as businesses and our responsibilities as journalists. Many journalists feel a sense of lost purpose. There is even doubt about the meaning of news, doubt evident when serious journalistic organizations drift toward opinion, infotainment and sensation out of balance with the news.[30]

Given this very brief outline of the history of the rise of the neoliberal model of democracy and its impact on the status of families and children and on the media industry, the question becomes, What vision of citizenship and democracy will we find, if any, in corporate-produced "news for kids?"

From the crisis of citizenship perspective this is a question that doesn't even bear asking. The "crisis" is a failure primarily taking place in the schools that must be addressed in the schools. Nearly every report detailing the "crisis" notes that not enough time is devoted in the classroom to "current events," meaning knowledge of timely events and debates over their significance to democracy. In addressing the political apathy and cynicism of youth, current events must be brought into the classroom in a meaningful way so that students can understand what is at stake in these events as well as their responsibilities in relationship to them.

Curiously, the word "news" is seldom used; "knowledge of current events" is the preferred phrasing in calling for links between the classroom and the world outside. The use of "current events" allows the advocates of civic education to sidestep the messy crisis of journalism—the sex, violence, sensationalism, celebrity worship, and growing economic concentration—that the word "news" calls to mind. "Current events" suggests that the teacher need only open the classroom door and allow students to peer out at an unblemished view of a blemished world. In this view, any "news" in the classroom is better than no "current events" at all. It represents either a naive vision of the politics of news or, equally likely, an unwillingness to directly challenge the corporate hegemony in the media and news businesses. To bring up-to-date news of the "war on terrorism" or the "California wildfires" into the classroom—especially in a way that fits into the grid of benchmark standards—would seem to be work enough for teachers already overburdened with narrowly defined accountability mandates—another new and disruptive assault on the classroom created as the politics and economics of neoliberalism work their way into the nooks and crannies of public life. Understanding these stories and initiating a study of the politics of news and media would seem more than any administrator could ask of a staff—especially when the critiques of news and media are likely to run parallel to the criticisms that could be leveled against the corporatization of public education and the rise of the neoliberal model of democracy.

The "crisis of empowerment" view of the crisis of citizenship suggests a very different frame of reference for considering the corporate production of news for kids. It suggests that there is an intersection in the social and economic crisis of families with the funding crisis and commercialization of schools, as well as with the corporate invasion of nearly every aspect of youth culture, including "news for kids." It requires that we carefully examine the news, not simply for its surface content but for the deeper lessons it teaches about the meaning of democracy, particularly with respect to the "free market" and for its definitions, direct and implied, about the meaning of citizenship. It also requires that we recognize, from a cultural pedagogy perspective, that youth learn as much, if not more, about what is going on from the context in which it is presented—the aspects of their experience that are engaged and the ones that are ignored, and if they are engaged, how.

From the crisis of empowerment view of the crisis of citizenship, news for kids must be viewed as yet another front in the culture war for the hearts and minds of our children, as they struggle with the postmodern avalanche of images and the hyperreality of information and symbols to understand themselves and create their own civic identities.

To begin to answer the question, What vision of citizenship and democracy will we find, if any, in corporate-produced news for kids? we need to begin mapping the current landscape of news for kids.

MAPPING THE LANDSCAPE OF NEWS FOR KIDS

What "News for Kids"?

For the most part, young people are not interested in traditional news and don't watch it. While this tends to hold true for adults as well, youth interest in news has dropped off precipitously. In 1990 the Times Mirror Center (now the Pew Research Center for the People and the Press) produced a report entitled *The Age of Indifference: A Study of Young Americans and How They View the News*.[31] The report found that young people had become significantly less interested in news in general and political news in particular and were less well-informed overall over the last twenty years.

Other reports by the Pew Research Center in 1996 and 1997 and the Center for Information and Research on Civic Learning and Engagement in 2002 confirm these trends and report them to be increasing.[32] Young people and youth are much less likely to watch television news or read a newspaper than older adults or their peers from twenty years ago. When they do watch or read, they are most likely to follow sports or entertainment news.

In one of the few studies that looked at what children have to say about news, conducted by Children Now and published in 1994, a number of surprising findings emerged.[33] Children are widely exposed to news, but not news produced for kids. In fact such a question was not even included in the study. Overall 65 percent of children reported watching television news, but this broke down to watching primarily adult local news (36 percent)—which tended to be the most violent, most sensational form of television news—and adult network news (17 percent). Nearly a third were regularly watching MTV News and television tabloid news shows. News for these youth *was* MTV—at least,

MTV "news" and the supersensational tabloids that mix fantasy, urban folklore, celebrity, and desire with selected bizarre moments of "reality." Nearly two-thirds (61 percent) saw kids their age primarily portrayed in a negative light, and 71 percent agreed that "sometimes I get sick and tired of seeing so much negative news on television. I wish they would cover more positive stories." Over 50 percent of children said they felt angry, sad, and depressed after watching the news, with nearly two-thirds of girls reporting these feelings.

If we as educators, parents, and civic leaders go looking for examples of news produced for kids in the marketplace—on the newsstands, on the broadcast networks, across the growing number of cable channels—what we find is mostly nothing.

There are no newsmagazines for young people on the newsstands. *Teen People* is available but not *Time for Kids*. *Cosmo Girl* but not *Upfront*, the newsmagazine produced jointly by the *New York Times* and Scholastic. One would be hard-pressed to find any youth television news programs on the major broadcast networks. ABC News, a division of the Disney Corporation, put up an ABC News 4 Kids Web site in 2000 but stopped updating it sometime in late 2001. In late 2003 the independent production company Kids News launched a joint venture with *Weekly Reader,* airing the weekly *Eyewitness Kids News* with an initial syndication to 150 television stations. The program carries national and local advertising and is being promoted as meeting the new, harsher FCC enforcement standard for what constitutes educational programming and as a vehicle for reaching the elusive "tweens" market demographic.

Cable television provides two programs: Nickelodeon, a subsidiary of the MTV Network, which in turn is a subsidiary of media giant Viacom, cable-casts on Sunday evening a half-hour news program, *Nick News,* and CNN, a subsidiary of Time Warner, cable-casts *CNN Student News,* a ten-minute news program at 3:00 A.M. Sunday through Thursday. While *Nick News* is considered a program for general distribution, teachers are expected to record *CNN Student News* and bring it into the classroom.

In 1989, cable companies and cable networks formed Cable in the Classroom, which represented, according to its mission statement, the cable telecommunications industry's "commitment to education—to improve teaching and learning for children in schools, at home, and in their communities. This is the only industry-wide philanthropic initiative of its kind."[34] This industry initiative claimed to be providing "free access to commercial-free, educational cable content and new technologies to 81,000 public and private schools, reaching 78 percent of K–12 students."

Critics are less enthused by the civic-minded rhetoric of the cable industry, noting that by the late 1980s a public backlash was growing to the deregulatory Cable Act of 1984. The industry felt it had to do something dramatic to bolster its public image. The programming, however, is not necessarily developed for the civic affairs needs of youth; it is simply an indexing of programs cable channels are already producing that might be relabeled as having some educational benefit. For instance, one can visit the Cable in the Classroom Web site, www.ciconline.com, go to their search engine, and type in "school funding" between November 2000 and November 2003, searching all of the programming provided by the thirty-eight member companies, which range from A&E, to Biography, to the Discovery Channel, to Disney, to the History Channel to the Learning Channel. That search will come up with "0 matches." If one clicks on the "other recommended sites" for this keyword search, the first five that appear are "Reducing School Shootings," "Reducing School Violence," "Murder in Another School," and "Dinosaur Halls: Elementary School Teacher's Guide" (listed twice). On the other hand, if one searches for "Ronald Reagan" for the same period, ten program listings are identified.

The Internet provides a somewhat different picture of news sources produced for kids. If one searches for "news for kids" using the Yahoo! search engine, one finds a category heading by the same name that lists thirteen featured Web sites, most linked to news magazines or video news programs, and links to other children's media, including magazines, radio programs, television programs, and a "media awareness site." In the magazine section, nine magazines are listed as most popular, with *Time for Kids* representing the only public affairs magazine. Number one is *Sports Illustrated for Kids*.

If we put together young people's lack of attention and interest in public affairs programming with the lack of easily available public affairs information production for youth by traditional news vendors, we can make two important observations. The first, mentioned above, is that this information is not only hard for students to find but is also nearly invisible to parents and other adults. The second is that the classroom and the Internet are the real pipelines for the distribution of news expressly produced for young people.

What these observations suggest for this discussion of kids, news, and citizenship is that the "crisis of citizenship" view, with its emphasis on addressing the crisis in the schools through bringing "current events" into the classroom, appears to be a positive contribution to the job of civic reengagement. On the other hand the findings can also be read, from the "crisis of empowerment" perspective, to indicate that the corporate news media is neglecting the work of providing meaningful and appropriate programming, particularly public affairs programming, to children.

The corporate media industry has been historically criticized for writing off children and the youth market because their demographics don't fit with their profit maximizing strategies. Cable has dramatically changed this equation by allowing the media industry to go after distinct niche markets. The rise and success of the Fox Network seems to prove that both the multibillion dollar youth market and the media industry's interest in that market have also substantially changed.

What kinds of programming has this new attention from the networks, the cable channels, and independents brought to the youth audience? A proliferation of quality children's programming that includes appropriate public affairs content, or child-pandering, low-quality, high "wow!" value images and stories? From a crisis of empowerment perspective, two key questions emerge. First, if the schools have emerged as the last best place to reach youth with critical public affairs programming, is this due to a market failure on the part of corporate media in providing this material outside of the classroom? Second, if the corporate media are failing children in providing appropriate current events knowledge outside of the classroom, why should we expect them to provide this material inside the classroom?

Civics Lessons from Corporate News

When we look at the growing presence of corporate media culture in our children's everyday lives, what effect is this likely to have on their civic health? Can multinational corporate media help parents and educators raise healthy democratic citizens? And more specifically, what vision of citizenship and democracy is encouraged by corporate-produced news for kids, the only news that young people are likely to see in their schools?

LESSONS FROM THE CORPORATE STRUCTURE OF KIDS' NEWS PROVIDERS

In its present form, the news is not good. Corporations have actively lobbied for the creation of a neoliberal model of democracy and have benefited enormously from its realization. Neoliberal politics and economics unleashed these media corporations to force open the doors of the public schools to corporate entrepreneurship, where they discovered the commodity value of the hearts, minds, and pocketbooks of children. These forces do not offer fertile grounds for imagining or advocating for a new vision of participatory democracy and active citizenship celebrating social and economic interdependence and social justice.

Clearly the idea of producing news is a small piece of the media industry market and is primarily an avenue to direct wayward audience members back to the more profitable domains of entertainment and escapist marketing. For corporations like Scholastic, the last decades have made it very clear that product marketing and in-school educational marketing are more lucrative business strategies than the production of news stories for fifth graders about problem pets. It is good business sense to keep these two enterprises linked in the minds of the civic and educational community.

At another level a lesson for youth is conveyed by the organizational structure of these news programs for kids and how they fit into the larger marketing and promotional webs of the parent companies. News and advertising/marketing go together as part of the postmodern media landscape. News about social responsibility, social and moral interdependence, and the fulfillment of respectful and caring human dialogue will always have a hard time competing against the morally and developmentally regressive seductions of immediate, self-indulgent gratification. More pictures and stories of starving babies from Africa versus a hair shampoo that promises something like an orgasm. Decades ago Marshall McLuhan recognized this postmodern twist on the news. To understand the phenomenon of modern news, he argued, is to recognize that both news and advertising are part of the news system. The "news" news is always bad. The "good news" can always be found in the accompanying ads. News produced in a commercial environment is always about consuming, not citizenship.

THE NEWS THAT'S NOT THERE

An examination of the specific content of news stories, news programs, news magazines, news Web sites, and the links between these news products and corporate empires is beyond the scope of this chapter. However, I will offer a few suggestive observations. In the many rousing calls to civic reengagement much is made about the need to provide youth with current events knowledge relevant to their immediate circumstances and experience. Taking this as a cue, one would expect news produced for kids to undertake a sustained examination of issues like school funding (No Child Left Behind Act), child poverty (debate over child tax credits for the working poor), health care for children and families, the wealth gap, the impact of globalization on the kinds and quality of jobs that will be available to them when they enter the workforce, and so on. In the argument developed in this chapter, little could be more relevant than understanding the transformations of democracy now under way and how they will affect the life chances of young people for decades to come. Thoughtful examinations of the rise of neoliberal democracy, the growing power of corporations, the success or lack of success of globalization for average U.S. citizens (as well as citizens of the world), and the status of media concentration in the United States are topics of critical concern to be addressed directly or in relationship to the various issues of the day, from campaign finance laws, the "war on terrorism," corporate wrongdoing—from cooking the books to manipulating energy prices and supplies to profiteering while ignoring employee and investor interests.

As mentioned earlier, in doing a search for "school funding" on the Cable in the Classroom site, representing 39 cable networks and 8,500 cable companies, the result was "0" hits. If we look at some of the top news sites, the results are fairly consistent.

A search of the Channel One site for "school funding" turned up one story that addressed the school-funding crisis in Oklahoma. The story had not been featured on a regular Channel One program. It was a student e-mail posting in the student exchange section. The story provided the only detailed description of the suffering being experienced by students and school districts across the nation. The student concluded, "One of the few pieces of proposed legislation that directly benefits education funding is a lottery. It is currently being debated by the Oklahoma Legislature, and will go to a popular vote later this year."[35] On the same page as the posting were two advertisements, an antidrug ad and an ad for *Surfing* magazine. There were also links to the day's top stories: A salute to the Wright Brothers, FDA approves an obesity drug for teens, *Lord of the Rings* fans brave movie marathon, and President Bush signs an antispamming bill.

A search for "child care" pulled up seven hits. The most closely related to the issue of child care were a story about a foster mother being arraigned for leaving two small boys to die in a sweltering SUV while she worked in a nearby day care center; schools being forced to move to a four-day week; and teens becoming more cynical about politics due to the California recall carnival.

The *Time for Kids* Web site fared about as well. No hits for "school funding." A search for "child care" turned up one seven-year-old article, "Welfare: Can We Make it Work?" "Children's tax credit" turned up no hits. Same for "media concentration" and "media ownership." Same for "sweatshops." "Child poverty" brought one hit. With the rates of children living in poverty in the United States on the rise since 2001, the only story posted was "First Ladies Fight Poverty," which focused on the efforts of "twenty-two first ladies from North, Central and South

America" promising to fight child poverty. The story was five paragraphs long, with most of the detailed information focusing on Mexico.[36] A search for "Britney Spears" turned up nearly forty hits.

And so on.

A BIT OF GOOD NEWS FROM THE PUBLIC SECTOR

Turning away from the blockbuster producers of youth news, Channel One, Scholastic, and *Time for Kids,* with their giant corporate parents and their student audiences that run into the millions, we find some encouraging news. Financially beleaguered PBS has managed to maintain the production of three important news series, all of them for adults, but all of them providing support resources for teachers and older students online: *The NewsHour with Jim Lehrer* with its Extra: News for Students, *Frontline* with Frontline's Teacher Center, and *Now with Bill Moyers* with its For Educators. In addition the PBS site maintains TeacherSource, a searchable database that provides content and lesson plans based on materials from hundreds of stand-alone documentaries and series aired on the network.[37]

PBS in general and *Newshour* in particular have come under increasing criticism as the double-edged assault by neoliberal ideology and market forces continues to transform their organizational structure, funding, and programming. Nevertheless, a search of *NewsHour*'s Extra: News for Students turns up thoughtful information on the No Child Left Behind Act, the debate over tax credits for the children of the working poor, and discussions of the growing gap between the rich and the poor. *Frontline*'s Teacher Center provides powerful resources on marketing to teenagers, growing media concentration, critical examinations of the two wars against Iraq, and so on. One can even find sophisticated examinations of the neoliberal challenge of privatizing the public schools, with documentaries and resources entitled *The Battle Over School Choice, Testing Our Schools,* and *Public Schools, Inc.*[38]

On the *Now with Bill Moyers* site one can even find, under For Educators, a lesson plan entitled "Corporate Governance," which addresses Standard 31 of the U.S. History Standards requiring that every student "understands social and cultural developments in the United States."[39] It addresses Benchmark 1 of Level IV: Understands how changes in the national and global economy have influenced the workplace (e.g., sluggishness in the overall rate of economic growth, the relative stagnation of wages since 1973, the social and political impact of an increase in income disparities, the effects of increased global trade and competition on the U.S. economy, the influence of new technology on education and learning, and the relation between education and earnings in the workplace).

This lesson plan and the additional materials from Bill Moyer's *Now* series provide sophisticated, contextual material on the critical tension between democracy and capitalism. At the same time, the site and resources provide a wealth of information for middle and high school students starting to develop a sophisticated understanding of the form of democracy currently in ascendance in the United States, as well as its shortfalls in terms of the promise of a participatory model of democracy. At the same time, and a search for "neoliberalism" on the entire PBS site turned up only two hits, and a search for "neoconservatism" turned up only three hits. For someone searching to understand the meaning of either term and its relationship to the new vision of democracy operating in the United States, there was only one link to relevant additional information, the neoconservative Irving Kristol's book, *Neoconservatism: The History of an Idea*.

The vocabulary to think, much less to think critically, about the conflicting models of democracy seems to have been erased from the press as a public forum. And it must be remembered that these small outposts which are producing news for youth provide the most rudimentary materials of history, ideas, and evidence for piecing together a critical consciousness. And they are under siege.

The Corporation for Public Broadcasting and the Public Broadcasting System were created under the Public Broadcasting Act of 1967 and have, for the most part, been under withering attack from conservatives and neoliberals ever since. In the early 1970s President Richard Nixon went after its federal funding base out of sheer outrage over its critical documentaries and reporting of the Vietnam War. These attacks had a substantial chilling effect on the political substance of the system for the remainder of the decade. In the early 1980s President Ronald Reagan, drawing on public broadcasting's fearful turn to depoliticized high culture, went after its federal funding base drawing on a twisted sense of populist rhetoric—why should the federal government subsidize a programming system that produced classical music concerts, operas, and ballets that only the rich cared about or watched?

This set the stage for the rise of the more sophisticated, long-running, and aggressive neoliberal critique. As Milton Friedman, the Nobel Prize–winning economist who has championed capitalism over democracy for nearly thirty years, said, public broadcasting is yet another area of public life that must be subjected to "market discipline."[40] The effect of these attacks has been to force the Corporation for Public Broadcasting and its state affiliates into closer relationships with corporate partners and to operate like commercial stations to garner audiences with the right demographics to allow them to survive with shrinking federal and state support.

Whether you call it ironic or an enormously successful propaganda coup, the structural, political, and economic forces transforming the current meaning of democracy remain for the most part unnamed. Even a television news program such as *Now with Bill Moyers*, which has done an outstanding job of criticizing the debilitating effects of the neoliberal attack on social justice, has failed to give a name to this antidemocratic model of democracy or to name a more progressive alternative. The same word, "democracy," is used for all stripes and colors of democratic philosophy, leaving citizens bewildered, cynical, and frustrated.

CORPORATE NEWS, CORPORATE SCHOOLS, AND RECLAIMING A DEMOCRACY OF THE PEOPLE

Can corporate news produced for students help regenerate an active, critically engaged citizenry? Can corporate news produced for students invigorate a positive and joyful sense of civic interdependence as opposed to a "survivor" mentality marked by a strange mix of hedonism and fear—a materially based sense of self and consumer desire? This survey of sources of news for kids makes it seem unlikely. Corporate news producers teamed up with corporate marketers, often part of the same corporation, have little to gain from making visible, much less questioning or challenging, the sea changes in the meaning of democracy that have taken place in the past twenty years. Currently corporate news for children is calculated to maintain, if not intensify, the belief among young people that politics is a place where only elites and corporations are major players. Civic ambitions are the dreams of losers. Better to collapse into slacker cynicism, become a "survivor" by adopting a combination social Darwinism/hit-the-jackpot view of entertainment and reality or become a neighborhood volunteer, doing critically needed social service but without a sense of the larger social and economic forces that created the need for social services in the first place.

What's a teacher, civic educator, or parent activist to do? First and foremost it is essential that we fight for and recover a language of democracy that enables us to recognize the historic struggles over what democracy should mean, could mean, and has come to mean. The story of democracy told in our schools, news media, and entertainment media greatly resembles religious fundamentalism. It is a story told to justify the present, not to explain the past or open up our imaginations to future possibilities. Our youth, as well as the public as a whole, need to have in their vocabulary the words that name the political and economic philosophies driving the battles over what democracy will mean tomorrow: neoliberalism, neoconservatism, participatory, strong, communitarian, and so on. The popular qualifiers of left versus right, democratic versus republican, and liberal versus conservative have become ideological distractions rather than useful categories helpful to understanding the national and international political and economic battles of our times. The word "democracy" has become dangerously empty and must be recharged with meaning. In the United States we increasingly live in a corporate state for which we have no name.

Second, the intersection of media power and political power and economic power must be a critical focus of any civic education curriculum. The corporate journalism we see, or as adults actually see very little of, in our schools is not so very different than the corporate journalism that surrounds the shrinking population of adults who follow the news. It is not journalism in the service of civic empowerment. It is, for the most part, infotainment in the service of a marketing system of growing complexity, sophistication, and effectiveness. As mainstream media icon Walter Cronkite put it, "I've been increasingly and publicly critical of the direction that journalism has taken of late, and of the impact on democratic discourse and principles. Like you, I'm deeply concerned about the merger mania that has swept our industry, diluting standards, dumbing down the news, and making the bottom line sometimes seem like the only line. It isn't and it shouldn't be."[41]

Many other journalists, including Bill Moyers, have also weighed in as advocates of participatory over neoliberal news reporting. Yet today, despite plenty of lip service on every ritual occasion to freedom of the press, radio, and TV, three powerful forces are undermining that freedom, damming the streams of significant public interest news that irrigate and nourish the flowering of self-determination. The first is the centuries-old reluctance of governments—even elected governments—to operate in the sunshine of disclosure and criticism. The second is more subtle: the tendency of media giants, operating on big business principles, to exalt commercial values at the expense of democratic values, running what Edward R. Murrow forty-five years ago called broadcasting's "money-making machine" at full throttle.

Add to that the censorship by omission of consolidated media empires digesting the bones of swallowed independents, and you've got a major shrinkage of the crucial information that thinking citizens need to act on. Regulators and regulated, media and government are supposed to keep a wary eye on each other, preserving the checks and balances that form the bulwark of our constitutional order.

What would happen if the contending giants of big government and big publishing and broadcasting joined hands and made the public's need for news secondary to free market economics? That's exactly what's happening now under the ideological banner of deregulation.[42]

Civic education and current events education that do not take media power as a crucial component for understanding the intersection of identity, politics, economics, and desire have completely missed the significance of our postmodern historical moment. It is not education but indoctrination.

Finally, the challenge that the neoliberal model of democracy poses to the fundamental idea of the "public" and the "public sphere" must be fully and carefully explored in the schools and in the media and challenged as necessary. For a democracy to exist, to maintain and recreate itself, not just as an abstract and symbolic idea but as an operating principle of self-government, there must be a place where the people can come together and form themselves as a public capable of self-rule. These free spaces, outside of the formal boundaries of government institutions and the grind of economic roles and relationships, are where we develop our civic identities and our capacities for dialogue, debate, critical reflection, mutual appreciation, toleration, self-rule, and justice. While these encounters can happen in many places, from volunteer organizations to churches to neighbor associations, two critical sites for the development of this sense of civic identity have been our public schools and our public media, and our media committed to the public good. In corporate kinderculture these two critical sites are rapidly being undermined as fertile ground for a public consciousness.

Corporate kinderculture inside and outside of the classroom has contributed to a crisis of citizenship. This crisis needs to be understood more fully in terms of its connection to the transformations of democracy, to the corporate assault on public education and public forms of communication. Both the civic education movement and the defenders of public education need to question the neoliberal model of democracy and refuse to allow the corporate news media to be the watchdog over corporate excess and public interests. Action can and must be taken in the classroom every day and at the level of policymaking. The struggle for current events knowledge that takes into account the ongoing war against children is central to creating a kinderculture that will make a participatory democratic future possible.

Chapter 4

MCDONALD'S, POWER, AND CHILDREN: RONALD MCDONALD/ RAY KROC DOES IT ALL FOR YOU

Joe L. Kincheloe

IN HIS BOOK *The Hawkline Monster: A Gothic Western*, the late Richard Brautigan develops the character of Cameron:

> Cameron was a counter. He vomited nineteen times on his way to San Francisco. He liked to count everything that he did. This had made Greer a little nervous when he first met up with Cameron years ago, but he'd gotten used to it by now.
>
> People would sometimes wonder what Cameron was doing and Greer would say, "He's counting something," and people would ask, "What's he counting?" and Greer would say, "What difference does it make?" and the people would say, "Oh."
>
> People usually wouldn't go into it any further because Greer and Cameron were very self-assured in that big relaxed casual kind of way that makes people nervous now. (Brautigan 1974, 11)

I can relate to Cameron, for I too am a counter. McDonald's is also a counter—and like the people who noticed Cameron's peculiar proclivity, most Americans don't go very far in analyzing McDonald's propensity for counting or, for that matter, anything else about the fast food behemoth. Like Greer and Cameron, McDonald's self-assurance (i.e., power) must make people a little nervous.

I was destined to write about McDonald's, for my life has always intersected with the golden arches. As part of my undergraduate comedy shtick, I told my listeners (truthfully) that I had consumed 6,000 McDonald's hamburgers before graduating from high school. In junior high and high school we were allowed to go off campus to eat. My friends and I (before we had driver's licenses) would tromp through the Tennessee woods rain or shine to McDonaldland; in high school we drove. After six years of three-hamburger lunches, not to mention three more on Wednesday nights with my parents and several on weekend nights after cruising with friends, the count began to mount. A secondary bonus for my fifteen-cent burgermania involved the opportunity to count my cholesterol numbers as they crept higher and higher. Ray Kroc, the man who made McDonald's a household name, would have been proud.

Somewhere in my small-town-Tennessee adolescent consciousness, I understood that McDonald's was the future. I couldn't name it, but the standardized hamburger was a symbol of some vague social phenomenon. Like Italian or Polish immigrants of another place and time, I was ethnic (hillbilly). And like all children of traditional ethnic parents, I struggled for an American identity free from the taint of ethnicity. Though it hadn't yet assumed the mantle of All-American symbol around the world, I knew that McDonald's of the early 1960s was mainstream American through and through. As such, my participation in the burger–fries ritual was an act of shedding my ethnic identity. Understanding McDonald's regulation of customer behavior, I complied readily, knowing the menu in advance and placing my order quickly and accurately. My parents, on the other hand, raised in the rural South of the early twentieth century, were lost at the ordering counter—lost in the Hamburger Patch. Never understanding the menu, always unsure of the expected behavior, they frustrated the effort to shape their customer conduct.

On a very different level, however, my parents were seduced by McDonald's. Students of media have come to understand that individuals' readings of film, TV, and TV commercials is idiosyncratic, differing significantly from individual to individual. So it was in my home. As victims of the Great Depression in southern Appalachia (a double economic whammy), my mother and father came to see excessive spending as a moral weakness. Eating out, when it was possible to prepare food at home, was especially depraved. My father would darken the door of McDonald's only if he was convinced of its economic "good sense." Indeed, advertisers struck an emotional chord when they pitted McDonald's fifteen-cent hamburgers and twelve-cent french fries as an alternative to the extravagant cost of eating out. To my self-identified working-class father, eating McDonald's was an act of class resistance. He never really cared much for the food—he would rather eat my mother's country ham and cornbread. But as we McDined, he spoke with great enthusiasm about how McDonald's beat the price of other burgers around town by fifty or sixty cents. Such statistics made him very happy.

Like others in peculiar social spaces around the world, my father consumed a democratic egalitarian ethos. French teenagers accustomed to the bourgeois stuffiness of French restaurants could have identified with my father's class-resistant consumption, as they revel in the informality and freedom of McDonald's "American atmosphere." The inexpensive fare, the informal dress, the loud talk are class signifiers (Leidner 1993). Such coding is ironic in light of McDonald's rightwing political history, its manipulations of labor, and its cutthroat competition with other fast food enterprises. That McDonald's continues to maintain an egalitarian image is testimony to the power and expertise of its public relations strategists. And here we find the major questions raised by this chapter: What is the nature of these PR strategies? What do they tell us about McDonald's? And how do they affect American culture—particularly its kinderculture?

SHAPING CULTURE, SHAPING CONSCIOUSNESS

Few Americans think about efforts by powerful interests in the larger society to regulate populations to bring about desired behaviors. In

America and other Western societies political domination shifted decades ago from police or military force to cultural messages. Such communications are designed to win the approval or consent of citizens for actions taken by power elites (Giroux 1988). The contributors to this book in their own ways are involved in efforts to expose the specifics of this process of cultural domination (often labeled hegemony). The process takes place in the everyday experience of our lives. The messages are not sent by a clandestine group of conspirators or devised by some secret ministry of propaganda; neither are they read by everyone in the same way. But some people understand their manipulative intent and rebel against their authority (Goldman 1992). The company's role in these power dynamics illustrates the larger process. If any organization has the power to help shape the lives of children, it is McDonald's.

The construction of who we are and what we believe cannot be separated from the workings of power. Americans don't talk much about power; American politicians don't even talk about power. When power is broached in mainstream sociology, the conversation revolves around either the macro level, the political relations of governments, nor the micro level, the personal relations between two people (Abercrombie 1994). Power, as the term is used in this essay, is neither macro nor micro, nor does it rely on legality or coercion. Power, as it has evolved in the first decade of the twenty-first century, maintains its legitimacy in subtle and effective ways.

Consider the power generated by McDonald's use of the media to define itself not simply as an American institution but as America itself. As the "land we love" writ small, McDonald's attaches itself to American patriotism and the cultural dynamics it involves. Ray Kroc understood from the beginning that he was not simply selling hamburgers—he was selling America a vision of itself (Luxenberg 1985). From the All-American marching band to the All-American basketball and football teams to the All-American meal served by All-American boys and girls, the All-American of the Year, Ray Kroc, labored to connect the American signifier to McDonald's. The American flag will fly twenty-four hours a day at McDonald's, he demanded. Using the flag as a backdrop for the hamburger count, Kroc watched the burger numbers supplant the Dow Jones closing average as the symbolic statistical index for America's economic health. In the late 1960s and early 1970s, Kroc saw the perpetually flying flag as a statement to the war protesters and civil rights "kooks" that McDonald's (America) would not stand for anyone criticizing or attempting to undermine "our" country (Kroc 1977).

One of the reasons Americans don't talk much about power is that it works in a subtle, hard-to-define manner. Ask Americans how McDonald's has shaped them or constructed their consciousness, and you'll draw blank stares. What does it mean to argue that power involves the ability to ascribe meanings to various features of our lives? Return to the McDonald's All-American ad campaign. Kroc and the McDonald's management sanctioned the costliest, most ambitious ad campaign in American corporate history (Boas and Chain 1976). All this money and effort were expended to imbue the hamburger—the McDonald's variety in particular—with a star-spangled signification. And it worked in the sense that Americans and individuals around the world began to make the desired connection. Described as the "ultimate icon of Americana," a "cathedral of consumption" where Americans practice their "consumer religion," McDonald's, like Disneyland, transcends status as mere business establishment (Ritzer 1993). When McDonald's or Disney speak, they speak for all of us. How could the Big Mac or Pirates of the Caribbean mislead us? They are us.

Just as Americans saw mystical implications in Thomas Jefferson and John Addams both dying on July 4, 1826—the fiftieth anniversary of the Declaration of Independence—contemporary Americans may see mystical ramifications in the fact that Ray Kroc and Walt Disney were in the same company in the U.S. Army. Having lied about their age, the two prophets of free enterprise-grounded utopian Americana fought the good fight for the American way. It takes nothing away from the mystery to know that Kroc described Disney as a "strange duck" (Donald? Uncle Scrooge? Daisy?) because he wouldn't chase girls (Kroc 1977).

No expenses were spared, no signifiers were left floating freely in the grand effort to transfer reverence for America to McDonald's. The middle-class cathedral was decorated as a shrine with the obligatory plastic eagle replete with powerful wings and glazed, piercing eyes. A banner held in the bald eagle's beak reads "McDonald's: The American Way" (Boas and Chain 1976). These legitimation signifiers work best when they go unnoticed, as they effectively connect an organization's economic power to acquire property, lobby Congress, hire lawyers, and so on to its power to ascribe meaning and persuade. In the process the legitimated organization gains the power to create and transmit a view of reality that is consonant with its larger interests—American economic superiority as the direct result of an unbridled free enterprise system.

A recent ad campaign paints a nostalgic, sentimentalized, conflict-free American family pictorial history. The purpose of the ad is to forge an even deeper connection between McDonald's and America by creating an American historical role for McDonald's where none ever existed. You can almost hear the male voice-over: "Though we didn't yet exist, we were there to do it all for you—McDonald's then, McDonald's now." We're all one big, happy family with the same (European?) roots. "We" becomes McDonald's and America—"our" family (Goldman 1992). The only thing left to buttress the All-American image would be a Santa Claus connection. Kroc's PR men quickly made their move, inducing Kroc himself to distribute hamburgers to Chicago's street corner Santa Clauses and Salvation Army workers. Newspapers noticed the event and, to Kroc's delight, linked Santa Claus to a chauffeur named McDonald's. The legend grew when the PR men circulated a story about a child who was asked where Santa had met Mrs. Santa. "At McDonald's," the child reportedly said. Wire services picked up the anecdote, sending it to every town in the country (Boas and Chain 1976). Big ad campaigns or bogus anecdotes, McDonald's has used the media to create an American mythology.

Like other giant international corporations of the contemporary era, McDonald's has used the media to invade the most private spheres of our everyday lives. Our national identifications, desires, and human needs have been commodified—appropriated for the purposes of commerce (Giroux 1994; Kellner 1992). Such media usage grants producers a level of access to human consciousness never imagined by the most powerful dictator. Such power is illustrated in the resistance Mc-

Donald's elicits as signifier for America. Time and time again in Mc-Donald's brief history, neighborhood organizers have reacted to the firm's efforts to enter their communities. Seeing McDonald's as a form of cultural colonization that overwhelms locally owned businesses and devours local culture, individuals have fought to keep McDonald's out. In the 1970s opposition became so intense in New York City that Kroc ordered high walls built around construction sites to keep them hidden from local residents. At the same time in Sweden, radicals bombed two restaurants in hopes of thwarting "creeping American cultural imperialism" (Boas and Chain 1976). In various demonstrations against the World Trade Organization in the early years of the twenty-first century demonstrators smashed McDonald's windows and vandalized stores (Kincheloe 2002). For better and for worse, McDonald's has succeeded in positioning itself as America.

MCDONALD'S, GLOBALIZATION, AND HEGEMONY: CONSTRUCTING KINDERCULTURE

Ironically, as McDonald's became America it outgrew U.S. borders. By the last quarter of the twentieth century the golden arches represented a global enterprise. In this transnational process, the company became the symbol of Western economic development. Often McDonald's was the first foreign corporation to penetrate a particular nation's market. Indian social critic Vandana Shiva (1997) found dark humor in the symbolism of the golden arches. They induce the feeling that when you walk into McDonald's, you are entering heaven. The corporate marketers want children around the world to view the "McDonald's experience" as an immersion in celestial *jouissance*—while they are actually eating junk. In terms reminiscent of the outlook of the Pentagon in the second Iraq war, McDonald's executives refer to their movement into foreign markets as the company's "global realization" (Schlosser 2001). When statues of Lenin came down in East Germany after reunification, giant statues of Ronald McDonald took their place almost overnight. Driving through that country in the late 1990s and the first decade of the twenty-first century, I imagined cartoon bubbles coming out of each Ronald's mouth as the clown proclaimed: "No Nikita, we buried you—the West has won."

In the city of Santos, Brazil, several schoolteachers told me that they worried about the impact of McDonald's on their pupils. One teacher contended: "The danger of McDonald's imperialism is that it teaches children to devalue Brazilian things and to believe that the U.S. is superior to all of us poor South Americans." The anger these women directed at McDonald's and the company's ideological impact on Brazilian children was inscribed on each word they spoke. Western so-cieties and the United States in particular have set up this corporate colonialism via the construction of corporatized governments (Kinche-loe 1999) over the past twenty-five years. Particular types of conscious-ness are needed for such political economic reforms to work. Individuals in Brazil, Mexico, Malaysia, and the United States need to dismiss from their consciousness questions of social justice, egalitarian-ism, and environmentalism. Corporatized, globalized governments and their corporate allies need well managed, socially regulated, consump-tion-oriented children and adults who understand that economic growth demands "good business climates," antiunion perspectives, and low wages for those lower in the hierarchy.

To gain the ability to introduce these ideas to children in the United States and around the world, corporations such as McDonald's continue to refine their appeal to the affective dimension. Their ability to produce entertainment for children that adults deem inappropriate is central to this enterprise. After decades of marketing research includ-ings, over the years, Ugly Stickers, Wacky Packs, Toxic High stickers, Garbage Pail Kids, Mass Murderer cards, and McDonald's cuisine, pro-ducers of kinderculture understand part of the appeal of children's con-sumer products lies in vociferous parental disapprove of them (Spigel 1998). Indeed, the more subversive the kinderculture, the better. Schools not only ignore the power of such influences on children but have allowed McDonald's and other marketers into their hallways and classrooms (Molnar 1996; Kenway and Bullen 2001).

In addition to selling its products in schools, McDonald's has al-most unlimited ideological access to elementary and secondary students by way of such ploys as, for example, "job interview seminars." Analysis of such seminars reveals that they are less about the interviewing process and more about inculcating particular beliefs about the social benefits of McDonald's and the unregulated free enterprise system. Creating a positive affective valence with the subversive kinderculture, McDonald's goes in for the knockout punch with its ideological treatises. In my research I found that students who were savvy enough to recognize the covert ideological dimensions of McDonald's seminars and brave enough to expose them to the school community were often punished for such "misbehavior" by school officials (see Kincheloe 2002 for an expansion of this theme).

A critical pedagogy of childhood cannot ignore these political, economic, social, and ideological dynamics. It is important for children around the world to understand the ways commercially produced children's culture (Kenway and Bullen 2001) in general and the subversive kinderculture in particular wins their consent to positions that serve the interests of multinational corporations and their allies, not young people or anybody else. Children are directly affected by corporate hegemonization and globalization—forces that are central players in the social construction of childhood in hyperreality (Jans 2002). As always in discussions of these hegemonic dynamics, it is important to outline the complex issues of the production and reception of ideology. Daniel Cook (2004) offers valuable insights in this context that are important in the reading of McDonald's impact on children. Arguing that we must reject the dichotomy of the exploited child and the empowered child, Cook maintains that children are inevitably positioned in market relations and are always empowered to make decisions in this context.

Such a point resonates with what Shirley Steinberg and I argue in the introduction to this volume: Researchers of childhood must always maintain a delicate balance between structure and agency. We cannot understand contemporary childhood(s) outside of their relation to the market, and children always make decisions in this context. Importantly, they are not free to make any consumption or ideological decision they want—they must make decisions based on their social, political, economic, and cultural terrain. In the twenty-first century, that terrain cannot be understood outside of the commodification of children's culture. The market does not snatch children from the innocent garden of childhood and transform them into crazed consumers. Concurrently it does not simply have to do with providing empowerment for self-sufficient agential children. Corporate producers and marketers must be exerting economic and ideological effects by their efforts, since they keep pouring billions of dollars into advertising directed at children from New Orleans to Nigeria, from Jacksonville to Jakarta. While children construct their own meanings, the corporate culture of power does exploit them—the corporate effort to ideologically construct children's consciousness is a cold reality.

Social scholars who do not value the importance of studying the effects of dominant power on the lived world often slam more critical takes on the effects of political economic structures on the lives of children. They often interpret critical charges of ideological exploitation with the assertion that the dominant power of McDonald's, for example, produces standardized and homogenized "corporate children." (See Kincheloe 2002 for examples of this dynamic in anticritical scholarship from various disciplines.) This is not what McDonald's and other producers of kinderculture do. Producers of commercial children's culture reshape everyday places and activities in ways that resonate with corporate economic and ideological interests. In this context, as parents of young children often describe, the relationship of children to, say, eating is reconfigured as children cry out for McDonald's hamburgers. For example, as I sat in the waiting room of a doctor's office I observed a young mother of a restless, frightened six-year-old boy struggle to contain him as they waited to see a pediatrician.

> MOTHER: Would you please sit still and stop crying. Stop it! Now! I'm not going to take you to McDonald's if you don't stop it.
> CHILD: (screaming) I want to go to McDonald's. Let's go, Mommy. Please . . . let's go now. (crying) I want to go to McDonald's.
> MOTHER: I'm going to brain you. Now you just stop it.
> CHILD: I want a coke and a cheeseburger. Please (screaming) McDonald's, McDonald's, McDonald's. Cheeseburger!
> MOTHER: (slapping child's face) You're not going to McDonald's, young man.

CHILD: (louder screams and hysterical crying) McDonald's, Mc-
Donald's, McDonald's.

McDonald's advertisers have tapped into this child's affect at a level
that transcends rational understanding. In his time of stress in the pediatrician's office the little boy seeks the comfort of his provider of pleasure. I can recall a similar moment at a similar age in my own
pre-McDonald's early childhood. In seeking the comfort of food from
the stresses of the doctor's office, I begged my mother to take me home
for some of her southern fried chicken and pinto beans. But this little
boy doesn't want to go home; he wants to visit the golden arches. Reading her child's reactions, the mother appeals to the most severe threat
she can formulate in the situation—the threat of not going to McDonald's. As the child breaks free from the mother's restraint, he runs
around the waiting room screaming, crying, and flailing his arms. She
chases him for several moments, finding it difficult to corral him. Finally catching him, she carries him back screaming, crying, and flailing
to her seat. Panting for breath, she reassesses her strategy in her attempt
to get control of the situation:

> MOTHER: I'm going to buy you two cheeseburgers and one of
> them hot apple pies.
> CHILD: (immediately calmed by the prospect of consumption at
> McDonald's) You are?!
> MOTHER: Yes, and I'm going to get you some of those animal
> cookies you like. Hippo-hippo-hippopotamus.
> CHILD: I love those cookies. I LOVE THEM! Cheeseburgers and
> cheeseburgers.

Everyday places and activities have been reshaped by McDonald's
kinderculture. There are no standardization and homogenization
processes at work here. A new relationship has emerged that will be
acted on in diverse ways by differing children and parents. The complexity of the relationship between corporate producer and child consumer is so powerful that I cannot produce a final interpretation of
what this vignette means. Though meaning here is loose and slippery, it

does not mean that my readings are irrelevant. I stand ready to argue their contribution to the effort to understand McDonald's social power and resulting impact on contemporary childhood. It could be argued that the vignette is a micropolitical reflection of a new knowledge order that decenters parents' roles as the primary providers of aid and comfort to their children. It may tell us that a new set of material realities, ideological assumptions, and configurations of power have made an impact on contemporary childhood. The little boy in the doctor's office possessed a detailed, if not expert, knowledge of McDonald's product line that he had learned via TV. Such knowledge shaped his behavior and his relationship to his mother. Undoubtedly the child's cultural identifications and affect had been rerouted by corporate marketers.

Consumption and pleasure are intimately connected in the life of this young boy and millions of other children. Corporate power has entered domains of life once free from market influences. Without their conscious awareness such children may eventually find that this power and the connections it forges exert a significant impact on their life choices. Young boys in China, for example, fantasize about opening chains of McDonald's restaurants in Beijing (Yan 1997). In a communist country such dreams are ideologically significant and alter the relationship between the young boy and Chinese politics. Like the U.S. military in Vietnam and Iraq, corporations work to win the hearts and minds of young consumers; the only difference is that corporate methods are more sophisticated and work much better than the military strategies. Subtle kinderculture is amazingly intrusive, working twenty-four hours a day to colonize all dimensions of lived experience (Kenway and Bullen 2001; Cook 2004).

MCDONALD'S IS A KIDS' KIND OF PLACE: E-I-E-I-O

Contrary to the prevailing positivist wisdom, we begin to understand in more detail that childhood is not and never has been an unchanging developmental stage of humanness. Rather, it is a social and economic construction tied to prevailing perceptions of what constitutes the "natural order" (Polakow 1992). Forces such as urbanization and industrialization have exerted significant influences on the nature of childhood—as have the development of media and the techno power it produces. By "techno power" I mean the expansion of corporate influence via the use of recent technological innovation (Kellner 1989; Harvey 1989). Using techno power, corporations like McDonald's have increased their ability to maximize capital accumulation, influence social and cultural life, and even help mold children's consciousness. Since childhood is a cultural construction shaped in the contemporary era by the forces of this media-catalyzed techno power, the need for parents, teachers, and community members to study it is dramatic. Let us turn now to McDonald's and the construction of childhood in contemporary globalized society.

Even the name, "McDonald's," is kid-friendly, with its evocation of Old MacDonald and his farm—E-I-E-I-O. The safety of McDonald's provides asylum, if not utopian refuge, from the kid-unfriendly contemporary world of child abuse, broken homes, and child-napping. Offering something better to escape into, McDonald's TV depiction of itself to children as a happy place where "what you want is what you get" is very appealing (Garfield 1992). By the time children reach elementary school, they are often zealous devotees of McDonald's who insist on McDonaldland birthday celebrations and surprise dinners. Obviously McDonald's advertisers are doing something right, as they induce phenomenal numbers of kids to pester their parents for Big Macs and fries.

McDonald's and other fast food advertisers have discovered an enormous, previously overlooked children's market. Children aged five to twelve annually spend almost $5 billion of their own money. They influence household spending of an additional $140 billion each year, more than half of which goes to soft drinks and fast food. Every month nineteen out of every twenty kids aged six to eleven visit a fast food restaurant. In a typical McDonald's promotion, where toys like Hot Wheels or Barbies accompany kids' meals, company officials can expect to sell 30 million to child customers. By the time they reach the age of three, over four out of five children know that McDonald's sells hamburgers. As if this level of child consciousness colonization were not enough, McDonald's, along with scores of other companies, has targeted the public schools as a new venue for child marketing and consumption. In addition to hamburgers for A's programs and advertising-based learning packets for science, foreign language, and other subjects, McDonald's and other fast food firms have gained control of school cafeterias, much to the consternation of many advocates of child health (Hume 1993; Ritzer 1993; Giroux 1994; Kincheloe 2002).

Make no mistake about it, McDonald's and its advertisers want to transform children into consumers; indeed, they see children as consumers in training (Fisher, et. al. 1991). Ellen Seiter (1993), however, warns against drawing simplistic conclusions about the relationship between advertisers and children, as have, she says, many well-intentioned liberal children's advocacy groups. The leading voice against corporate advertising for children, ACT (Action for Children's Television), fails to capture the subtle aspects of techno power and its colonization of childhood, the complicated interactions of structure and agency. Seeing children as naive innocents who should watch only "good" TV, meaning educational programs that portray middle-class values, the ACT has little appreciation of the complexity of children's TV watching. As argued in this chapter and in the introduction, children are not passive, naive TV viewers. As advertising professionals have learned, children are active, analytical viewers who often make their own meanings of both commercials and the products they sell. These social and psychological dynamics between advertiser and child deserve further analysis.

One important dynamic is advertisers' recognition that children feel oppressed by the middle-class view of children as naive entities in need of constant protection. By drawing on the child's discomfort with middle-class protectionism and the accompanying attempt to "adjust" children to a positivist "developmentally appropriate" norm, advertisers hit on a marketing bonanza. If we address kids as kids—a dash of anarchism and a pinch of hyperactivity—they will love our commercials even though parents (especially middle-class parents) will hate them. By the end of the 1960s, commercial children's TV and advertising were grounded on this premise. Such video throws off restraint, discipline, and old views that children should be seen but not heard. Everything, for example, that educational TV embraces—earnestness, child as an incomplete adult, child in need of correction—commercial TV rejects. In effect, commercial TV sets up an oppositional culture for kids.

One doesn't have to look far (try any middle-class home) to find that children's enthusiasm for certain TV shows, toys, and foods often isolates them from their parents. Drawing on this isolation, children turn it into a form of power—they finally know something that Dad doesn't. How many dads or moms understand the relationship between Mayor McCheese and the French Fry Guys? Battle lines begin to be drawn between children and parents, as kids want to purchase McDonald's hamburgers or action toys. Conflicts in lower-middle-class homes may revolve around family finances; strife in upper-middle-class homes may concern aesthetic or ideological concerns. Questions of taste, cultural capital, or self-improvement permeate child–adult interactions in such families. The child's ability to negotiate the restrictions of adult values is central to the development of an independent self. A common aspect of this developing independence involves the experience of contradiction with the adult world. Children of upwardly mobile, ambitious parents may find it more difficult to negotiate this experience of contradiction because of the parents' strict views of the inappropriateness of TV-based children's culture. Thus the potential for parent–child conflict and alienation may be greater in this familial context.

PLAY IN HYPERREALITY: MCDONALD'S COLONIZATION OF FUN

In this context play is placed in cultural conflict. Over the past several decades psychologists and educators have come to recognize the importance of play in childhood and child development. With this in mind, our examination of McDonald's opens a window into what can happen when the culture and political economy of play begins to change. With a changing culture of play, we begin to discern different effects of play on the construction of children's identities and with their cognitive development. New forms of play may accelerate particular forms of intellectual development while concurrently limiting the imagination—a dynamic that holds interesting implications for universalist perspectives on child development. With the corporate colonization of play in hyperreality, play begins to lose its imaginative dimensions. Contemporary children's play occurs in the same public spaces as adult labor, as children enter into cyberspace using the same hardware and software that their parents use in their professional lives.

McDonald's is, of course, just one producer in an expanding children's commercial culture. Again, it is important to note that children in their interactions with McDonald's and other manifestations of this commercial kinderculture use its symbolic and material dimensions in often unique and idiosyncratic ways. McDonald's and other corporations worry about this idiosyncratic agential dynamic of childhood play. Like other marketers McDonald's wants children to engage its products and company-produced meanings in an "appropriate" manner. Such engagement would not include "playing" with environmental and health concerns by developing cyber communities of like-minded children calling for corporate responsibility. McDonald's and other corporations do not want power-savvy children engaging in socially conscious use of their products—such as the ones who formed the organization Children Against McDonald's. Corporate marketers and other protectors of the status quo fear the agential, empowered child. Media corporations and companies like McDonald's work hard to control and structure the way consumers interact with their products. Indeed, child consumers do not experience the freedom and empowerment some advocates of the agential childhood claim for them. Play as political resistance must be opposed at all costs (DuBois-Reymond, Sunker, and Kruger 2001; Hengst 2001; Nations 2001; Cassell and Jenkins 2002; Mouritsen 2003; Jenkins 2003).

A covert children's culture has always existed on playgrounds and in schools. The children's culture of the past, however, was produced by children and propagated through child-to-child contact. The postmodern children's culture of today is increasingly created by adults and dispersed via television for the purpose of inducing children to consume. (Children's use of the Internet may provide a countervailing trend in this context.) As they carefully subvert middle-class parents' obsession with achievement, play as a serious enterprise, and self-improvement oriented "quality time" (a subversion that in my opinion probably contributes to the public good), advertisers connect children's culture to their products. McDonald's commercials reflect these themes, although less blatantly than many advertisers.

Attempting to walk a tightrope between tapping the power of children's subversive culture and offending the middle-class guardians of propriety—a walk that has become increasingly difficult in the first decade of the twenty-first century—McDonald's developed a core of so-called "slice-of-life" children's ads. Casting no adults in the commercials, advertisers depict a group of preteens engaged in "authentic" conversations around a McDonald's table covered with burgers, fries, and shakes. Using children's slang ("radical," "dude," "we're into Barbie") to describe toys in various McDonald's promotions, children discuss the travails of childhood with one another.

In many commercials children make adults the butt of their jokes or share jokes that adults don't get (Seiter 1993; Goldman 1992). McDonald's subtly attempts to draw some of the power of children's subversive culture onto their products without anyone but the kids knowing. Such slice-of-life ads are opaque to the degree that adults watching them don't get it—they don't see the advertiser's effort to connect McDonald's with the subversive kinderculture. This "oppositional aesthetic" (Jenkins 1998) has fueled numerous aspects of children's commercial culture (e.g., several Nickelodeon shows, Paul Reuben's transgressive Pee-wee's Playhouse, many video games, etc.) that play on children's differences from adults. It is a key weapon in the corporate construction of childhood.

THE BLOODY FIGHT FOR CONFORMITY, COURTESY, AND ESTABLISHED VIRTUE: MCDONALDLAND, RONALD, AND RAY

TV ads often serve as postmodern myths, as they resolve cultural contradictions, portray models of identity, and glorify the status quo. While all McDonald's ads accomplish these mythic functions to some degree, none do it better than ads and promotions involving McDonaldland. To understand the mythic dynamics of McDonaldland, one must appreciate the psychological complexity of Ray Kroc. Born in 1902 in a West Side Chicago working-class neighborhood into what Kroc called a "Bohunk" (Bohemian) family, Kroc was obsessed throughout his life with proving his worth as both a human being and a businessman. Having failed in several business ventures in his twenties and thirties, Kroc had much to prove by the time the McDonald's opportunity confronted him at the age of fifty-two (Boas and Chain 1976). Kroc defined McDonaldland the same way he defined himself—through consumption. Driven by an ambition to own nice things, Kroc's autobiography is peppered with references to consumption: "I used to comb through the advertisements in the local newspaper for notices of house sales in the wealthier suburbs . . . I haunted these sales and picked up pieces of elegant furniture . . . " (Kroc 1977, 27). Watched over by the messianic Ronald McDonald, McDonaldland is a place (your kind of place) where consumption functioned as the means through which its inhabitants gained their identities.

McDonaldland is a kid's text fused with Kroc's psyche that emerges as an effort to sell the system, to justify consumption as a way of life. As central figure in McDonaldland, Ronald McDonald emerges as a multidimensional clown deity, virgin-born son of Adam Smith, press secretary for free enterprise capitalism. He is also Ray Kroc's projection of himself, his ego creation of the most loved prophet of utopian consumption in the McWorld. Ronald's life history begins in Washington, D.C., with *Today Show* weatherman Willard Scott. Struggling to make it as a junior announcer at WRC-TV in D.C. in the early 1960s, Scott agreed to play Bozo the Clown on the station's kid show. When Scott donned the clown suit, he was transformed from Clark Kent to Superman, bumbling Willard to superclown. The local McDonald's franchisees recognized Scott's talent and employed Bozo as a spokesperson for McDonald's. When the Bozo show was canceled by WRC, McDonald's lost a very effective advertiser. The local D.C. McDonald's owners worked with Scott to create Ronald McDonald (Scott's idea), debuting him in October 1963. Ronald created traffic jams every time he appeared in public, and local operators suggested to the Chicago headquarters that Ronald go national (Love 1986).

After a lengthy debate over whether they should employ Ronald McDonald as a clown, a cowboy, or a spaceman, corporate leaders and advertisers settled on the clown Ronald. Dumping Scott because he was deemed too fat for the image they wanted to promote, the company in 1965 hired Coco, an internationally known clown with the Ringling

Bros. and Barnum & Bailey Circus. Beginning with his first national appearance in the Macy's Thanksgiving Day parade on November 25, 1966, the deification of Ronald began. The press releases on Ronald issued by the McDonald's Customers Relations Center are sanctification documents cross-pollinated with frontier tall-tale boasting. "Since 1963, Ronald McDonald has become a household name, more famous than Lassie or the Easter Bunny, and second only to Santa Claus" (McDonald's Customer Relations Center 1994).

The other characters in McDonaldland, the company's promotional literature reports, revere Ronald (a.k.a. Kroc). He is "intelligent and sensitive . . . he can do nearly anything . . . Ronald McDonald is the star." If children are sick, the promos contend, Ronald is there. Even though he has become an "international hero and celebrity," Ronald is the same friend of children he was in 1963. Ninety-six percent of all children, claimed a bogus "Ronald McDonald Awareness Study" fed to the press, can identify this heroic figure (Boas and Chain 1976). Ronald was everything Kroc wanted to be: a beloved humanitarian, an international celebrity, a philanthropist, a musician (Kroc made his living for a while as a piano player; Ronald has cut children's records). Even the sophisticates loved Ronald, Kroc wrote in his autobiography—a group whose affection Kroc sought throughout his life. Unfortunately he had to settle for it vicariously through Ronald. Abe Lincoln too was rejected by the sophisticates of his day; as a twentieth-century Lincoln, Kroc prominently displayed the bust of Ronald adjacent to the bust of Lincoln on a table behind his desk at the Chicago headquarters (McCormick 1993; Kroc 1977).

According to the promotional literature designed for elementary schools, Ronald "became a citizen of [the McDonald's] International Division" in 1969 and soon began to appear on TV around the world. Kroc was propelled to a new level of celebrity as the corporation "penetrated" the global market. Now known everywhere on earth, Kroc/Ronald became the grand salesman, the successful postindustrial Willie Loman—they love me in Moscow, Belgrade, and New York. Stung by a plethora of critics, Kroc was obsessed with being perceived as a moral man with a moral company that exerted a wholesome influence on children around the world. Kroc wrote and spoke of his noble calling, establishing his "missions" with the golden arches as part of his neo-white man's burden. I provide a humanitarian service, Kroc proclaimed: "I go out and check out a piece of property [that's] not producing a damned thing for anybody," he wrote in his epistles from California. The new franchise provides a better life for scores of people: "out of that bare ground comes a store that does, say, a million dollars a year in business. Let me tell you, it's great satisfaction to see that happen." Kroc/Ronald personified the great success story of twentieth-century capitalism. The fortunes that were made by Kroc and his franchisees came to represent what happens when one works hard in the free enterprise system. McDonaldland and the McWorld—signifiers for the McDonaldization of the planet.

The convergence of the growth of international mega-corporations with the expanding technological sophistication of the media has prompted a new era of consumption. Some analysts argue that the central feature of the postmodern lifestyle revolves around the act of consuming. In McDonaldland Ronald McDonald serves as CEO/archduke over his fiefdom of consumer junkies. The Hamburglar is "cute" in his addiction to hamburgers. According to the literature provided to schools about McDonaldland the Hamburglar's "main purpose in life is the acquisition of McDonald's hamburgers." Grimace is described as "generous and affectionate . . . [his] primary personality attribute is his love for McDonald's shakes." The most important passion of Captain Crook is his love of McDonald's Filet-O-Fish sandwiches.

As a free enterprise utopia, McDonaldland erases all differences, all conflicts; social inequities are overcome through acts of consumption. As such messages justify existing power relations, conformity emerges as the logical path to self-production. The only hint of difference in McDonaldland involves Uncle O'Grimacey, the annual Irish visitor who speaks with a brogue and is defined by his obsession with Shamrock shakes. The emphasis on standardization and "sameness" is so intense that all Ronald McDonalds go to school to learn a uniform image. The training system is so rationalized that students are tracked into one of two groups; throughout pre-service and in-service experiences the clowns are either "greeting Ronalds" or "performing Ronalds." The most compelling manifestation of conformity in Mc-

Donaldland involves the portrayal of the French Fry Guys. As the only group of citizens depicted in the Hamburger Patch, these faceless commoners are numerous but seldom seen:

> They tend to look, act, and think pretty much alike. Parent French Fry Guys are indistinguishable from children, and vice versa. They are so much alike that, so far, no individual French Fry Guy has emerged as a personality identifiable from the others. They resemble little mops with legs and eyes and speak in squeaky, high-pitched voices, usually in unison. They always move quickly, scurrying around in fits and starts, much like the birds one sees on sandy beaches. (McDonald's Customer Relations Center 1994)

As inhabitants of a McDonalidized McWorld, the French Fry Guys are content to remove themselves from the public space, emerging only for brief and frenetic acts of standardized consumption—their only act of personal assertion.

Life in McDonaldland is free of conflict—the Hamburger Patch is a privatized utopia. It is contemporary America writ small, corporate-directed and consumer-oriented. Questions such as distribution of income among classes, regulation of corporate interests, free trade, minimum wage, and collective bargaining traditionally elicited passion and commitment—now they hardly raise an eyebrow. The political sphere where decisions are made concerning who gets what and who voted for what is managed by a small group. Their work and the issues they confront are followed by a shrinking audience of news watchers tuned to CNN and C-SPAN. Politics, Americans have concluded, is not only useless but, far worse in the mediascape, boring. It can't be too important; it gets such low Nielsens. The political structure of McDonaldland reflects this larger depoliticization with its depiction of the inept, superfluous Mayor McCheese. The school promotional literature describes him as a "silly" character not "to be taken seriously." As a "confused and bumbling" politician, the mayor would rather spend his time in the privatized space of McDonald's eating cheeseburgers. The lesson is clear to children—politics doesn't matter; leave McDonald's alone; let these businessmen run their business the way they see fit.

The benign nature of capitalist production with its freedom from serious conflict of any type portrayed by McDonaldland and Kroc/Ronald is a cover for a savage reality. Business analysts, for example, liken McDonald's operations to the Marine Corps. When a recruit graduates from basic training (Hamburger University), he believes that he can conquer anybody (Love 1986). Motivated by an econo-tribal allegiance to the McFamily, store operators express faith in McDonald's as if it were a religion. Kroc openly spoke of the Holy Trinity—McDonald's, family, and God in that order (Kroc 1977). Released from boot camp on a jihad for a success theology, these faceless French Fry Guys have forced thousands of independent restaurant owners out of business (Luxenberg 1985). Competing fast food franchisees tell of their introduction to recent Hamburger University graduates and other McDonald's managers with amazement. "We will run you out of business and bury you," these Khrushchevs of fast food proclaim.

No matter how ruthless business might become, there is no room for criticism or dissent in McDonaldland. "I feel sorry for people who have such a small and wretched view of the system that made this country great," Kroc (1977) wrote in his autobiography. The "academic snobs" who criticized McDonald's tapped a sensitivity in Kroc's psyche that motivated counterattacks until the day he died. This love-it-or-leave-it anti-intellectualism finds its McDonaldland expression in the Professor. Described as the proud possessor of various degrees, the Professor is a bumbling fool with a high-pitched, effeminate voice. As none of his theories or inventions ever work, he meets Kroc's definition of an overeducated man: someone who worries about inconsequential affairs to the degree that he is distracted from the normal problems of business. Kroc never liked books or school and saw little use for advanced degrees: "One thing I flatly refuse to give money to is the support of any college" (Kroc 1977, 199). Intellectuals don't fit into the culture of the Hamburger Patch.

As much as the Professor is effeminate, Big Mac, McDonaldland's policeman, is manly. The promotional literature describes him as "the strong, silent type. His voice is deep and super-masculine; his manner is gruff but affectionate . . . his walk is a strut. His stance is chest out, stomach in." The gender curriculum of McDonaldland is quite explicit:

Big Mac as the manly man; Birdie, the Early Bird, as the pert, nurturing female. As the only female in McDonaldland, Birdie is faced with a significant task. She is the cheerleader who encourages the male residents to jump into the activities of the new day. "Her enthusiasm and energy are infectious . . . her positive attitude is emphasized by her bright, perky, cheerful voice" (McDonald's Customer Relations Center 1994). Once the McDonaldlanders have gobbled down their Egg McMuffins and are off to their respective occupations, Birdie retires to the sidelines as a passive observer.

The Kroc influence is alive and well in the gender dynamics of the corporation. Referring to himself in the third person as Big Daddy, Kroc expressed a sometimes disturbing misogyny in his handling of company affairs. Ray's personality, one colleague observed, would never allow a woman to gain power (Love 1986). To Kroc women were to take care of frills, leaving the important work to men:

> Clark told me I should hire a secretary. "I suppose you're right," I [Kroc] said. "But I want a male secretary . . . I want a man. He might cost a little more at first, but if he's any good at all, I'll have him doing sales work in addition to administrative things. I have nothing against having a pretty girl around, but the job I have in mind would be much better handled by a man. . . . My decision to hire a male secretary paid off when I was hospitalized for a gall bladder operation and later for a goiter operation. [The male secretary] worked between our office and my hospital room, and we kept things humming as briskly as when I was in the office every morning. (Kroc 1977, 48–49)

June Martino was a very talented woman who had been with Kroc from the earliest days of his involvement with McDonald's. Corporate insiders described her as a gifted businesswoman whose expertise often kept the company going during difficult times. Kroc's view of her reflected his view of women in general:

> I thought it was good to have a lucky person around, maybe some of it would rub off on me. Maybe it did. After we got McDonald's going and built a larger staff, they called her "Mother Martino." She kept track of everyone's family fortunes, whose wife was having a baby,

who was having marital difficulties, or whose birthday it was. She helped make the office a happy place. (Kroc 1977, 84)

Such attitudes at the top permeated all levels of the organization, expressing themselves in a variety of pathological ways. Management's sensitivity to sexual harassment was virtually nonexistent well into the 1980s. Interviews with women managers reveal patterns of sexual misconduct involving eighteen- and nineteen-year-old women employees being pressured to date older male managers. Reports of sexual harassment were suppressed by the company bureaucracy; women who complained were sometimes punished or forced to resign. One successful manager confided that after she reported harassment, company higher-ups stalked her both on and off the job. She was eventually forced to leave the company. Not surprisingly, such an organization was not overly concerned with women's complaints about the exaggerated gender roles depicted in McDonald's commercials and promotions. From Birdie as cheerleader to Happy Meals with Barbies for girls and Hot Wheels for boys, McDonald's has never escaped Kroc's gender assumptions (Hume 1993).

McDonald's perpetuates what Allen Shelton (1993) refers to as a hegemonic logic—a way of doing business that privileges conformity, zealously defends the middle-class norm, fights to the death for established virtue, and resists social change at all costs. As a passionate force for a Warren G. Harding "normalcy," McDonald's is the corporation that invites the children of prominent civic, military, and business leaders to the opening of its first McDonaldland Park—but leaves the daughters and sons of the not so rich and famous off the list. This hegemonic logic holds little regard for concepts such as justice or morality—McDonald's morality is contingent on what sells. This concept is well illustrated in McDonald's emphasis on the primacy of home and family values in its advertising.

WE'VE GOT OURSELVES A FAMILY UNIT: HOME IS WHEREVER RONALD MCDONALD GOES

Kroc and his corporate leaders unequivocally understood their most important marketing priority—to portray McDonald's as a "family kind of place." As they focused on connecting McDonald's to America and the family, they modified the red and white ceramic take-out restaurants to look more like the suburban homes that sprang up throughout America in the late 1950s and 1960s. Ad campaigns proclaimed that McDonald's was home, and that anywhere Ronald goes "he is at home." Like many other ads in American hyperreality, McDonald's home and family ads privilege the private sphere, not the public sphere, as the important space where life is lived. As an intrinsically self-contained unit, the family is removed from the public realm of society; such a depiction, however, conceals the ways that politics and economics shape everyday family life. The greatest irony of these ads is that even as they isolate the family from any economic connections, they promote the commodification of family life. A form of doublespeak is discernible in this situation: The family is an end in itself; the family is an instrumental consumption unit whose ultimate purpose is to benefit corporate profits and growth.

McDonald's ads deploy home and family as paleosymbols that position McDonald's as the defender of "the American way of life." Kroc (1977) never knew what paleosymbols were, but he understood that McDonald's public image should be, in his words, a "combination YMCA, Girl Scouts, and Sunday School." Devised to tap into the right-wing depiction of the traditional family under attack from feminists, homosexuals, and other "screwballs," these so-called legitimation ads don't sell hamburgers—they sell social relations. Amid social upheaval and instability, McDonald's endures as a rock of ages, a refuge in a world gone mad. McDonald's brings us together, provides a safe haven for our children. The needs the legitimation ads tap are real, but the consumption panacea they provide is false (Goldman 1992). After its phenomenal growth in the 1960s, McDonald's realized that it was no longer the "cute little company" of the 1950s (Love 1986). The antiwar, civil rights, and other social movements of the late 1960s were repugnant to Kroc's American values. Such views, when combined with the marketing need for McDonald's to legitimate itself now that it was an American "big business," made home and family the obvious battlefield in the legitimation campaign. As the public faith in corporations declined, McDonald's used the paleosymbols to create an environment of confidence. Going against the grain of a social context, perceived to be hostile to big business, the ads worked. The lyrics of accompanying music read:

> *You, you're the one.*
> *So loving, strong, and patient.*
> *Families like yours*
> *made all the states a nation.*
> *Our families are our past,*
> *our future and our pride.*
> *Whatever roots we come from,*
> *we're growing side by side.*
> (quoted in Goldman 1992, 95)

The world of home and family portrayed by the McDonald's legitimation ads is a terrain without conflict or tension. In an ad produced in the early 1980s as the Reagan family values agenda was being established, a typical white, middle-class family is returning to the small town of Dad's childhood. Excited to show his preteen son and daughter his childhood world, Dad tells the family that his old house is just up the street. As the "Greek chorus" sings "things have changed a bit since you've been around" as background music, Dad is shocked to discover new condominiums have replaced the old house. Dismayed but undaunted, Dad tells the family that his old friend Shorty's house is just around the corner. Shorty's house is also gone, replaced by a car wash. From the backseat the daughter tells her disappointed father that she hopes the place he used to eat at is still standing because she's hungry. Dad immediately begins to look for the unnamed eating place; the background chorus sings: "In the night, the welcome sight of an old friend." The camera focuses on Dad as his eyes brighten and a smile explodes across his face. Camera cuts to car pulling into McDonald's. The chorus sings: "Feels so right here tonight at McDonald's again."

Once again consumption at McDonald's solves the problem of change. The consumptive act in this case serves to affirm family values in a world where the larger society threatens them. Nothing has changed at McDonald's, as Dad tells the perky counter girl that he had

his first Big Mac at this McDonald's. The camera focuses across the din-
ing room to a short man expressing surprise and disbelief. Of course, it
is Shorty. As Shorty embraces Dad, we find out that Dad's childhood
name was Curly—ironic in the fact that he is now bald. The camera retreats to frame the old friends embracing in the light cast by the golden
arches. Dad is at McDonald's; he is home with old friends and family.
McDonald's made it all possible (Goldman 1992). The turbulent 1960s
are finally over. We (America) have "come home" to the traditional
family values that made us great. The chorus has already reminded us
that it "feels so right . . . at McDonald's again," the key word being
"again." Reagan, whose candidacy Kroc and the McDonald's management fervently supported, has brought back traditional values—Mc-
Donald's wants viewers to know that McDonald's is an important
aspect of the traditional family values package.

In the final scene of this "Home Again" commercial, the camera
shoots a close-up of the son and daughter. Having just watched the embrace between Dad and Shorty, the daughter turns to her brother and
says with ironic inflection, "Curly?" Her brother shrugs and rolls his
eyes in recognition of the generational rift between Dad's understanding of the scene as compared to their own. The reunion is irrelevant to
the son and daughter, the camera tells us as it focuses on the attention
they pay to the hamburgers sitting in front of them—the only time
McDonald's food is displayed in the ad. McDonald's wants it both
ways: the adult identification with Reagan, America, and the return to
traditional family values, as well as child identification with the subversive kinderculture described previously. The subversive kindercultural
subtext of this ad involves the children's shared recognition of the father's fatuous pursuit of a long dead past and his embarrassing public
display of emotion. Dad blows his "cool pose." The "Curly irony" is the
overt signifier for these deeper generational divisions—differentiations
described by advertisers as market segments.

The grand irony of this and many other subversive kindercultural
ads is that under the flag of traditional family values McDonald's actually undermines the very qualities it claims to promote. The Mc-
Donald's experience depicted does not involve a family sharing a
common experience—each market segment experiences it in a differ-

ent, potentially conflicting way. The family depicted here, like so many American middle-class families, is an isolated unit divided against itself. In terms of everyday life McDonald's does not encourage long, leisurely, interactive family meals. The seats and tables are designed to be uncomfortable to the point that customers will eat quickly and leave. In the larger scheme of things, family values, America, and home are nothing more than cynical marketing tools designed to legitimate McDonald's to different market segments. Kroc made his feeling about family very clear—work comes first, he told his managers. "My total commitment to business had long since been established in my home" (Kroc 1977, 89). The cynicism embedded in ads by McDonald's and scores of other companies undermines the social fabric, making the culture our children inhabit a colder and more malicious place. Such cynicism leads corporations to develop new forms of techno power that can be used to subvert democracy and justice in the quest for new markets. Such cynicism holds up Ronald McDonald/Ray Kroc as heroes, while ignoring authentic heroes—men and women who struggle daily to lead good lives, be good parents, and extend social justice.

REFERENCES

Abercrombie, N. 1994. "Authority and Consumer Society." In R. Keat, N. Whiteley, and N. Abercrombie, eds., *The Authority of the Consumer*. New York: Routledge.

Boas, M., and S. Chain. 1976. *Big Mac: The Unauthorized Story of McDonald's*. New York: Dutton.

Brautigan, R. 1974. *The Hawkline Monster: A Gothic Western*. New York: Pocket Books.

Cassell, J., and H. Jenkins. 2002. "Proper Playthings: The Politics of Play in Children." web.media.mit.edu/~andrew_s/andrew_sempere_2002_politics_of_play.pdf.

Cook, D. 2004. *The Commodification of Childhood: The Children's Clothing Industry and the Rise of the Child-Consumer*. Durham, N.C.: Duke University Press.

DuBois-Reymond, M., H. Sunker, and H. Kruger, eds. 2001. *Childhood in Europe*. New York: Peter Lang.

Fischer, P., et al. 1991. "Brand Logo Recognition by Children Aged 3 to 6 Years." *Journal of the American Medical Association* 266, no. 22: 3145–3148.

Garfield, B. 1992. "Nice Ads, But That Theme Is Not What You Want." *Advertising Age* 63, no. 8: 53.

Giroux, H. 1994. *Disturbing Pleasures: Learning Popular Culture*. New York: Routledge.

_____. 1988. *Teachers as Intellectuals: Toward a Critical Pedagogy of Learning*. Granby, Mass.: Bergin & Garvey.

Goldman, R. 1992. *Reading Ads Socially*. New York: Routledge.

Harvey, D. 1989. *The Condition of Postmodernity*. Cambridge, Mass.: Basil Blackwell.

Hengst, H. 2001. "Rethinking the Liquidation of Childhood." In M. du Bois-Reymond, H. Sunker, and H. Kruger, eds., *Childhood in Europe*. New York: Peter Lang.

Hume, S. 1993. "Fast Food Caught in the Middle." *Advertising Age* 64, no. 6: 12–15.

Jans, M. 2002. "Children and Active Citizenship." www.surrey.ac.uk/education/etgace/brussels-papers/march-paper-jans.doc.

Jenkins, H. 2003. "The Poachers and the Stormtroopers: Cultural Convergence in the Digital Age." web.mit.edu/21fms/www/faculty/henry3/pub/stormtroopers.htm.

Keat, R., N. Whiteley, and N. Abercrombie. 1994. Introduction to R. Keat, N. Whiteley, and N. Abercrombie, eds., *The Authority of the Consumer*. New York: Routledge.

Kellner, D. 1989. *Critical Theory, Marxism, and Modernity*. Baltimore: Johns Hopkins University Press.

_____. 1992. "Popular Culture and the Construction of Postmodern Identities." In S. Lash and J. Friedman, eds., *Modernity and Identity*. Cambridge, Mass.: Blackwell.

Kenway, J., and E. Bullen. 2001. *Consuming Children: Entertainment, Advertising, and Education*. Philadelphia: Open University Press.

Kincheloe, J. 1999. *How Do We Tell the Workers? The Socio-Economic Foundations of Work and Vocational Education*. Boulder: Westview.

Kroc, R. 1977. *Grinding It Out: The Making of McDonald's*. New York: St. Martin's Paperbacks.

Leidner, R. 1993. *Fast Food, Fast Talk: Service Work and the Routinization of Everyday Life*. Berkeley: University of California Press.

Love, J. 1986. *McDonald's: Behind the Arches*. New York: Bantam.

Luxenberg, S. 1985. *Roadside Empires: How the Chains Franchised*. New York: Viking Penguin.

McCormick, M. 1993. "Kid Rhino and McDonald's Enter Licensing Agreement." *Billboard* 105, no. 8: 10–11.

McDonald's Customer Relations Center. 1994. Handout to Schools.

Molnar, A. 1996. *Giving Kids the Business: The Commercialization of America's Schools.* Boulder: Westview.

Mouritsen, F. 2003. *Project Demolition: Children's Play-Culture and the Concept of Development.* www.hum.sdu.dk/projekter/ipfu.dk/online-artikler/mouritsen-demolition.pdf.

Nations, C. 2001. "How Long Do Our Children Have to Wait? Understanding the Children of the Twenty-first Century." pt3.nmsu.edu/edu621/cynthia 2001.html.

Palakow, V. 1992. *The Erosion of Childhood.* Chicago: University of Chicago Press.

Ritzer, G. 1993. *The McDonaldization of Society.* Thousand Oaks, Calif.: Pine Forge.

Schlosser, E. 2001. *Fast Food Nation: The Dark Side of the All-American Meal.* Boston: Houghton Mifflin.

Seiter, E. 1993. *Sold Separately: Parents and Children in Consumer Culture.* New Brunswick, N.J.: Rutgers University Press.

Shelton, A. 1993. "Writing McDonald's, Eating the Past: McDonald's as a Postmodern Space." *Studies in Symbolic Interaction* 15: 103–118.

Shiva, V. 1997. "Vandana Shiva on McDonald's Exploitation and the Global Economy." www.mcspotlight.org/people/interviews/vandanatranscripts.html.

Yan, Y. 1997. "McDonald's in Beijing: The Localization of Americana." In J. Watson, ed., *Golden Arches East: McDonald's in East Asia.* Stanford: Stanford University Press.

Chapter 5

THE BITCH WHO HAS EVERYTHING

Shirley R. Steinberg

THIS IS THE BOOK OF THE generations of Barbie. In the day that Ruth created her, in the likeness of Ruth's daughter and a German whore, she made Barbie. (2) Female first she created her, and blessed her and called her name Barbie after her firstborn. (3) And Barbie lived three years and Ruth created Ken, male and female she created them both. (4) And Barbie begat Skipper and friends, by the year of our lord nineteen hundred and sixty four, they were three. (5) And Barbie lived thirty and seven years until this record. Within those years, ten friends were created for Skipper; Midge was created to be Barbie's best friend. (6) And in the year nineteen hundred and sixty eight, Christie was created. Christie was unlike any other creation; her skin was black. (7) And these are the years and days of Barbie, the days of Barbie and the Rockers; the days of Barbie and her pets, including puppy Sachi and horse Rosebud; and the years of Barbie's family, cousins Francie and Jazzie; siblings Tutti, Todd, and Stacie. (8) And through Stacie, friends were born, Whitney and Janet. (9) And through Ken, multiple male friends were born, and like Ken, none of them ever married, and verily their manhood was always in question. (10) However, Barbie was most plentiful with friends, by the year nineteen hundred and ninety four, having twenty and six new girlfriends. Among them Cara, who was also black, Teresa, who was made Hispanic, and Kira, who was Asian.

(11) Hence Barbie was known through the land as diverse and multi-cultural. (12) And these were the days of Barbie; and it came to pass, when Barbie and her friends began to multiply on the face of the earth, little girls began to buy, as verily, one doll was never enough.

Okay, maybe I am taking an artist's license in rewriting scriptures. It only seemed appropriate, as Mattel has been rewriting history and children's play for years.

Playing Barbies in the fifth grade consisted of lugging plastic cases laden with "outfits" to the playground and constructing scenarios around Barbie and "getting" Ken. I knew at this early age that Barbie (as a female) must have an "outfit" for every occasion and that wearing the same thing within some unspoken frame of time was just not done.

When I was twelve or thirteen I began meticulously recording what I wore each day on a calendar. I made sure that at least a month went by before I wore an outfit again. While a high school teacher, my students called attention to my idiosyncrasy by applauding the first day that I duplicated an outfit in the classroom. Did Barbie construct this behavior, or do I just love clothes?

Where does the text of Barbie begin? Thirty-seven years ago, Mattel invested in the production of a slim, blonde doll who (that?) wore a variety of coordinated "outfits." While on vacation in Europe, Mattel co-founder Ruth Handler discovered Lily. Lily was a prominent star of comics—a sexy blonde with loose morals who adorned dashboards throughout Germany and Switzerland. Her origin is not well documented, although her lineage has been traced back to a *Lily* comic strip. Handler decided to take the model of Lily back to the States and create a doll that could wear multiple outfits. She named her Barbie, after her daughter, Barbara. The promotional "hook" that Handler cited was the possibility that the doll could have multiple outfits and girls could just own one doll.

Physiologically, Barbie had perfect breasts (although no nipples), a tiny waist and long, slender legs. Much has been written in a feminist framework about Barbie, discussing the unrealistic body shape, and so on. I won't "go there." Barbie was made slim so that layers of designer fabric would flow nicely and realistically on her body. She was, first and foremost, a model—fabric by Dior, designs by Mackie, nothing was beyond reach for her. I am not offended by her figure; I do wonder, however, about her poorly constructed private parts.

Speaking of private parts, four years later, Barbie was given a boyfriend, Ken—he had no genitals. Ken's crotch was (and is) as flat and smooth as Barbie's. I remember specifically my disappointment in disrobing my first Ken—nothing to see. Possibly that physical defect is in line with the personality that Ken has displayed throughout the years (although Earring Ken had a certain flair). Ken and Barbie have gotten as far as their wedding but never past it. The couple has never had a wedding night and Barbie is always seen pushing a stroller of cousins, younger siblings, or friends. Only Ken's friends of color, Derek and Steve, radiate any machismo sexuality—still crotchless.

Within months of her creation, Barbie was a sensation. Mattel had transformed toys, especially dolls, and Barbie became "us." Little girls were frenzied to own a Barbie, each one coming in her own long, thin box, wearing a black-and-white striped swim suit. Barbie had a blonde ponytail and earrings. She was a teen model. Girls moved from cradling baby dolls to demanding the latest in haute couture à la Mattel. Barbie was sexy, although most of her owners were not even aware of the genre of sexiness—they just loved their Barbies.

FROM RESEARCH TO OBSESSION

I take my work seriously. Indeed, I think I am a superb researcher. I love the challenge of finding strange and wonderful factoids of trivia in little known academic nooks and crannies. However, this chapter has caused havoc in my life. Four years ago, I became fascinated with Barbie's effect on little girls. I started to pick up Barbies, Barbie furniture, Barbie comics, Barbie books, Barbie jewelry, and Barbie toys wherever I went. I even found the Benetton Barbie in the Istanbul airport (under the sign featuring the Marlboro man).

In order to do thorough textual analyses of Barbie and Barbie accoutrements, I needed to purchase my artifacts. I sit now, with great embarrassment, in an office with no less than forty Barbies, ten Kens, several Skippers (including a beauty princess and a cheerleading Skipper), and a plethora of "ethnic" and "special edition" Barbies. I have three Barbie watches, a $300 Barbie jacket from F.A.O. Schwartz, a Barbie McDonald's playset, Christmas playset, and bakery set. I have two Barbie board games, one computer game—Barbie Goes Shopping—and a floppy disk game, Barbie Design Studio. My life is out of control. I am only thankful that this research came long after my children stopped playing with toys—consequently I am the only one in the family who lays claim to this Mattel treasure trove. However, when children come to visit, they plow through my Barbies in an hour and then inquire, "Do you have anything else?" Obviously I don't have enough. My thoughts roam to my colleagues; does Doug sleep under a canopy of Buffy posters? Does Joe really idolize Macauley Calkin? I know he desires McDonald's Arch Deluxes constantly. Does John Weaver wear baggy hip-hop pants along with Greg Dimitridis? Does Ruthann secretly see herself as Hermione? Or is this all just rock and roll?

My ownership of Barbies and paraphernalia qualifies me as an expert. I am a consumer and a scholar; there is no better combination. Historically, I come by the expertise naturally: I have had Barbies since she was invented. However, as I trace my Barbie autobiography, I am only able to single out my fetish for outfits as a permanent influence à la Barbie. I remain untouched from other taint . . . unless one looks at my research.

WHAT BARBIE DOESN'T HAVE

Discussing what Barbie doesn't have is easier than what she does have. The list is much shorter. Barbie doesn't have a locomotive, a battleship (although she is a sailor), a rocket (although she is an astronaut), or an Uzi (although she is a soldier). Thematically Mattel still has not invented the Homeless Barbie, the Abortion Barbie, the Alcoholic Barbie, or the S&M Bondage Barbie. As far as special editions, Barbie still has not come out as a criminal—she has, however, come out in special editions of fairy tales (never a witch), "true" history, careers, and in different ethnicities—different from white, that is. There is no northern

Barbie, but the Southern Beauty Barbie features "today's Southern belle with charm and style!"

Barbie doesn't have holes in her clothes (unless placed there by Bob Mackie), she doesn't ever walk because she has a plane, boat, Corvette, bicycle, horse, roller blades, and Ken. Barbie doesn't have a favorite color other than hot pink; she has one logo and no last name. Actually, I once heard her last name is Roberts; so, where are her people from? Barbie does not have holiday sets for Chanukah or Ramadan, although she does have them for Easter and Christmas. Kmart does not have a Kmart Barbie, but there is a Wal-Mart, Saks Fifth Avenue, Gap, Bloomingdales, Avon, and Nichole Miller Barbie (the designer whose ties cost $60).

It is also easier to look at what Barbie isn't. Barbie is never sad, is always available, and "saves the day" in every story written about her. Barbie is timeless; she existed in the days of the Mayflower, she was in Oz as Dorothy, and has run for president in several U.S. elections. She has never been a cook but has been a chef; has never been a construction worker but has been a fashion designer. She has been a soloist, a rock star, and the mythical tooth fairy. Barbie is exclusively thematic; Ken, Christie, and the rest are occasionally given professions.

THE BITCH HAS EVERYTHING

She does. From the pink condo, to the swimming pool, to the RV, to the recording stage, to more friends than anyone. Everyone loves Barbie and Barbie loves everyone. Barbie proves to us that if we try hard enough, we can own anything and everything. Barbie always succeeds. She becomes whatever she sets her mind to—she influences generations of children and adults and is a perpetual reminder of all that is good, wholesome, and pink in our lives. Barbie is a true American. She stands for the family values that our country holds dear. She is strictly heterosexual, self-providing, philanthropic, and moral. She is also ready to bring "other" people into her life, no matter what color or ethnicity.

Barbie moves in and out of social circles with ease. Her plate is always filled with charity organizations and doing "good." The "Love to

Read" Barbie comes with two children (one black and one white) and a book; for every LTR Barbie sold, Mattel donates a dollar to the Reading Is Fundamental organization. As consumers, we are able to support reading by purchasing this doll. That makes all the difference.

INTERCOURSE BARBIE

As much as Barbie is a virgin in sexual relationships, she is a whore in the corporate world. Barbie has "been in bed" with more Fortune 500 members than anyone. She has worked in and owned her own Pizza Hut and McDonald's, she is a special Wal-Mart edition; she is also the star of *Baywatch* and a perennial guest in Happy Meals. Disney's Epcot Center features a Magical World of Barbie show, complete with dancers, singers, and fireworks. Avon regularly offers a special edition Barbie, and Hallmark has Barbie Christmas ornaments, a new one issued each year. I already mentioned the Benetton Barbie, my unlikely find in a broken-down Turkish airport. eBay is filled with bidding searchers for the rare Holiday Barbie each year. Barbie wanders in and out of corporate headquarters with ease. Companies know that if they tap into her resources, it is a quick ride to higher profits. No one really wants the tiny hamburger in the child's meal; they all are looking for the Barbie—which one is she? the Kenyan? the ballerina? or the wedding Barbie? As a professional, Barbie chooses from her cellular phone, her video camera, and numerous pink briefcases for "just the right thing" for breaking that glass ceiling.

As a professional, Barbie has set records for changing vocations. In the early days, she was featured as a nurse, a baby-sitter, and a secretary. Within months of political correctness, she became a doctor, a pilot, and a businesswoman. Naturally, many of her careers still smack of nurturing; how can one avoid it with a perpetual pink motif? One of my favorite fashion sets is the Caring Careers Fashion Gift Set. These "play pieces for Barbie at work" include a firefighter suit with pink trim, a teacher set, and a veterinarian's smock. Dr. Barbie is a pediatrician with a little black child and a little white child, all adorned in pink and blue. Astronaut Barbie came out in the 1980s and reappeared in the late

1990s. As a part of the Career Collection, this Barbie first appeared as a space pioneer. A newer version highlights Space Week and NASA and "encourages children of all ages to discover the past and future of the exploration in space." All of the boxes featuring careers have the slogan We Girls Can Do Anything! ribboned across the front. Police Officer Barbie is a "friend to all in the community! In her glittery evening dress, Police Officer Barbie shines with pride at the Police Awards Ball. Everyone applauds as she receives the Best Police Officer Award for her courageous acts in the community." PO Barbie comes with a badge and a short formal gown for the ball.

No group of careers could be complete without acknowledging our armed forces. As sergeants and majors, these booted girls march to the beat of proud, patriotic America. Choosing a favorite would be hard, but, well, okay, I guess mine was the Desert Storm Barbie. "Wearing authentic desert battle dress uniforms" of camouflage material—Sergeant Barbie is a medic, and she's ready for duty! Staff Sergeant Ken is ready too! Their berets bear the distinctive 101st Airborne unit insignia with the motto: Rendezvous with Destiny. Both are proud, patriotic Americans serving their country wherever they are needed."

Rounding up the professions, 1992 ushered in the Barbie for President Gift Set. This was a Toys R Us limited edition. "Barbie hits the campaign trail in spectacular style! Dressed in her winning red and gold suit she's the picture perfect candidate to get out the vote. Then, at her inaugural ball, the festive crowd cheers as Barbie enters in a sensational sparkling gown sprinkled with silver stars!" We girls can do anything. How about the $75 Statue of Liberty Barbie? Holding the torch of freedom, this golden-haired doll stands perched on a plastic island, adorned with a shimmery crown, beckoning all who will listen to join her in liberty and justice for all. Of course, it may be the only way we can see Lady Liberty, as all visits to her shores are now forbidden.

HERSTORY

Barbie's other identities lie in ethnic and historical roots. Not satisfied with the existential Barbie, Mattel allowed Barbie to revisit, ergo, rewrite the past through a series of historical dolls. Each doll belongs to a collector's set, usually priced from $5 to $100 more than a regular Barbie. A collector's doll should be kept in her box, appreciating in value as the ages tick by.

One must take a little boat down It's a Small World in Disneyland or Disneyworld to understand how ethnicity is defined by a corporation. Sailing down that channel, listening to hundreds of little dolls sing—constantly—we see different peoples grouped together on their continents. Northern countries show a preponderance of buildings and clothing—countries from south of the equator seem to exhibit dolls wearing scant clothing, selling vegetables, taking a siesta, or climbing trees. No buildings are evident in Africa, and only huts appear in the South American countries. Taking It's a Small World seriously as a metaphor for The World, we are able to understand the consciousness that constructed Mattel's line of ethnic Barbies.

Imagine we are sailing through our own small world and meeting these diverse Barbies; we hear their words describing their heritage. Each Barbie is distinct in native dress and manner. The Jamaican Barbie comes with large hoop earrings and a red bandanna. Many exclaim how like Aunt Jemima or a slave she looks. Jamaican Barbie claims that her people speak patois, "a kind of Jamaica talk" filled with English and African words. She also insists Jamaicans are a very "happy" people and are "filled with boonoonoonoos, much happiness." Culturally, this Barbie teaches us that her country is filled with higglers (women merchants) who sell their food in open markets. Along with pictures of Bob Marley, sugar cane, and palm trees, the Jamaican Barbie is prettily packed in hot pink.

In keeping with the island theme, we move to the Polynesian Barbie. The box never mentions which island she is from, somewhere within the thirteen groups of tropical islands. We are told that people live closely together and are kind to one another. Polynesians like luaus and like to eat.

Another Barbie "of color" is the Indian Barbie. Unlike her island cousins, her box shows a picture of a building, the Taj Mahal. We are reminded that India is a very old country and that most people eat only vegetables and rice "with their fingers." It is not mentioned whether or not Indians are happy or kind. None of these Barbies discuss their skin color or hair texture, and there is no mention of physical attributes. Naturally, they are all standing on tiptoe. Puerto Rican Barbie is dressed all in white as she readies herself for, dare I say? Her confirmation. No self-respecting Puerto Rican girlfriend I have has ever done anything but shriek in horror at this plastic sista.

As we visit northern Europe, we do not meet amalgamated Barbies. For instance, there are no British Isles Barbies or Scandinavian Barbies. Each has her own country. The German Barbie looks splendid in her milkmaid's outfit with long blonde braids. We are welcomed to a country that is known for its "breathtaking beauty and hard-working people." Evidently the south of the equator Barbies do not work, or at least not hard. Mentioned on the box are modern cities, museums, art galleries, and industries. The Norwegian Barbie tells us of her mythological tradition and describes her people as "tall, sturdy, fair-skinned, blonde and blue eyed." Food is not mentioned nearly as often on northern Barbies as on the southern counterparts. Evidently the farther north one moves, the less people talk or think about food.

There is no specifically American Barbie. However, there is a Native American Barbie in the Dolls of the World Collection. NA Barbie is a part of a "proud Indian heritage, rich in culture and tradition." Long ago her people belonged to a tribe. Her dress is that of a Plains Indian, yet she describes homes like those constructed by eastern Indians. Three times she mentions her pride in her people.

What's going on here? Mattel has defined ethnicity as other than white. Regular blonde Barbie is the standard from which the "others" come. As it emulates the dominant culture, the norm is Barbie, without a title. All other Barbies are qualified by their language, foods, and "native" dances. Attempting to be multicultural, parents buy these dolls for their children to teach them about "other" people. No "regular" Barbie ever talks about her regular diet, the personality of "her" people, and her customs. Only the designated "ethnic" dolls have those qualifications. Much like the sign in the local Kmart that designates the location of ethnic hair products, Barbie has otherized dolls into dominant and marginal cultures. Barbie's whiteness privileges her to not be questioned; she is the standard against which all others are measured.

THE NEW SOCIAL STUDIES

A couple of years after the ethnic Barbie line, Mattel introduced the American Stories Collection, which featured a Civil War Nurse Barbie, a Pilgrim Barbie, a Pioneer Barbie, and an American Indian Barbie (there she is again). Each doll comes with a storybook that places Barbie in the middle of essential historical action. Each book ends with Barbie "saving the day" and changing history for the better.

As you have probably guessed, the Pilgrim Barbie meets Squanto and he teaches her how to plant corn: "he wasn't savage at all." She grows a successful crop of corn and decides to share it with her neighbors; hence, the first Thanksgiving. And Barbie was there. Conveniently neglected are the Pilgrims' grave robbing, confiscation of Indian lands, and, yes, the sticky matter of genocide.

Since Betsy Ross already made the flag in 1776, Colonial Barbie decides to make a quilt to celebrate the thirteen colonies. The quilt was embroidered "Happy Birthday America" and Barbie and her female helpers were congratulated for it and treated "with great respect." Western Barbie cleverly brings dried apples on the long journey during the westward expansion. When her friends get hungry, the apples are produced to make a delicious apple pie. American Indian Barbie takes care of a papoose, parentage unknown, and tells stories to the little Indian villagers. I will stop here, fearing an overload of saccharine.

Each book is signed on the back with a personal note from the author. History becomes firm in the eyes of the reader as it is legitimized by the author. Here are a few excerpts:

During my research for Western Promise, I learned a lot about pioneers. The more I read, the more I admired these courageous, self-reliant people.

Even though it's fun to read books, I still love to hear someone tell a good story! In the early days of the American Indians, there were no books or schools like there are today.

In writing this story for you, I have learned so much! What I noticed most about the story of the Pilgrims and Thanksgiving is how the Native Americans became their friends and helped these strangers in a new land.

I hope you enjoyed imagining Barbie as a colonial girl. Perhaps you will think of her on the next 4th of July and what it must have been like during the early days when America was first "born."

Consumers are told that history is being taught in a friendly way through Mattel. Children now place Barbie within historical contexts in order to understand what really happened.

Fairy tales and fiction are not immune from Mattel's rewriting. The Children's Collection Series features heroines from different stories. "Childhood favorites 'come to life' with Barbie. Play out the story of Rapunzel." Barbie as Scarlett O'Hara promises to be one of the most successful dolls of the decade. Promoted in a thirty-minute infomercial by Cathy Lee Gifford (a TV Barbie), the doll is sold as essential for anyone who was affected by the novel or movie version of *Gone with the Wind*: "See Barbie as your favorite character, Scarlett," Cathy Lee advises us. She recalls that when she was a little girl, Barbie was her favorite doll and there is nothing more special than having her best friend become Scarlett. The line between reality and fantasy is blurred. Barbie acting as a character?

BARBIE AS LITERARY TEXT

In its merchandising Mattel recognizes the importance of reading and education, creating hundreds of types of reading materials that feature Barbie. Not satisfied with the toy market, Mattel has branched out to themes in magazines, books, newspapers, and film.

The Adventures with Barbie book series features a set of paperback books in which "Barbie stars in her own series of fabulous adventures that tie inspiring messages in with action, suspense and fun with friends—and set an example of independence, responsibility and kindness for young girls everywhere." *Barbie,* the magazine for girls, gives fashion tips, promotes new Barbie themes, teaches fun crafts, and gives beauty advice. The comic market promotes *Barbie Fashion* and *Barbie.* Both comics are monthly and tell "stylish stories" and give "trend-setting tips." Little Golden Books for toddlers include several Barbie titles, including *Very Busy Barbie* (Barbie as a model who gives up her career), *A Picnic Surprise* (Barbie finding an old lady's puppy instead of having fun), and *Barbie, the Big Splash* (Barbie's photo shoot is spoiled, but she is able to take disappointment). We constantly are bombarded by the altruistic blonde (in the books she is usually monocolored) giving up something sensational for the good of all humankind. Little girls are taught at an early age that it is more important to give up one's own goal than to disappoint someone else. Disney did it well with *The Little Mermaid* and *Beauty and the Beast.* It is a female's place to sacrifice for the good of others. What about Pocahontas? Esmeralda? You get the point.

Not to be outdone by three-foot-tall competitors, adults have their own Barbie literature: *Barbie Collector's Magazine* and several weekly and monthly newspapers, the most circulated paper being *Miller's Market Report: News, Advice and Collecting Tips for Barbie Doll Investors.* The tabloid features Barbie events; in an April issue, nineteen "don't miss" gatherings were advertised, including the Great Barbie Show of Southern California, Barbie Comes to Bloomingdale's, Seventh Annual Barbie Grants-A-Wish, and many regional conventions. Barbie clubs adorn the United States from sea to sequined shining sea. There is an annual Barbie world convention, classes on Barbie, and, a couple of years ago, a Barbie summit in New York. To emulate a global consciousness, Mattel organized this summit for women and girls to caucus about their needs and desires from Mattel for the twenty-first century. Always the educator, Barbie proves to us that reading and schooling cannot be left behind. Math becomes essential in order to add up the values of vintage dolls and collectors' items. Barbie, for many, is a full-time occupation. Barbie is the only nonhuman figure in the famed wax museum of Hollywood. Naturally, she has her own Barbie Boutique on Fifth Avenue adjoining F.A.O. Schwartz, a store that provides myriads of books, magazines, videos, and objects devoted to Barbie. The market flourishes.

What could possibly be next?

Are Barbies good for children? Should our girls play with them? How many Barbies should a child own? Do the dolls teach us what true beauty is? Can a child have self-esteem and not look like Barbie? Should we bend to peer pressure and allow our children to reside in pink-trimmed junior condos, dreaming of far-away places and exotic men? Does Barbie assist in constructing childhood consciousness?

Of course she does—just like any other feature of kinderculture. The effect of the Barbie curriculum is idiosyncratic—for some it facilitates conformity; for others, it inspires resistance. Multiple readings aside, Barbie does operate within the boundaries of particular cultural logics. She does celebrate whiteness, blonde whiteness in particular, as a standard for feminine beauty; she does reify anorexic figures coupled with large breasts as objects of male desire. She does support unbridled consumerism as a reason for being. She never questions American virtue and supports the erasure of the colonial genocide in America's past. Make no mistake, she is a Christian, not a Jew, and certainly not a Muslim—mainstream and not countercultural. No poor girl is Barbie as she repetitively displays her upper-middle-class credentials. Again, the curriculum may not take, no effect is guaranteed, but we must be aware of the terrain on which Barbie operates.

Barbie enthusiasts feel great anticipation about the next line of Barbies. Having featured professions, movie stars, stories, sports, and fashion, could Barbie ever run out of themes? By maintaining authenticity, Mattel is able to continue rewriting history and life.

Following the popular Baywatch Barbie, we found an X-Files Barbie complete with unknown blobby substance and missing/replaceable metal limbs. After Barbie has been Scarlett, will she be offered the part of Lady Chatterly? Following Rapunzel, will we see a hairless Barbie? In keeping with real-life professions, wouldn't we be wise to wait for a factory worker Barbie, a prostitute Barbie, a drug pusher Barbie—can a pimp Ken be far behind? What about more politically active Barbies? Protest Barbie, chained to her dream house, Bisexual Barbie, complete with both Ken and Midge (or Steve and Christie)?

The mind wearies with the possibility. One knows for certain, however, Barbie is with us: (13) Yea, verily, she who is known as Barbie will walk the earth through the millennium, being praised by both women and men and ushering in a new day for all humankind.

In 2004, as George W. Bush began his assault on gay and lesbian marriage, Mattel announced the breakup of Barbie and Ken. Although they would always remain "close friends," their romance was over. It seemed proof that the last days are upon us.

Chapter 6

ARE DISNEY MOVIES GOOD FOR YOUR KIDS?

Henry A. Giroux

Though it appears to be a commonplace assumption, the idea that culture provides the basis for persuasive forms of learning for children was impressed on me with an abrupt urgency during the past decade. As a single father of three young boys, I found myself somewhat reluctantly being introduced to the world of Hollywood animation films, and in particular those produced by Disney. Before becoming an observer of this form of children's culture, I accepted the largely unquestioned assumption that animated films stimulate imagination and fantasy, reproduce an aura of innocence, and, in general, are good for kids. In other words, such films appeared to be vehicles of amusement, a source of fun and joy for children. However, it soon became clear to me that the relevance of such films exceeded the boundaries of entertainment. Animated films operate on many registers; one of the most persuasive is the role they play as the new "teaching machines," as producers of culture or what I call forms of public pedagogy. I soon found out that for my children, and I suspect for many others, these films appear to inspire at least as much cultural authority and legitimacy for teaching specific roles, values, and ideals as more traditional sites of learning such as public schools, religious institutions, and the family.

The significance of animated films as a site of learning is heightened by the widespread recognition that schools and other public sites are increasingly beset by a crisis of vision, meaning, and motivation. The mass media, especially the world of Hollywood films, on the contrary, constructs a dreamlike world of childhood innocence where kids increasingly find a place to situate themselves in their emotional lives. Unlike the often hard-nosed, joyless reality of schooling, children's films provide a high-tech, visual space where adventure and pleasure meet in a fantasy world of possibilities and a commercial sphere of consumerism and commodification.

The educational relevance of animated films became especially clear to me as my kids experienced the vast entertainment and teaching machine embodied by Disney. Increasingly as I watched a number of Disney films, first in the movie theater and later on video, I became aware of how necessary it was to move beyond treating these films as transparent entertainment in order to question the messages behind them.

At the same time I recognized that any attempt to take up Disney films critically rubbed against the grain of American popular opinion. After all, the "happiest place on earth" has traditionally gained its popularity in part through a self-proclaimed image of trademark innocence that has protected it from the interrogating gaze of critics. Of course, there is more at work here than a public relations department intent on protecting Disney's claim to fabled goodness and uncompromising reverence. There is also the reality of powerful economic and political power that staunchly protects its mythical status as a purveyor of American innocence and moral virtue.[1] Quick to mobilize its monolith of legal institutions, public relations spokespersons, and professional cultural critics to safeguard the borders of its Magic Kingdom, Disney has aggressively prosecuted violations of its copyright laws, controlled access to the Disney archives, and attempted to influence the uses of material researched in the archives. In its zeal to protect its image and extend its profits, Disney has taken legal action against a small day care center that used Disney cartoon characters in its advertising. In this instance Disney, a self-proclaimed defender of family values, compromised its Dan Quayle philosophy for an aggressive endorsement of property rights. Similarly, Disney has a harsh reputation for applying pressure on authors critical of the Disney ideology and enterprise. But the power of Disney's mythological status comes from other sources as well.

Disney's image as an icon of American culture is consistently reinforced through the penetration of the Disney empire into every aspect of social life. Children experience Disney's cultural influence through a maze of representations and products found in home videos, shopping malls, classroom instructional films, the box office, popular television programs, and family restaurants. Through advertising, displays, and use of public visual space, Disney inserts itself into a network of commodities that lends itself to the construction of the world of enchantment as closed and total category. Disney goes to great lengths to boost its civic image. Defining itself as a vehicle for education and civic responsibility, Disney sponsors Teacher of the Year Awards, provides scholarships to students, and offers financial aid, internships, and educational programs to disadvantaged urban youth through a number of programs.

Disney no longer simply provides the fantasies through which childhood innocence and adventure are produced, experienced, and affirmed. Disney now produces prototypes for model schools, families, identities, communities, and the way the future is to be understood through a particular construction of the past. From the seedy urban haunts of New York City to the spatial monuments of consumption shaping Florida, Disney takes full advantage of refiguring the social and cultural landscape while spreading the ideology of its Disney Imagineers. For instance, not only has Disney taken over large properties on West 42nd Street in New York City in order to produce a number of musicals, it has also constructed Celebration, a town covering 5,000 acres of property in Florida that is designed to accommodate 20,000 citizens. According to Disney, this is a "typical American small town . . . designed to become an international prototype for communities."[2] In actuality, Celebration has turned out to be less a lesson in new urbanism than a community for largely privileged whites. What Disney leaves out of its upbeat promotional literature is the rather tenuous notion of democracy that informs its view of municipal government, since the model of Celebration is "premised upon citizens not having control over the people who plan for them and administer the policies of the city."[3] But Disney does more than provide prototypes for upscale communities; it also makes a claim on the future through its nostalgic view of the past and its construction of public memory as a metonym for the Magic Kingdom.

The French theorist Jean Baudrillard has captured the scope and power of Disney's influence by arguing that Disneyland is more "real" than fantasy because it now provides the image on which America constructs itself. For example, the Houston airport models its monorail after the one at Disneyland. Towns throughout America appropriate a piece of nostalgia by imitating the Victorian architecture of Disneyland's Main Street USA. It seems that the real policymakers reside not in Washington, D.C., but in California, calling themselves the Disney Imagineers. The boundaries between entertainment, education, and commercialization collapse through the sheer omnipotence of Disney's reach into diverse spheres of everyday life. The scope of the Disney empire reveals both shrewd business practices and a sharp eye for providing dreams and products through forms of popular culture in which kids are willing to materially and emotionally invest.

Popular audiences tend to reject any link between ideology and the prolific entertainment world of Disney. And yet Disney's pretense to innocence appears to some critics as little more than a promotional mask that covers over its aggressive marketing techniques and influence in educating children to the virtues of becoming active consumers. Eric Smooden, editor of *Disney Discourse*, a book critical of Disney's role in American culture, argues that "Disney constructs childhood so as to make it entirely compatible with consumerism."[4] Even more disturbing is the widespread belief that Disney's trademarked innocence renders it unaccountable for the diverse ways in which it shapes the sense of reality it provides for children as they take up particular and often sanitized notions of identity, culture, and history in the seemingly apolitical cultural universe of the Magic Kingdom. For example, Jon Wiener, a professor of history at the University of California at Irvine, argues that Disneyland's version of Main Street America harks back to an image of small towns characterized by "cheerful commerce, with barbershop quartets and ice cream sundaes and glorious parades." For Wiener this view not only fictionalizes and trivializes the history of real Main Streets at the turn of the century, it also represents an appropriation of the past to legitimate a present that portrays a world "without tenements or poverty or urban class conflict. . . . [I]t's a native white Protestant dream of a world without blacks or immigrants."[5]

I want to venture into the contradictory world of Disney through an analysis of selected animated films. These films, all produced within two decades, are important because they received enormous praise and achieved blockbuster status. For many children these films represent their first introduction into the world of Disney. Moreover, the success and popularity of these films, rivaling many adult features, do not engender the critical analyses often rendered on adult films. In short, popular audiences are more willing to suspend critical judgment about such children's films. Animated fantasy and entertainment appear to collapse into each other and as such fall outside of the world of values, meaning, and knowledge often associated with more pronounced educational forms such as documentaries, art films, or even wide circulation adult films. Given the influence that the Disney ideology has on children, it is imperative for parents, teachers, and other adults to understand how such films attract the attention and shape the values of the children who view and buy them.

In what follows, I will argue that it is important to address Disney's animated films without either condemning Disney as an ideological reactionary deceptively promoting a conservative worldview under the guise of entertainment or simply celebrating Disney as the Hollywood version of Mr. Rogers doing nothing more than providing sources of joy and happiness to children all over the world. In part, Disney does both. But the role that Disney plays in shaping individual identities and controlling the fields of social meaning through which children negotiate the world is far too complex to be reduced to either position. Disney inscribes itself in a commanding way on the lives of children and powerfully shapes the way America's cultural landscape is imagined. Disney's commanding cultural authority is too powerful and far-reaching to simply be the object of reverence. What Disney deserves is respectful criticism, and one measure of such respect is to insert Disney's scripted view of childhood and society within a critical dialogue regarding the meanings it produces, the roles it legitimates, and the narratives it uses to define American life.

The question of whether Disney's animated films are good for kids has no easy answers but necessitates examining such films outside of the traditional register of fun and entertainment. Disney's most popular films, which include *The Little Mermaid, Aladdin, Beauty and the Beast,* and *The Lion King,* provide ample opportunity to address how Disney constructs a culture of joy and innocence for children out of the intersection of entertainment, advocacy, pleasure, and consumerism. While I have not addressed all of Disney's films, such as *Finding Nemo* and *Haunted Mansion,* I think it is crucial to understand how these films operate within a broader nexus of power and circulation linked less to matters of entertainment than to the dynamics of consumerism and profit making, on the one hand, and the legitimation of particular narratives, stories, values, and identities on the other. These films have been high-profile releases catering to massive audiences. Moreover, their commercial success is not limited to box office profits. Successfully connecting the rituals of consumption and moviegoing, Disney's animated films provide a "marketplace of culture," a launching pad for an endless number of products and merchandise that include videocassettes, sound track albums, children's clothing, furniture, stuffed toys, and theme park rides.[6] In some cases, theme park attractions such as Haunted Mansion provide the basis for the film, which then offers up a host of toys and other forms of merchandise to be peddled to kids and adults.

On a positive note, the wide distribution and popular appeal of these films provide diverse audiences and viewers the opportunity to challenge assumptions that allow people to suspend judgment regarding Disney's accountability for defining appropriate childhood entertainment. Critically analyzing how Disney films work to construct meanings, induce pleasures, and reproduce ideologically loaded fantasies is not meant as an exercise in disparagement. On the contrary, Disney, which made $1.27 billion in profits in 2003, wields corporate and cultural influence so far-reaching that it should go neither unchecked nor unmediated.[7]

The films Disney made under the leadership of CEO Michael Eisner embody structuring principles and themes that have become the trademark of Disney animation. As sites of entertainment, Disney films work because they put children and adults in touch with joy and adventure. They present themselves as places to experience pleasure, even when we have to buy it. Hollywood glitz, colorful animation, and show-stopping musical scores combined with old-fashioned cheer create a celluloid zone of aesthetic and emotional comfort for children and adults alike. The rousing calypso number "Under the Sea" in *The Little Mermaid* and the "Be Our Guest" Busby Berkeley-inspired musical sequence in *Beauty and the Beast* are indicative of the musical talent at work in Disney's animated films. All four of the films draw on the amazing talents of songwriters Howard Ashman and Alan Menken, and the result is a series of musical feasts that provide the emotional glue of the animation experience. Fantasy abounds as Disney's animated films produce a host of exotic and stereotypical villains, heroes, and heroines. While Ursula, the large black and purple squid in *The Little Mermaid*, gushes with evil and irony, the heroine and mermaid, Ariel, appears as a cross between a typical rebellious teenager and a Southern California fashion model. Disney's representations of evil and good women appear to have been fashioned in the editorial office of *Vogue* magazine. The wolflike monster in *Beauty and the Beast* evokes a rare combination of terror and gentleness while Scar, the suave and scheming feline, adds a contemporary touch to the meaning of evil and betrayal. The array of animated objects and animals in these films is of the highest artistic standards. For example, the Beast's enchanted castle in *Beauty and the Beast* becomes magical as household objects are transformed into dancing teacups, a talking teapot, and dancing silverware. *Finding Nemo* offers up a rich mix of dazzling characters and undersea wonderland that is as complex as it is dazzling. Such characters are part of larger narratives of freedom, rites of passage, intolerance, choices, the injustice of male chauvinism, father and son rivalry, and the mobilization of passion and desire that are just some of the many themes explored in these animated films. But enchantment is not without its price if it seduces its audience into suspending critical judgment on the messages produced by such films. Even though these messages can be read through a variety of interpretations and are sometimes contradictory, there are a number of assumptions that structure many of these films that represent the hidden face of Disney.

One of the most controversial messages that weave in and out of Disney's animated films concerns the portrayal of girls and women. In both *The Little Mermaid* and *The Lion King*, the female characters are constructed within narrowly defined gender roles. All of the women in these films are ultimately subordinate to men, and they define their sense of power and desire almost exclusively in terms of dominant male narratives. For instance, modeled after a slightly anorexic Barbie doll, Ariel, the woman-mermaid in *The Little Mermaid,* at first glance appears to be struggling against parental control, motivated by a desire to explore the human world and willing to take a risk in defining the subject and object of her desires. But in the end, the struggle to gain independence from her father, Triton, and the sense of desperate striving that motivates her dissolves when Ariel makes a Mephistophilean pact with the sea witch, Ursula. In this trade, Ariel gives away her voice to gain a pair of legs so that she can pursue the handsome Prince Eric. While children might be delighted by Ariel's teenage rebelliousness, they are positioned to believe in the end that desire, choice, and empowerment are closely linked to catching and loving handsome men. Ariel in this film becomes a metaphor for the traditional housewife-in-the-making narrative. When the sea witch Ursula tells Ariel that taking away her voice is not so bad because men don't like women who talk, the message is dramatized when the prince attempts to bestow the kiss of true love on Ariel even though she has never spoken to him. Within this rigidly defined narrative, womanhood offers Ariel the reward of marrying the right man and renouncing her former life under the sea as a telling cultural model for the nature of female choice and decision-making in Disney's worldview. It is difficult to see how a film such as this does more than reinforce negative stereotypes about women and girls. Unfortunately, this type of stereotyping is reproduced, in varying degrees, in all of Disney's animated films.

In *Aladdin* the issue of agency and power is centered strictly on the role of the young street tramp, Aladdin. Jasmine, the princess he falls in love with, is simply an object of his immediate desire as well as a stepping-stone to social mobility. Jasmine's life is almost completely defined by men; in the end her happiness is ensured by Aladdin, who finally receives permission to marry her.

The gender theme becomes a bit more complicated in *Beauty and the Beast*. Belle, the heroine of the film, is portrayed as an independent woman stuck in a provincial village in eighteenth-century France. Considered odd because she always has her nose in a book, she is pursued by Gaston, the ultimate vain, macho male typical of Hollywood films of the 1980s. To Belle's credit she rejects him, but in the end she gives her love to the Beast, who holds her captive in the hopes she will fall in love with him and break the evil spell cast on him as a young man. Belle not only falls in love with the Beast, she "civilizes" him by instructing him on how to eat properly, control his temper, and dance. Belle becomes a model of etiquette and style as she turns this narcissistic, muscle-bound tyrant into a model of the "new" man, who is sensitive, caring, and loving. Some critics have labeled Belle a Disney feminist because she rejects and vilifies Gaston, the ultimate macho man. Less obviously, *Beauty and the Beast* can also be read as a rejection of hypermasculinity and a struggle between the macho sensibilities of Gaston and the reformed sexist, the Beast. In this reading Belle is less the focus of the film than prop or "mechanism for solving the Beast's dilemma."[8] Whatever subversive qualities Belle personifies in the film, they seem to dissolve when focused on humbling male vanity. In the end, Belle simply becomes another woman whose life is valued for solving a man's problems.

The issue of female subordination returns with a vengeance in *The Lion King*. All of the rulers of the kingdom are men, and they reinforce the assumption that independence and leadership are tied to patriarchal entitlement and high social standing. The dependency that the beloved Mufasa engenders from the women of Pride Rock is unaltered after his death when the evil Scar assumes control of the kingdom. Lacking any sense of outrage, resistance, or independence, the women felines hang around to do his bidding. Given Disney's purported obsession with family values, especially as a consuming unit, it is curious as to why there are no mothers in these films. The mermaid has a domineering father; Jasmine's father is outwitted by his aides; and Belle has an airhead for a father. So much for strong mothers and resisting women.

Jack Zipes, a professor of German at the University of Minnesota and a leading expert on fairy tales, claims that Disney's animated films celebrate a masculine type of power and reproduce "a type of gender stereotyping . . . that [has] an adverse effect on children in contrast to what parents think. . . . Parents think they're essentially harmless—and they're not harmless."[9] Disney films are seen by enormous numbers of children in both the United States and abroad. Disney's view of the relationship between female agency and empowerment is not merely nostalgic but borders on being overtly reactionary.

Racial stereotyping is another major issue that surfaces in many Disney animated films. But the legacy of racism does not begin with the films produced since 1989; on the contrary, there is a long history of racism associated with Disney's work, and it can be traced back to denigrating images of people of color in films such as *Song of the South* (1946) and *The Jungle Book* (1967).[10] Moreover, racist representations of native Americans as violent "redskins" were featured in Frontierland in the 1950s. In addition, the main restaurant in Frontierland featured the real-life figure of a former slave, Aunt Jemima, who would sign autographs for the tourists outside of her "pancake house." Eventually the exhibits and the Native Americans running them were eliminated by Disney executives because the "Indian" canoe guides wanted to unionize. They were displaced by robotic dancing bears. Complaints from civil rights groups led to the elimination of the degrading Aunt Jemima spectacle.[11]

The most controversial example of racist stereotyping associated with the Disney publicity machine occurred with the release of *Aladdin* in 1992, although such stereotyping reappeared in 1994 with the release of *The Lion King*. *Aladdin* was a high profile release, the winner of two Academy Awards, and one of the most successful Disney films ever produced. Playing to massive audiences of children, the film's opening song, "Arabian Nights," begins its depiction of Arab culture with a decidedly racist tone. The song states: "Oh, I come from a land—From a faraway place—Where the caravan camels roam. Where they cut off your ear—If they don't like your face. It's barbaric, but hey, it's home." In this characterization, a politics of identity and place associated with Arab culture magnifies popular stereotypes already primed by the media through its portrayal of the Gulf War. Such racist representations are further reproduced in a host of supporting characters who are portrayed as grotesque, violent, and cruel. Yousef Salem, a former spokesperson for the South Bay Islamic Association, characterized the film in the following way:

> All of the bad guys have beards and large, bulbous noses, sinister eyes and heavy accents, and they're wielding swords constantly. Aladdin doesn't have a big nose; he has a small nose. He doesn't have a beard or a turban. He doesn't have an accent. What makes him nice is they've given him this American character. . . . I have a daughter who says she's ashamed to call herself an Arab, and it's because of things like this.[12]

Jack Shaheen, a former professor of broadcast journalism at Southern Illinois University of Edwardsville, along with radio personality Casey Kasem, mobilized a public relations campaign protesting the anti-Arab themes in *Aladdin*. At first Disney executives ignored the protest, but the rising tide of public outrage prompted them to change one line of the stanza in the subsequent videocassette and worldwide film release; it is worth noting that Disney did change the lyrics on its popular CD release of *Aladdin*.[13] Disney executives were not unaware of the racist implications of the lyrics when they were first proposed. Howard Ashman, who wrote the main title song, submitted an alternative set of lyrics when he delivered the original verse. The alternative set of lyrics, "Where it's flat and immense—And the heat is intense" eventually replaced the original verse, "Where they cut off your ear—If they don't like your face." Though the new lyrics appeared in the videocassette release of *Aladdin*, many Arab groups were disappointed because the verse "It's barbaric, but hey it's home" was not altered. More importantly, the mispronunciation of Arab names in the film, the racial coding of accents, and the use of nonsensical scrawl as a substitute for an actual written Arabic language were not removed.

Racism is a powerful but subtle structuring principle in Disney's animated film *Pocahontas*. In the Disney rendition of history, Pocahontas is converted into a brown Barbie doll, a supermodel with an hourglass figure whose relationship with Aryan hunk John Smith transforms an act of colonial barbarism into a sentimental romance. In this romantic allegory, the rapacious, exploitative narrative of colonialism is rewritten as a multicultural love affair in which issues of human conflict, suffering, and exploitation are conveniently erased. Captain John Smith, whose historical reputation was founded on his unrelenting murderous pursuit of "Indians," is mystified in Disney's *Pocahontas*. Rather than portrayed accurately as part of a colonial legacy that resulted in the genocide of millions of Native Americans, Disney turns John Smith into a morally uplifted, white male who ends up being Mr. Right for an ill-fated brown-skinned version of Calvin Klein model Kate Moss. While Disney's rendition of Pocahontas as a strong-willed woman may seem too politically correct for conservatives, the film is, in actuality, a deeply racist, sexist portrayal of Native Americans.

Racism in Disney's animated films does not simply appear in negative imagery or through historical misrepresentation; racist ideology also appears in racially coded language and accents. For example, *Aladdin* portrays the "bad" Arabs with thick foreign accents, while the Anglicized Jasmine and Aladdin speak in standard American English. A hint of the unconscious racism that informs this depiction is provided by Peter Schneider, president of feature animation at Disney, who points out that Aladdin was modeled after Tom Cruise. Racially coded language is also evident in *The Lion King*, as members of the royal family speak with posh British accents while Shenzi and Banzai, the despicable hyena storm troopers, speak through the voices of Whoopi Goldberg and Cheech Marin in racially coded accents that take on the nuances of the discourse of decidedly urban black and Latino youth. The use of racially coded language in Disney films occurs in an early version of *The Three Little Pigs, Song of the South,* and *The Jungle Book*.[14] Astonishingly, these films produce a host of representations and codes which teach children that cultural differences are deviant, inferior, ignorant, and a threat to be overcome. There is nothing innocent in what kids learn about race as portrayed in the magical world of Disney. The race card has always been central to Disney's view of cultural and national identity. Yet the issue of race only warrants public discussion when it appears in the discourse of civil rights to benefit black people either through affirmative action or in the outcry over the O.J. Simpson verdict. But when the race card is used to denigrate African Americans and other people of color, the issue of race as an act of racism seems to disappear from public discourse.

Another central feature common to many of Disney's animated films is the celebration of deeply, antidemocratic social relations. Nature and the animal kingdom provide the mechanism for presenting and legitimating social hierarchy, royalty, and structural inequality as part of the natural order. The seemingly benign presentation of celluloid dramas in which men rule, strict discipline is imposed through social hierarchies, and leadership is a function of social status suggests a yearning for a return to a rigidly stratified society modeled after the British monarchy of the eighteenth and nineteenth centuries. For children, the messages offered in Disney's animated films suggest that social problems such as racism, the genocide of Native Americans, sexism, and crisis of democratic public life are simply willed through the laws of nature. Clearly, this is a dangerous lesson for powerlessness and a highly conservative view of the social order and relations of the contemporary world.

Does this mean that Disney's children's films should be ignored or censored? I think there are a number of lessons to be learned from recognizing the deeply ideological messages behind Disney's view of the world. First, it is crucial that the realm of popular culture that Disney increasingly uses to teach values and sell goods be taken seriously as a site of learning, especially for children. This means, at the very least, that it must be incorporated into schools as a serious object of social knowledge and critical analysis. Second, parents, community groups, educators, and other concerned individuals must be attentive to the messages in these films in order to both criticize them when necessary and, more importantly, to reclaim them for more productive ends. The roles assigned to women and people of color, along with a rigid view of family values, history, and national identity, need to be challenged and transformed. Such images and their claim to public memory need to be rewritten as part of the script of empowerment rather than simply dismissed because they undermine human agency and democratic possibilities. Third, Disney's all-encompassing reach into the spheres of economics, consumption, and culture suggest that we analyze Disney in a range of relations of power. Eric Smoodin argues correctly that the American public needs to "gain a new sense of Disney's importance, because of the manner in which his work in film and television is connected to other projects in urban planning, ecological politics, product merchandising, United States domestic and global policy formation, technological innovation, and constructions of national character."[15] This suggests undertaking new analyses of Disney that connect rather than separate the various social and cultural formations in which the company actively engages. Clearly, such a dialectical position provides a more theoretically accurate understanding of Disney's power; it also contributes to forms of analysis that rupture the notion that Disney is primarily about the pedagogy of entertainment. Equally important, research about Disney must be at once historical, relational, and multi-faceted.[16] It is perfectly suited for cultural studies, which can employ an interdisciplinary approach to such an undertaking, one that makes the popular the object of serious analysis, makes the pedagogical a defining principle of such work, and inserts the political into the center of the project.[17]

Fourth, if Disney's films are to be viewed as more than narratives of fantasy and escape, as sites of reclamation and imagination that affirm rather than deny the long-standing relationship between entertainment and pedagogy, cultural workers and educators need to insert the political and pedagogical back into the discourse of entertainment. In part, this suggests analyzing how entertainment can be rendered as a subject to work on rather than be passively consumed. This suggests a pedagogical approach to popular culture that engages how a politics of the popular works to mobilize desire, stimulate imagination, and produce forms of identification that can become objects of dialogue and critical investigation. At one level, this suggests addressing the utopian possibilities in which children often find representations of their hopes and dreams. At another level, cultural workers need to combine a politics of representation with a discourse of political economy in order to understand how Disney films work in a broad network of production and distribution as teaching machines within and across different public cultures and social formations. In this type of discourse, the messages, forms of emotional investment, and ideologies produced by Disney can be traced through the various circuits of power that both legitimate and insert the "culture of the Magic Kingdom" into multiple and overlapping public spheres. Moreover, such films need to be analyzed for not only what they say but also how they are used and taken up by adult audiences and groups of children within diverse national and international contexts. Cultural workers need to study these films intertextually and from a transnational perspective. Disney does not represent a cultural monolith ignorant of different context; on the contrary, its power in part rests with its ability to address different contexts and be read differently by transnational formations and audiences. Disney engenders what Inderpal Grewa and Caren Kaplan have called "scattered hegemonies."[18] It is precisely by addressing how these hegemonies operate in particular spaces of power, specific localities, and differentiated transnational locations that progressives will be able to understand more fully the specific agendas and politics at work as Disney is both constructed for and read by different audiences.

Fifth, pedagogically it is imperative that parents, educators, and cultural workers be attentive to how these Disney films and visual media are used and understood differently by diverse groups of kids. This provides an opportunity for parents and others to talk to children about popular culture; it also creates the basis for better understanding how young people identify with these films, what issues need to be addressed, and how such discussions would open up a language of pleasure and criticism rather than simply shut down such a conversation. This suggests that we develop new forms of literacy, new ways of critically understanding and reading the electronically produced visual media. Teaching and learning the culture of the book is no longer the staple of what it means to be literate. Children learn from exposure to popular cultural forms and these provide a new cultural register to what it means to be literate. Educators and cultural workers need to recognize the need to take seriously the production of popular art forms in the schools; there can be no cultural pedagogy without cultural practices that both explore the possibilities of different popular forms and bring out students' talents. Students should not merely analyze the representations of electronically mediated, popular culture; they must also be able to master the skills and technology to produce it. This means making films, videos, music, and other forms of cultural production. Needless to say, this suggests giving students more power over the conditions for the production of knowledge; but a cultural pedagogy also involves the struggle for more resources for schools and other sites of learning.

Sixth, I think it is crucial to understand that Disney's cultural identity cannot be separated from its identity as a corporate power and that its corporate identity must be understood within a larger framework of neoliberal capitalist relations. Disney is one of the largest global corporations in the world, and the real threat it poses does not reside in its ability to commercially carpet-bomb children with its endless appeals to commercialism. Nor does it reside in its utterly racially scripted view of the world, a world in which a bleached, conflict-free history and a suburban zeitgeist offers up a one-dimensional view of both the United States and the rest of the globe. The real threat from Disney comes from its power to monopolize public space, shape policy, enact media censorship, and shape the world of politics. All in all, Disney's presence in the global infrastructure of neoliberalism is a threat to democracy itself. As the democratic state is transformed into the corporate state, government begins to look more like entertainment and citizens act more like spectators.

Finally, I believe that since the power and influence of Disney is so pervasive in American society, parents, educators, and others need to find ways to make Disney accountable for what it produces. The defeat of the proposed theme park in Virginia suggests that Disney can be challenged and held accountable for the so-called Disnification of American culture. While Disney provides both children and adults with the pleasure of being entertained, Disney's public responsibility does not end there. Rather than being viewed as a commercial public sphere innocently distributing pleasure to young people, the Disney empire must be seen as a pedagogical and policymaking enterprise actively engaged in the cultural landscaping of national identity and the "schooling" of the minds of young children. This is not to suggest that there is something sinister behind what Disney does as much as it points to the need to address the role of fantasy, desire, and innocence in securing particular ideological interests, legitimating specific social relations, and making a distinct claim on the meaning of public memory. Disney needs to be held accountable not just at the box office, but also in political and ethical terms. And if such accountability is to be impressed on the Magic Kingdom, then parents, cultural workers, and others will have to challenge and disrupt the images, representations, and values offered by Disney's teaching machine. The stakes are too high to ignore such a challenge and struggle, even if it means reading Disney's animated films critically.

Chapter 7

GOT AGENCY? REPRESENTATIONS OF WOMEN'S AGENCY IN HARRY POTTER

Ruthann Mayes-Elma

And shall we just carelessly allow children to hear any casual tales which may be devised by casual persons, and to receive into their minds ideas for the most part the very opposite of those which we should wish them to have when they are grown up? We cannot!

—Plato, 340 B.C.

Since *Harry Potter and the Philosopher's Stone*, the first book in the Harry Potter series, was published in Great Britain in 1997, "Pottermania" has taken the world by storm. Indeed, there may be no other twentieth-century book read by more children worldwide. Many have analyzed the "Harry Potter phenomenon," addressing questions such as, Why is Harry Potter so beloved by children? What made this the best-selling children's book of all time? What are the occult messages embedded in this text? Although the Harry Potter series has been critiqued and analyzed by journalists and academics alike, there are fascinating gaps in the analyses. Perhaps the most rousing of these gaps is the virtual lack of attention to the ways in which J.K. Rowling has constructed gender and the agency of the female characters in these texts.

THE HARRY POTTER PHENOMENON

Harry Potter and the Philosopher's Stone was published in Great Britain in 1997. The instant success of the first and subsequent books, as well as Rowling's quick rise to fame, has amazed scholars. Nicholas Tucker noted how rapidly the Harry Potter books became a household name:

> The phenomenal commercial and critical success of the first three Harry Potter stories is without precedent in twentieth-century British children's literature. Other best selling writers have made a lot of money quickly, but none had managed in a first novel to prove so instantly acceptable both to critics and to a vast international child and adult readership. In just two years, after being refused by at least two major publishers, J.K. Rowling is now the hottest property in children's literature and serial prize-winner to boot. (1999, 221)

By 2000, the more than two dozen languages into which Harry Potter had been translated had risen to thirty-five languages (Grossberg 2000, 1); it was last reported to be translated into forty-seven languages in late 2001 (Puig 2001, 1E).

Since the first book, retitled *Harry Potter and the Sorcerer's Stone,* came out in the United States in 1997, it and the three subsequent volumes have been on the *New York Times* bestsellers list continuously. This is the first time since *The Wizard of Oz* was published in 1900 that a children's book has resided on the *New York Times* best-seller list. Harry Potter dominated the list to such a degree that in 2000 publishers of adult books demanded that the *New York Times* exclude children's literature and make it a separate list. When the first children's literature list came out in December 2000, the Harry Potter novels topped it off (Jenkins 2001, 1).

By 2002 the first four books, *Harry Potter and the Sorcerer's Stone* (1997), *Harry Potter and the Chamber of Secrets* (1999), *Harry Potter and the Prisoner of Azkaban* (1999), and *Harry Potter and the Goblet of Fire* (2000), had sold 175 million copies (Majendie 2002, 1). The great success of the books is especially intriguing given the length of the novels. One of the complaints the publishers had of the first manuscript Rowling submitted was that it was too long for a children's book at an overwhelming 309 pages. They did not think the book would be read if it stayed at 309 pages, and as a result they were unwilling to sign a contract with Rowling to publish her book. Eventually Rowling did get a contract with Bloomsbury Books, and after the success of *Harry Potter and the Philosopher's Stone* she received a contract with Scholastic for $105,000, which is the highest sum ever paid for a children's book.

Since the first book Rowling has increased the length of each successive book, with the longest being almost nine hundred pages. However, children do not seem to have a problem with the page length; they are still coming out in droves to get their hands on the newest copy. Beach and Willner (2002) found that children liked the length of the Harry Potter books. Nathan, a young boy, stated, "I was glad to get to read that big book. It made me feel important" (105). Not only does being able to read such lengthy books make children feel important, it makes children who did not like to read want to read. Ten-year-old Jennifer stated, "I don't usually like to read, matter of fact I don't like to read. I thought Harry Potter was going to be an ordinary book, but it isn't. . . . When my teacher says that it [is] time to stop reading, me and my classmates would groan" (102). This positive attitude toward reading has not gone unnoticed by adults. In a 2002 issue of the *Toledo Blade* an editorial cartoon by Kirk Walters appears with a father standing over his son who is reading a Harry Potter book, while, in the background, the television set is black. The father asks his son, "If Harry Potter is such a cool wizard, what's his greatest achievement?" to which his son replies, "Getting me to turn off the TV and open a book."

Not only have adults taken notice of the Harry Potter phenomenon, teachers have incorporated the books into their lessons. It is now standard practice at the elementary school at which I used to teach that all fifth graders read *Harry Potter and the Sorcerer's Stone*. At a Cincinnati high school, freshmen are required to read *Harry Potter and the Sorcerer's Stone*. Scholastic publishing company has even created a teacher's guide for each Harry Potter novel, giving teachers multiple resources to use in their classrooms.

Harry Potter is not just for K–12 education anymore. Adults have also designed courses around the books at the collegiate level. The University of Cincinnati in Ohio and Boise State University in Idaho began classes centered on the Harry Potter books in 2001. The University of Cincinnati offered *Harry Potter: A Cultural Phenomenon* in June 2001. This group looked at the philosophy that the Harry Potter novels were promoting to children and the parallels that run through the novels. Boise State University offered Harry Potter: Mythology/Fantasy Worlds in the Education and Library Science Departments.

THE CRITIQUE OF HARRY POTTER

Clearly Harry Potter is a worldwide phenomenon. And while garnering great acclaim, it has also come under intense criticism. Interestingly, much of this criticism has condemned the Harry Potter books because they are said to be "dangerous, evil and perverted" (Gibson 2001, 1). Harry Potter has been attacked by many evangelical Christians as "glamorizing the occult" (Yahoo online 2002, 1). "Pottermania is corrupting the minds of young people" has been preached in Christian churches. Pastors in a variety of denominations have given sermons to their congregations about the dangers of allowing their children to read the Harry Potter books or watch the movie *Harry Potter and the Sorcerer's Stone* (Gibson 2001; Yahoo online 2002). Christian officials have discussed many characteristics of the Harry Potter books, from Harry's broomstick to Harry's scar to Harry's mother's death, as representations of the occult.

When Ms. Post, a current teacher, first heard of the controversy over the Harry Potter books, she raced out and bought a copy to read. "Whenever I hear a book is controversial I go out and read it right away. I figure it's my duty to read it and be able to talk about it intelligently with my students" (Rosendale 2001, 2). Rushing out to buy the Harry Potter books was not the first time Ms. Arden, another teacher, had raced out to purchase a "controversial" book. She bought a Dr. Seuss book, *Bartholomew and the Oobleck* (1970), when it was said to be "controversial" because of its use of magicians as characters in the book, and she bought Roald Dahl's *Matilda* (1988) when it came out and was considered inappropriate because of the lack of respect Matilda showed her parents. Arden believes that people are overreacting to the Harry Potter books and their use of wizards and witchcraft:

> It's fantasy and lots of children's books involve fantasy. Children know that to read is to lose themselves in another world. Yes, there are evil spirits and witchcraft and some think the Harry books promote witchcraft, but I see them as simply describing a fantasy life and doing that very well. (Rosendale 2001, 2)

In the controversy surrounding the Harry Potter books, the construction of gender, and other social locations, is rarely if ever critiqued. This is very disconcerting; why aren't critics discussing the overt messages of sexism in these texts? One notable exception is Heilman (2003), who critiques Harry Potter in terms of family unit, ethnicity, class, and gender. In her analysis of the Harry Potter books Heilman finds male characters depicted as wiser, braver, more powerful, and more fun than their female counterparts. Female characters are depicted as anti-intellectual, fearful, and emotional (2003, 223–224).

Such messages of sexism and the representations of gender must be critically examined. It is ironic that people would rather discuss "subliminal" messages of evil in Harry Potter than overt messages of sexism. It is of dire importance that we investigate what is being taught to children through children's literature. Children begin hearing these stories sometimes before they are even born, in the womb, and begin reading children's literature starting at a very early age. Children hearing such sexist stories over and over again become desensitized to the sexist content and believe it to be normal. If we, as a society, want to end sexism, I believe a good place to start is to teach students to read critically. Both boys and girls need to be shown that neither gender needs to be oppressed by the other.

With ushering in the twenty-first century, we have also continued to usher into our lives the postmodern child/childhood, as described by Shirley Steinberg and Joe Kincheloe (1998). Children have been and are still being bombarded with social, cultural, political, and economic forces that delegate to them to promote the oppressive nature that has plagued our society for way too long. That oppressiveness is taken out on minorities, whether they are defined by race, ethnicity, culture, sexual orientation, gender, and so on. Although gender analysis and reconceptualization have been talked about and researched over the past years, not much has changed in the culture of children, or kinderculture. Steinberg and Kincheloe (1998) pointed out that "where as the gender analysis of popular culture advances and grants important insights into media construction of gender, kinderculture continues to promote delineated gender roles" (25). This is why it is so important to promote understanding of these atrocities in hopes of leading to pedagogies that promote social justice for childhood at every level of existence.

That having been said, reflecting and analyzing the interpretations and explanations across the myriad examples of female characters' use of agency in Harry Potter reveals common themes. Five themes predominate: rule following and breaking, intelligence, validating/enabling, mothering, and "bounded" resistance.

THEME 1: RULE FOLLOWING AND BREAKING

One of the overarching themes was that of rules. In researching the Kevin character in *Home Alone*, Kincheloe found that rule breaking is a postmodern construct of childhood. No longer do children in movies and books have a "simpleminded the-policeman-is-our-friend view of the world" (Kincheloe 1998, 48). Instead, children in the postmodern world see themselves as adults and with that comes the right to break the rules. No longer is the hero a Dudley Do-Right type of character. On the contrary, in a postmodern world the hero is the wisecracking, rule-breaking character. Kincheloe refers to this hero as the "hero of the subversive kinderculture" (49). The characters that do not break the rules are seen by the postmodern child as "antimatter reflections of themselves" (48).

While the female characters in *Harry Potter* generally enforced or were concerned with following the rules, the male characters generally broke the rules. This role of rule enforcement begins in the very first scene where the primary female protagonist, Hermione, appears. When Hermione first met Harry and Ron on the train bound for Hogwarts, she was very disturbed that "people outside are behaving very childishly, racing up and down the corridors." No one else was represented as caring about the train rules (Rowling 1997, 110). Hermione was seen by the boys as not being fun-loving or carefree, but instead boring because she was so concerned with the rules.

Professor McGonagall also enacts her agency through enforcing the rules. When Harry, Ron, and Hermione are found out of their beds in the middle of the night helping Hagrid's dragon Norbert escape, Professor McGonagall punishes them: "She [Professor McGonagall] looked more likely to breathe fire than Norbert as she towered over the three of them. . . . 'I'm disgusted,' said Professor McGonagall. . . . 'All three of you will receive detentions . . . nothing gives you the right to walk around school at night, especially these days, it's very dangerous— and fifty points will be taken from Gryffindor'" (Rowling 1997, 243).

Many times during the book women are exerting their agency in order to maintain the status quo, by enforcing or following the rules. Although this may not be the most exciting form, it is an "accepted" form of agency for a woman to enact (Luke and Freebody 1997). The problem with this form of agency is that it perpetuates what is constructed in dominant discourse as appropriate or inappropriate for different groups of people.

The status quo the women in the text are trying to maintain has deemed women as the "other." So in essence they are maintaining a patriarchal system in which they are the outsider. As Foucault (1978) said, being the other is constructed in the dominant discourse as deviant, thus not what you are "supposed" to want to be. This holds true in this text; the other (female characters) is not a part of the group but is usually outside of the group and is as deviant because of concern with the rules of the institution. Women and girls try to maintain the status quo in the text but are resisted by the male characters. This sets up an interesting binary opposition of women–men and rule enforcers–rule breakers.

The men are the ones in the book, and usually in society as a whole, who make the rules; men set up the system of power, yet they do not want to play by the rules. Women have been largely silent when it comes to making rules or even questioning the rules; instead they have followed the rules (de Beauvoir 1949; hooks 2000a,b; Kristeva 1974; Woolf 1929). So, if women are supposed to follow the rules but men are not held to that same standard, who are the rules set up for? The answer to that would have to be "women" (Woolf 1929). If men, in a patriarchal society, set up the system of power, thus setting up the rules and preaching about how important they are, but are at the same time consciously breaking the rules in various ways, men are shown to be "above" the system/rules. The individuals who are not "above" the rules are women. Both Druxes (1996) and Foucault (1978) believe that women and minorities go along with and follow the rules that the patriarchal system of power sets forth because they have internalized various types of control regimes and in some instances have become "no more than a docile body, unconsciously reproducing repressive power relations" (Druxes 1996, 9). Various feminists, such as Butler (1993), would disagree with this idea of a "docile body." Butler believes that many women understand the system of power to be oppressive, but feel the need to maintain the status quo because of negative consequences that might occur if they used their agency to go against dominant societal power.

In a few scenes in the text female characters do break the rules, thus enacting a form of their agency and going against the dominant system of power. Hermione is shown in the second half of the text as breaking some rules, but only to help or enable the male characters in some way; she is never shown to break rules for her own interest. For example, Hermione put a spell on Neville, petrifying him, to keep him from following Harry, Ron, and her on their quest to find the Sorcerer's Stone (Rowling 1997, 273). Although Hermione knew it was against school rules to use magic outside of the classroom, she did anyway in order to better serve the interest of the group, not her self-interest.

Although girls are shown in a minority of scenes breaking the rules and enacting their agency, such female rule breaking only occurs within specific boundaries. Harry and Ron state that they like Hermione much better when she breaks the rules (Rowling 1997, 181), perhaps because she breaks the rules to help them. Would they like Hermione if she broke the rules for her own sake? I don't think so. When boys in the text break the rules, they act in their own interest, but girls break the rules as a selfless act that serves the boys' interest, which again maintains the dominant patriarchal system of power. There is not one scene in the text that shows a female character breaking the rules on her own behalf or for another female. Enacting agency for the good of the "group," or shared agency, is for the betterment of the male characters, not the female characters. The male characters compose the "group"; females are not portrayed as ever being in this group, which again shows this sense of woman as the other. And as the "other," at least in this text, Hermione tries to help the male characters by using her agency to resist, but never using her agency to resist her own otherness and oppression. This is also often perpetuated in society with the idea of the woman helping to further the man, but never vice versa. This concept of shared agency is consistent with May's definition, which states it is "two or more people act[ing] together to produce a common result" (1992, 53). Although Hermione does break the rules on occasion, her goal is shared with Harry and Ron; they all want the same result. What needs to be added to May's definition is the idea of whose interests shared agency serves.

Not only do boys and girls have different roles to play in the text when it comes to rule following and rule breaking, they are also reacted to differently by teachers when they break the rules. A male character who breaks the rules is usually not punished or not punished as severely as the rules say the student should be; in some cases the boys are even rewarded. When Hermione lied to Professor McGonagall, telling her that she had gone out of the dorm to capture the troll, when in fact it was Harry and Ron who had done this, Hermione was just in the wrong spot at the wrong time and she was punished. On finding out what

Hermione supposedly did, Professor McGonagall said, "Miss Granger, you foolish girl, how could you think of tackling a mountain troll on your own?" and then took five points from Hermione's house, or dorm, saying she was "very disappointed" in her (Rowling 1997, 178). Although to the true rule breakers, Harry and Ron, Professor McGonagall said, "You were lucky, but not many first years could have taken on a full-grown mountain troll. You each win Gryffindor five points" (178). This double standard of what is acceptable for boys to do is not what is acceptable for girls to do and vice versa is perpetuating the traditional construction of genders. This again shows that there are clear-cut boundaries in the text around rule breaking for women and men, and these boundaries are set up according to patriarchal systems of power.

Finally, on the off chance that women do enact their agency and break the rules, they are shown to be remorseful and ashamed afterward, as Hermione was after she was caught sneaking out of the dorm to help Norbert (Hagrid's dragon) be rescued. She felt so badly that she withdrew from her classes, which she is shown to be highly invested in (Rowling 1997, 245). Boys on the other hand are not shown to be remorseful or ashamed; they do not seem to be affected in any way. This differential reaction to breaking the rules further perpetuates traditional gender constructions, where the woman is supposed to be sorry for what she has done, but the man is not supposed to give it enough thought to be sorry or regretful.

In summary, women in this text enacted their agency through following the rules, which is not necessarily a bad thing. When women broke the rules, though, their consequences were much more severe. Women are shown to be the rule enforcers, as well as the rule followers; men, on the other hand, are seen to be the rule breakers. By enforcing the rules, women are maintaining the status quo system of power, which oppresses women, but at the same time women are enacting their agency through one of the few "accepted" forms by enforcing the rules.

THEME 2: INTELLIGENCE

Intelligence was a second overarching theme. The most frequent way in which the two main female characters in the text, Hermione and Professor McGonagall, enacted their agency was through their intelligence. Unlike the theme of rule enforcing, the use of intelligence to show agency can be used to further both the girl's own interest and the interests of others. There are scenes in the text where both Hermione and McGonagall enact their agency through intelligence in order to accomplish their own goals. For example, Hermione is obsessed with studying for final exams months before they are given. She wants to do well on her exams because she has set that as one of her goals. She does not study because it would be best for others, but because it would be best for her. She takes her education very seriously and accepts responsibility for it (Rowling 1997, 228–229, 234, 263). Hermione prides herself on being intelligent and puts great time and effort into being so, and has created her whole identity around it. But at the end of the text, when Harry tries to praise her for being smart and tell her that she is smarter than he, she downplays it, just as society would have her do. "'Me!' said Hermione. 'Books! And cleverness! There are more important things— friendship and bravery and—oh Harry—be careful!'" (Rowling 1997, 287). Even though Hermione is proud of her intellect, she downplays it and states that there are more important things, which is ironic indeed. Hermione has struggled and worked for everything she has gotten, but when the boy (her master) praises her she retreats and puts him back up on the pedestal from which he had climbed down, where society has told girls boys should be. Of course this sort of traditional gendered construction is not surprising. Throughout the text traditional constructions of males and females prevail time and time again.

Professor McGonagall is no different when it comes to enacting her agency through intelligence. She takes great pride in her intelligence, and throughout the text she is in positions of power due to her intellect. In one scene in particular, Professor McGonagall is one of the few people who knows Dumbledore has left the school due to urgent Ministry of Magic business. Harry, Ron, and Hermione go to her asking to see Dumbledore because they believe the Sorcerer's Stone is in danger of being stolen. Professor McGonagall promptly tells them that Dumbledore has left Hogwarts for the day, but rest assured the Stone is very safe (Rowling 1997, 267–268).

Although there are scenes in which the female characters in the text enact their agency through their intelligence for their own interest, more often than not they further the interests of others. This concept is no different from that of rule breaking, when the female characters broke the rules in order to help serve the interests of others instead of their own. Of course, this allows the oppressive patriarchal system of power to remain intact.

The way women's intelligence is constructed in the text is very different from the way men's intelligence is constructed. The representation of an intelligent man in the text is multifaceted. On the one hand, Dumbledore is a distinguished-looking man who has many friends and confidants, a man who is not made fun of or intimidated by others, and a man whom everyone would like to know. Throughout the text he is shown to always know the "correct" answer/information when many people do not. He is shown to have a lot of responsibilities but handles them with the greatest of ease, and he is shown to be well-liked by most everyone in the wizarding community. On the other hand, Professor Snape is shown to be of great intelligence, but his appearance is described as "a teacher with greasy black hair, a hooked nose, and sallow skin" (Rowling 1997, 126). Therefore Rowling presents the figure of an intelligent man as having differing variations; the boundaries for men around what it means and looks like to be intelligent are much wider than the boundaries for women in the text. This is not surprising, since it is a patriarchal power system that sets up these boundaries.

Both Professor McGonagall and Hermione are shown to be intelligent women, but they are traditionally constructed to represent "nerds." Both are physically unattractive. McGonagall is described as being "a rather severe-looking woman who was wearing square glasses . . . her black hair was drawn into a tight bun. She looked distinctly ruffled" (Rowling 1997, 9). Hermione is described as having "a bossy sort of voice, lots of bushy brown hair, and rather large front teeth" (105). The women in the text have a restricted range of looks if they are intelligent, whereas men do not. A man can be attractive or unattractive and be considered intelligent, whereas a woman must be unattractive to be considered intelligent. A man in the text can also be shown to be intelligent whether or not he is well liked by others, but an intelligent woman in the text is not permitted to have many friends. This particular representation of intelligence for women leads to the belief that women's intelligence is a negative. When women in the text enact their agency through their intelligence, it results in a negative view of them, since the other characters in general see them as "bossy and nosey." An intelligent woman is described as a hissing goose (155) and a "bossy know-it-all" (164).

The different representations of the intelligence of women and men in the text reflect what is constructed in the dominant discourse. Our patriarchal society accepts men as being intelligent, but not women. It is not the norm for women to be intelligent, and those who are must be physically unattractive and have few friends. On the other hand, it is the "norm" for men to be intelligent; their attractiveness or unattractiveness is not really an issue. The boundaries around gendered intelligence are much wider and more accommodating for men than for women. As with the theme of rule making/rule breaking, there is a double standard presented in the text.

These representations of the intelligence of men versus women support the power hierarchy of a patriarchal system. Men are allowed intelligence in myriad forms, whereas women's intelligence must occur within strict boundaries. Such constructions allow women to have some power (their intelligence) but at a cost (must be unattractive and unpopular). A rather insidious aspect of patriarchy is convincing the oppressed that they do indeed have some power and control, and simultaneously restricting this power to prevent true equality.

Ironically, de Beavoir (1949) and Tong (1998) both emphasize that the way women can transcend their oppressed state, and empower themselves, is by becoming intellectuals. De Beavoir and Tong emphasize critical analysis of texts as part of this intelligence. While Hermione and Professor McGonagall enact their agency and become empowered through their intelligence, they are not allowed to fully transcend male oppression or critique their own oppression and the institutions that support it. Rather, they are granted "partial power" that supports the oppressiveness of the patriarchal institutional system.

THEME 3: VALIDATING/ENABLING

A third theme that emerged from my interpretation and explanation of agency was validating/enabling. In various scenes throughout the text female characters ask male characters to validate what had been told to the female characters. At no point did the male characters know more about the situation or problem than the female characters did, but the female characters still asked for the male characters' validation. At first I saw this as a lack of agency, but as I delved deeper into the interpretation and explanation I realized that this was yet another form of "bounded" agency. By asking questions the female characters are trying to learn more about the situation they are in. Various scenes in the text include women questioning what had occurred in order to gain some kind of understanding and to become more informed.

When the women in the text enact their agency through questioning, they are represented as weak and unintelligent, which is quite the contrary to how they are portrayed in other scenes. Even though they are enacting their agency, they are shown enacting it through traditional constructions of gender. Women characters in the text are permitted to question, but just as in other themes they are only permitted to go so far and then they must stop. Women do not ask questions of other women, only of men. In a patriarchal society why would a woman ask validation of another woman when men hold the knowledge and power?

An example of agency through validation would be when Voldemort killed Harry's parents but could not kill Harry; thus it was rumored that Harry had defeated Voldemort. After hearing this, Professor McGonagall enacted her agency and asked Dumbledore if the rumors or what she had heard were true. Even though Professor McGonagall knew just as much about the situation as Dumbledore, she still felt the need to ask for his validation of it.

The interesting part of this theme is that Professor McGonagall has been shown to be a very intelligent woman, but in situations or scenes where Dumbledore is present she becomes a person who constantly questions her intelligence and therefore must ask Dumbledore for validation. This again, just as in the other themes, sets up a binary opposition of male–female, validator–questioner. The text shows women enacting their agency through questioning what they hear and thereby questioning their own intelligence. Men do not need to question what they hear; instead, they rely on their own intelligence to determine for themselves if what they have heard is true or false. Although the women in the text constantly ask men for validation, which is a traditional construction of woman, the men never know more than the women, which goes against the traditional construction of man. By setting up this binary opposition of validator–questioner, society has constructed a patriarchal society in which women are socialized to be reliant on men, which reinforces and reproduces women's oppression. It is expected for women to ask men questions, but not to question the man's response to the question. Just as with the previous themes, the boundaries around who is constructed in the dominant discourse as being "permitted" to ask questions are much wider for men than for women.

Coupled with validation is the theme of enabling; here, women enact their agency in order to enable men's agency or triumph. Again this brings up how women are permitted to enact agency, but only in certain ways. As long as a woman is enacting her agency in order to help or further the interests of the man, it is all right. But women enacting agency in order to help or further their own interests is not permitted.

An example of this would be when Hermione helped Harry find the Sorcerer's Stone by playing a game of "Wizard's Chess" in which she was a piece on the chess table. By playing, Hermione risked her life because in Wizard's Chess if your piece loses you die. Without her help Harry would not have been able to finally conquer Voldemort and capture the Sorcerer's Stone, thus becoming the triumphant hero.

This form of agency aids in the traditional construction of woman as inferior. Although Hermione is shown to be intelligent, she is consistently put in the position of aiding Harry, which constructs her as the inferior or the other; she is not permitted to enact her agency on her own behalf. Hermione is never seen in the text as enacting agency for her own triumph. She is instead constructed as being a means to Harry's end, so to speak. This is in keeping with the previous literature, which stated that binary oppositions are set up in order for the dominant group to remain dominant and in power by oppressing the other (Glenn 2000). This allows the institutionalized system of power to remain intact, thus maintaining the empowerment of men but not women.

THEME 4: MOTHERING

The fourth theme that reoccurred in the text was mothering. Throughout the text there are multiple examples of female characters enacting their agency to be a mother and a mothering figure. The only women in the text to have children are Mrs. Weasley (Ron's mother) and Petunia Dursley, who take on the traditional role of mother: caring, nurturing women who devote themselves to their biological children. Even though Mrs. Weasley's children play tricks on her and say things to upset her, she is always concerned about their well-being. In one scene she sends Harry a hand-knitted sweater for Christmas because she didn't want him to be the only child without anything to open on Christmas morning. Ron sees the sweater and groans "'oh, no,' . . . 'she's made you a Weasley sweater'" (Rowling 1997, 200). Ron then explains to Harry that every year his mother knits awful-looking sweaters for her children, but of course she sees them as beautiful. For all the loving care that she puts into the sweaters, they are made fun of and go unappreciated.

Even the youngest generation at Hogwarts is not without its construction of mothering; Hermione enacts her agency through mothering many times throughout the text. When Harry or Ron is sick or injured, Hermione is the caregiver, helper, and worrier. In one scene Hermione tries to get Harry to eat before the big Quidditch game, "'just a bit of toast', wheedled Hermione" (Rowling 1997, 184). Although her "wheedling" was to no avail, she still tried to make Harry feel better. Another scene in the text shows Hermione trying to calm Ron down because he was in a lot of pain while he was in the hospital. "'It'll all be over at midnight on Saturday,' said Hermione, but this didn't soothe Ron at all" (238). Again, her mothering quality did not help the situation.

Professor McGonagall and Madam Hooch are two other women in the text who enact their agency through being motherlike figures, even though they do not have children of their own. The two women often help students with both school work and personal problems, take them to the nurse when they are hurt or don't feel well, and worry about the students' safety. Even though the two women are not mothers, they are constructed in this mothering role.

The mothering in the text is not always effective. Both Mrs. Weasley and Petunia Dursley nurture their own sons but are ineffective and thus get taken advantage of by them. Petunia's son, Dudley, does not appreciate his mother and in most cases is not consoled or comforted by her persistent caring and coddling. In many scenes throughout the text Dudley takes advantage of his mother's caring nature in order to get what he wants.

> Dudley began to cry loudly. In fact, he wasn't really crying—it had been years since he'd really cried—but he knew that if he screwed up his face and wailed, his mother would give him anything he wanted. "Dinky Duddydums, don't cry, Mummy won't let him [Harry] spoil your special day!" she cried, flinging her arms around him. "I . . . don't . . . want . . . him . . . t-t-to come!" Dudley yelled between huge, pretend sobs. "He always sp-spoils everything!" He shot Harry a nasty grin through the gap in his mother's arms. (Rowling 1997, 23)

Without regard for their feelings, both sets of sons use their mothers' good-natured, caring demeanor for their own advantage. What is interesting in this particular text is that daughters are not described as acting this way, only sons.

Noddings notes that being the caretaker is a joyful experience. The effect of that joy is that "it accompanies our recognition of relatedness and reflects our basic reality. Its occurrence and recurrence maintain us in caring and, thus, contribute to the enhancement of the ethical ideal" (1984, 147). I do not see how Petunia and Mrs. Weasley are having a joyful experience when they are so ineffective and their sons are taking advantage of them. Caring comes from a place inside that is "good," as Noddings suggests; although you enact your agency through care, you may not receive the kind of response you intended. In this text many of the women enact their agency through caring for male characters, but only a few of them are appreciated for doing so; instead, caring is something they are expected to do because they are women.

These representations of woman as mother are in keeping with Nancy Chodorow's (1978) research. She stated that women's mothering is a product of "feminine role training and role identification" (31). She notes that girls identify with their mothers as they grow up, and this produces the girl as a mother. This social construction of mothering does not happen in isolation, though. Margaret Polatnick (1973) also believes that woman's role as mother is a social construction and men use their power to enforce the perpetuation of mothering. Since men are usually the ones who hold the power in society, it is in their best interest to keep women in the mothering and caregiving role. With this construction of woman, both in society and in the text, there is no sense of the disciplinarian, as there would be with a fatherlike construction. Woman as mother does not enact her agency in order to discipline others; if disciplinary action is taken, it is not by a woman.

Traditionally, a woman who is not seen as a mothering figure is a cold, heartless, selfish person; but men are not seen in this binary way. There is a middle ground for men that is not permissible for women; the boundaries are much wider for men and much narrower for women. Men do not have to be the nurturer or the self-centered person; they can also be a combination of the two and find a happy medium. Women are either the nurturer, which is traditionally what women are supposed to want to be, or the self-centered bitch.

In this text there are two exceptions to the mothering figure: the stepmother and the teacher. When a woman is in one of these two roles, and only these two roles, she is "permitted" to step out of the mothering role. The construction of the evil stepmother, which is not new to readers of fairy tales, is splendidly represented by Petunia, Harry's aunt. She hates Harry and resents his presence in her family, to the point of loathing him. She is of course jealous of Harry, as all evil stepmothers are traditionally represented, and goes to all ends to make sure he has a miserable life. But at the same time she makes the other people in her life have a wonderful life (Bettelheim 1975).

This construction of the evil stepmother is consistent with Giroux's research on the postmodern children's work of Disney. The lack of mothers in children's lives creates a romantic notion of the absence of mothers, and stepmothers take on the persona of the evil stepmother. Giroux find this absence of "strong mothers and resisting women" to be yet another example of the patriarchal system in which the stories are created (1998, 60).

Although Petunia participated in what society believed her to be, she also actively constructed her own identity by enacting her agency and continuing to perpetuate herself as the evil stepmother. She at no time tried to resist this construction of herself. The one way in which Petunia does not follow the construction of the evil stepmother and in turn uses her agency to resist is when she does not connive behind her husband's back; instead she takes his word as law.

Identity construction is a two-way street; you are acted on by society, but at the same time you can enact your own agency to accept or resist society's construction. This is in keeping with the previous literature on identity and agency, which states that on a daily basis people must take in what society tells them they need to be, filter it through their own beliefs, and expel what they do not agree with (Adams 1992). In this text Petunia uses her agency and constructs her own identity by choosing to follow the stepmother representation that society has constructed. Even though Petunia does not make the best choice in how she decides to treat Harry, she is enacting her agency nonetheless.

It is also acceptable for a woman to step out of her mothering role when she is a teacher. As I stated previously, women as mother do not perform such actions as disciplining the children/students, although these same women become the disciplinarians when they take on constructions of teacher. In the text, the role of teacher carries with it some very traditional ideals of what a teacher is to be. Professor McGonagall is at various points in the text described as wearing her hair in a bun and her glasses on the tip of her nose. Society constructs many representations of teachers with these same characteristics. And as always, the teacher is the person in power in the classroom and enacts her agency through such means. This same woman may be a mothering figure in certain situations, but she is also the "in control" teacher in other situations. Professor McGonagall enacts her agency by handing down punishments to both boys and girls when she feels they have broken the rules, although many times the consequences for boys and girls can be very different, and very unfair. The role of teacher gives Professor McGonagall permission to enact her agency as the disciplinarian, while her gender does not. The male characters do not seem to worry about such things as permission; the boys and men transcend role and gender, and their boundaries are a lot less rigid than girls' and women's boundaries, which follows the patriarchal system of power that has been set up in society.

Schools and families construct teaching and mothering in the ways they do in order to serve the interests of men. If women are taking care of the children's needs in the family and at school, men are free to take care of their own interests. Keeping women busy with family, school, church, and so on allows men to remain in power. The institutions of power perpetuate the social constructions of gender through such means as family and school in order to maintain the patriarchal power system.

THEME 5: "BOUNDED" RESISTANCE

The fifth and final theme that emerged from the analysis was the female characters' bounded resistance. By "bounded" I mean that the female characters would resist but only up to a certain point and only on certain issues. Throughout the text women find themselves in situations that they do not agree with, but instead of questioning the situation they are in and enacting their agency they allow men to dictate what will occur. For example, when Hermione, Harry, and Ron finished their exams, Hermione wanted to discuss what each had put down as answers to the questions. She is described as liking "to go through their exam papers afterwards," but Harry and Ron did not want to (Rowling 1997, 263). Even though Hermione took great joy in discussing exams afterward, and Harry and Ron both knew this, she did not question, or resist, Harry and Ron as to why they wouldn't discuss the exams. Instead she did what they wanted to do, which was sit under a tree and relax.

When the female characters do enact their agency and resist, they only resist up to a point and then they back down and go along with whatever the male characters want. For example, Petunia finally tells Vernon that they should turn around and go home, after spending several hours in the car driving away from all the harassing, enchanted letters from Hogwarts addressed to Harry. Vernon "didn't seem to hear her" (Rowling 1997, 43), so Petunia drops the subject and sits back in the car while Vernon continues to drive. She does not persist in turning the car around; she doesn't even persist in having Vernon acknowledge her.

These constructions of the female characters in *Harry Potter* are in keeping with the dominant discourse that "permits" women to enact their agency to question men, but not to go too far. If the scene had been reversed and Petunia was driving and Vernon was questioning her, traditionally Vernon would have been shown to persist in his questioning until he finally got his way and Petunia agreed to turn the car around and go home. It would not have been acceptable for Petunia to pretend not to hear him or brush him off because society tells us that women are supposed to hang on every word the man says. In the same instance it would not have been acceptable for Vernon to stop his persistence in turning the car around because society has not constructed maleness to give up; it would instead be seen as a form of weakness.

When women in the text do use their agency to resist, what they are resisting is not the construction of gender that society has "handed" them but instead the evil forces in the book. At no time in the text does a character resist her or his own gender construction. In our society this is very typical. Gender constructions are not supposed to be questioned; instead, they are a set of rules that an individual is supposed to follow to maintain the patriarchal system of power. When people do enact agency and resist society's construction of gender, which in and of itself is a rarity, they are seen as other, as noted in previous literature (de Beauvoir 1949; Foucault 1978; Tong 1998). In order for institutionalized systems of power to remain intact, we must not question rules related to gender; but in order to empower ourselves we must question them. At the same time it is important to remember that questioning gender and disrupting the system of power will trigger consequences and sanctions. Individuals who currently hold power are loath to give it up or share it, and institutions such as family, school, church, and workplaces have been constructed over hundreds of years to ensure that our patriarchal systems stay in place. "Bounded" resistance is one of these very systems; allowing the oppressed some freedom to resist provides a sense of control, while keeping such resistance "bounded" keeps the oppressed person in check.

CONCLUSION

The construction of women's agency that J.K. Rowling presents to the reader in *Harry Potter and the Sorcerer's Stone* is very much in keeping with the dominant discourse on gender. We do see images of intelligent, take-charge women, but more frequently we see images of women who doubt themselves, feel the need to comfort or take care of men, and need validation from the men in their lives. On the whole we see far more images of weak, needy women than strong, independent women. Although there are instances of women resisting, they never resist the most prevalent and complicated type of oppression in the text—gender oppression. The characters, both male and female, do not resist gender constructions but instead perpetuate the traditional gender constructions that are so prevalent in our society.

As media constructions of gender continue to perpetuate the oppressive gender roles of women, boys and girls alike continue to define their reality based on such oppressiveness. Steinberg and Kincheloe point out that "such a patriarchal form obviously holds serious implications for women, but it distorts male development as well" (1998, 25). Boys are encouraged by these different forms of kinderculture and thus take on the patriarchal, oppressive personas that are displayed throughout the various forms. They can then "enjoy the rewards of privilege through their domination of subordinates" (Steinberg and Kincheloe 1998, 25).

Institutions have been created in our society to maintain a patriarchal system of power. This institutional power is carried out in multiple arenas: schools, families, communities, churches, places of employment, and so on. The power relations that have been set up are not easily changed. If one disrupts workplace systems of power, there might be repercussions in all other institutional systems. This is why women enacting their agency are engaging in "border work," as Carlson (2002) deems it. Women must be very careful when crossing borders due to the consequences they will face, just as Hermione did when breaking the rules.

In *Harry Potter* we see border crossing as a very delicate matter. A woman who crosses the border is automatically told to back away. In the book Rowling allows women to resist up to a certain point but then always has them retreat. Rowling's construction of "resist and retreat" could be viewed in two very different ways. On the one hand, it is positive in that women and girls in the text are allowed to resist; they are allowed to be intelligent, caring, and agentic. On the other hand, Rowling is reinforcing the binary constructions and institutions of power relationships. Her text reflects the fact that patriarchal society needs women to back down in order to maintain the patriarchal institutionalized system of power and kinderculture. Women in the book are allowed to resist a bit, which shows the progression of women's roles and power from earlier days, but it also shows that the glass ceiling is still intact. They are allowed to resist, but they soon find themselves hitting the glass ceiling and are unable to pass through it. Is the power that women are given, only to be stopped by the glass ceiling, really power or is it an illusion of power? Is this power false? Or is it a tease, hoping that women will eventually back down and learn their lesson to not act in such a manner again?

If the patriarchal institutionalized system of power needs women to back down in order to maintain its power, then why give women any power to begin with? Women might seek out more power with this little bit of power they are "allowed" to enact, whether or not it was intended to be an illusion or false. This could begin the process of empowerment and eventually the entire system of power could crumble.

Certainly Rowling's text reflects a notion of power dynamics between men and women that is characterized by give-and-take, change, and interplay. Agency here is not static; it is held at times by both women and men. Questioning, empowerment, and resistance do occur, and women characters are constructed as agentic. However, their agency is embedded in the very traditional institutions of family, school, and wizarding community. Women and girls are allowed to cross some borders, but only with the permission of men and boys. A very important question arises: Has Rowling pushed the boundaries of gender constructions far enough to begin a process of female empowerment, or has she reinforced the status quo? I conclude that the text comes down in favor of status quo and kinderculture.

How then do we effect change? In order for society as a whole to change constructions of traditional gender roles and for individuals to construct their own identities, we must unpack these potentially harmful images of women and men. One of the most critical places to begin this process of deconstruction, and to learn the tools of critical thinking, is in the schools. It is imperative that children learn to critically deconstruct "texts" of various forms. Without strong agentic women figures in books and as models in society, how will girls learn to be strong agentic women?

REFERENCES

Adams, G. R. 1992. Introduction and overview to G. R. Adams, T. Gullotta, and R. Montemayor, eds., *Adolescent Identity Formation*, 1–8. Newbury Park, Calif.: Sage.

Alton, A. 2002. "Here's Harry! Why Not Harriette?" Symposium conducted at the annual meeting of the Popular Culture Conference, Toronto, Canada, March.

Beach, S. A., and E. H. Willner. 2002. "The Power of Harry: The Impact of J. K. Rowling's Harry Potter Books on Young Readers." *World Literature Today* 76: 102–106.

Bettelheim, B. 1975. *The Uses of Enchantment: The Meaning and Importance of Fairy Tales*. New York: Random House.

Bosworth, M. 1999. *Engendering Resistance: Agency and Power in Women's Prisons*. Hampshire, U.K.: Ashgate.

Butler, J. 1993. *Bodies That Matter: On the Discursive Limits of Sex*. New York: Routledge.

_____. 1999. *Gender Trouble: Feminism and the Subversion of Identity*. 10th ed. New York: Routledge.

Carlson, D. 2002. *Leaving Safe Harbors: Toward a New Progressivism in American Education and Public Life*. New York: Routledge Falmer.

Cherland, M. R., and C. Edelsky. 1993. "Girls and Reading: The Desire for Agency and the Horror of Helplessness in Fictional Encounters." In L. K. Christian-Smith, ed., *Texts of Desire: Essays on Fiction, Femininity, and Schooling*, 28–44. Bristol, Pa.: Falmer.

Chodorow, N. 1978. *The Reproduction of Mothering*. Berkeley: University of California Press.

Dahl, R. 1988. *Matilda*. New York: Viking.

Davidson, L., and L. K. Gordon. 1998. *The Sociology of Gender*. 2d ed. Boston: Houghton Mifflin College Press.

De Beauvoir, S. 1949. *The Second Sex*. Translated and edited by H. M. Parshley. New York: Vintage.

Druxes, H. 1996. *Resisting Bodies: The Negotiation of Female Agency in Twentieth-Century Women's Fiction*. Detroit: Wayne State University Press.

Foucault, M. 1978. *The History of Sexuality*. New York: Pantheon.

Freire, P. 1970. *Pedagogy of the Oppressed*. New York: Seabury.

Gibson, D. 2001. "Good, Evil, and Harry Potter: Boy Wizard Wins Over Some Members of the Christian Community." *Star-Ledger*, November 15.

Giroux, H. A. 1998. "Are Disney Movies Good for Your Kids?" In S. Steinberg and J. Kincheloe, eds., *Kinderculture*, 53–67. Boulder: Westview.

_____. 1999. *The Mouse That Roared: Disney and the End of Innocence*. Boulder: Rowman & Littlefield.

Glenn, E. N. 2000. "The Social Construction and Institutionalization of Gender and Race." In M. M. Ferree, J. Lorber, and B. B. Hess, eds., *Revisioning Gender*, 3–43. New York: Alta Mira.

Golombok, S., and R. Fivush. 1994. *Gender Development*. New York: Cambridge University Press.

Heilman, E. E. 2003. *Harry Potter's World: Multidisciplinary Critical Perspectives*. New York: Routledge Falmer.

hooks, b. 2000a. *Feminist Theory: From Margin to Center*. Cambridge, Mass.: South End.

_____. 2000b. *Feminism Is for Everybody: Passionate Politics*. Cambridge, Mass.: South End.

Hunt, P., ed. 1999. *Understanding Children's Literature*. New York: Routledge.

Kabeer, N. 1999. "Resources, Agency, Achievements: Reflections on the Measurement of Women's Empowerment." *Development and Change* 30, no. 3: 435–464.

Kilbourne, J. 1999. *Can't Buy My Love: How Advertising Changes the Way We Think and Feel*. New York: Simon & Schuster.

Kincheloe, J. L. 1998. "Home Alone and 'Bad to the Bone': The Advent of a Postmodern Childhood." In S. Steinberg and J. Kincheloe, eds., *Kinderculture*, 31–52. Boulder: Westview.

Kristeva, J. 1974. *Revolution in Poetic Language*. Translated by Margaret Waller. New York: Columbia University Press.

Lippa, R. A. 2002. *Gender, Nature, and Nurture*. Mahwah, N.J.: Erlbaum.

Luke, A., and P. Freebody. 1997. "Critical Literacy and the Question of Normativity: An Introduction." In S. Muspratt, A. Luke, and Freebody, eds., *Constructing Critical Literacies*, 1–18. Cresskill, N.J.: Hampton.

May, L. 1992. *Sharing Responsibility*. Chicago: University of Chicago Press.

Noddings, N. 1984. *Caring: A Feminine Approach to Ethics and Moral Education*. Berkeley: University of California Press.

Orenstein, P. 1994. *Schoolgirls: Young Women, Self-Esteem, and the Confidence Gap*. New York: Anchor.

Paechter, C. 2001. "Using Poststructuralist Ideas in Gender Theory and Research." In B. Francis and C. Skelton, eds., *Investigating Gender: Contemporary Perspectives in Education,* 41–51. Philadelphia: Open University Press.

Plato. 1955. *The Republic.* 2d ed. Translated by A. Bloom. New York: Viking. Plato wrote *The Republic* in 340 B.C.

Polatnick, M. 1973. "Why Men Don't Rear Children: A Power Analysis." *Berkeley Journal of Sociology* 18: 60.

Puig, Claudia. "Harry Potter Could Conjure Record." *USA Today,* October 22, 2001.

Rosendale, L. B. 2001. "There's Something About Harry." Calvin College *Spark* on-line edition. publications/spark/fall01/harry.html. Retrieved October 28, 2002.

Rowling, J. K. 1997. *Harry Potter and the Sorcerer's Stone.* New York: Scholastic.

———. 1999. *Harry Potter and the Chamber of Secrets.* New York: Scholastic.

———. 1999. *Harry Potter and the Prisoner of Azkaban.* New York: Scholastic.

———. 2000. *Harry Potter and the Goblet of Fire.* New York: Levine.

———. 2003. *Harry Potter and the Order of the Phoenix.* New York: Scholastic.

Seuss, T. G. 1970. *Bartholomew and the Oobleck.* New York: Random House for Young Readers.

Shotter, J. 1998. "Agency and Identity: A Relational Approach." In A. Campbell and S. Muncer, eds., *The Social Child,* 271–291. East Sussex, U.K.: Psychology Press.

Steinberg, S. R., and J. L. Kincheloe, eds. 1998. *Kinderculture: The Corporate Construction of Childhood.* Boulder: Westview.

Tong, R. 1998. *Feminist Thought.* Boulder: Westview.

University of Cincinnati. 2001. "E-Briefing Summer Reading for Fun and Profit." University of Cincinnati News Online. www.uc.edu/news/ebriefs/summread. html. Retrieved November 15, 2001.

Woolf, V. 1929. *A Room of One's Own.* London: Hogarth.

Chapter 8

PROFESSIONAL WRESTLING AND YOUTH CULTURE: TEASING, TAUNTING, AND THE CONTAINMENT OF CIVILITY

Aaron D. Gresson

MY DAUGHTER, ARIANE, was two years old when she saw her first professional wrestling match. We were traveling away from home and had spent the night in a motel. Trying to find a suitable children's show for her while my wife and I readied for the next leg of our journey, we came upon Saturday morning wrestling. Wanting to see the latest cast of characters, I left the show on and Ariane was immediately mesmerized by the match of the moment: a huge black male, Papa Shango, was working voodoo on his handsome, courageous, clearly overwhelmed white opponent. Dressed in native costume, complete with his staff and human skull, this fearsome creature called forth fire and smoke (stage effects), making his opponent spit forth some kind of greenish liquid reminiscent of Linda Blair in *The Exorcist*. The arena audience screamed and jeered, my daughter's eyes bulged in their sockets, and I only just managed to free myself to change the channel and break the spell that held both her and me.

I cannot say with certainty what my daughter saw or understood by this encounter with professional wrestling. I do know that when I reached for her, after changing the television channel, she initially recoiled from me. Was I momentarily Papa Shango? Had she seen me as she watched him, inflicting great, although faked, pain on his hapless opponent? It would be fruitless to speculate long on these questions. They are obviously unanswerable. Still, while we cannot know what Ariane saw and felt, there are some related questions worth asking that might allow conjecture. What place does professional wrestling have in the lives of the young? Is the effect of these constructed dramas largely benign, or is there an unhealthy dimension to this sport?

In this chapter I consider these questions by exploring some of the psychological and cultural dimensions of professional wrestling in the construction of consciousness in youth. I first briefly describe the structure and function of professional wrestling. Here I will consider the peculiar constructions it has taken within recent American history as a prelude to examining the ways in which wrestling engages youth's self-understanding. Next I reflect on the psychosocial implications of wrestling's organizing themes for youth. I conclude with a reading of the possibly unintentional role wrestling has in reactionary cultural politics.

PROFESSIONAL WRESTLING: ITS STRUCTURE AND FUNCTION

Somewhere around the age of fourteen I discovered the world of wrestling. This was a remarkable event, as I reflect on it some thirty-five years later. After all, back in 1960 wrestling had not yet become the multimillion-dollar, multimedia drama it is today. When I attended those Thursday night matches at the Norfolk, Virginia, arena, I was often the only black in the audience. Back then—as now—professional wrestling was working-class, white entertainment. Few racial minorities appeared as wrestlers: BoBo Brazil and Chief Big Heart were the notable tokens. Virtually no racial minorities were present at the live arena fights. (Even in the 1970s, one critic of the sport could declare: "To their credit blacks don't participate much inside or outside the ring" [Mano 1974, 705].) For the most part, wrestlers portraying white ethnics made up the local arena cards as promoters sought to provide identifiable heroes for the hometown crowds.

Still, there is a logic to why I, despite the relative nonparticipation of African Americans in the wrestling ritual, was turned on by this entertainment: Professional wrestling engages something primal in humans. This primal quality, passion, is triggered by the twin cultural themes encoded in the professional drama of wrestling: There is goodness in the world, but evil seems to be ubiquitous. Perhaps this is a first clue to the significance of professional wrestling in the United States and how its structure and function have evolved to the present forms.

MODERN PROFESSIONAL WRESTLING:
THE STRUGGLE OF GOOD AND EVIL

Most wrestlers are cast as either good or evil. In their carnival world, the wrestlers themselves call the good guy a "face" and the bad guy a "heel." The referee is the judge; he stands for justice. But justice can be conveniently blind, and the referee often sides with the "evil" wrestlers. This "unholy alliance" is what stacks the odds in favor of evil. By managing, routinely, to miss blatant "illegal acts" (which are perfectly evident to the audience), the referee induces the audience to identify with the "face." Roland Barthes has argued:

> But what wrestling is above all meant to portray is a purely moral concept: that of justice. Justice is the embodiment of a possible transgression. It is therefore easy to understand why out of five wrestling matches, only about one is fair. One must realize, let it be repeated, that "fairness" here is a role or a genre, as in the theater: the rules do not at all constitute a real constraint; they are the conventional appearances of fairness. In actual fact a fair fight is nothing but an exaggeratedly polite one. One must understand, of course, here, that all these polite actions are brought to the notice of the public by the most conventional gestures of fairness: shaking hands, raising the arms, ostensibly avoiding a fruitless hold which would detract from the perfection of the contest. (1972, 21–22)

The drama described by Barthes is a modern invention. Prior to the mid-nineteenth century, wrestling was largely a participant sport. It was almost solely controlled and attended by those participating in it (Ball 1990, 52). Only after 1900 did the audience become directly involved in the sport; only then were good and evil organizing themes for the passions and performances of audience and wrestlers alike.

When wrestlers themselves were largely the audience, personal development was an important motivation for participation: "The building of skill, physical agility, and general health, the learning of sportsmanship, the excitement of competition and the development of self-defense techniques . . . were all stressed" (Ball 1990, 52). Today professional wrestling has virtually no emphasis on personal development. It is orchestrated for an audience whose main interest seems to be the spectacle of brutality and violence. What took place with this shift from amateur to professional wrestler was a shift from personal development to communal celebration of certain basic yet largely destructive proclivities. This is perhaps best seen in the teasing and taunting that the drama calls forth in the audience. To achieve this level of audience involvement, wrestling promoters stereotyped the wrestlers. For example, professional wrestling traditionally engaged the audiences by staging battles between local favorites and a variety of "aliens" or "others."

A favorite stop among promoters at this time was the ethnic communities of large cities where wrestlers could play in school auditoriums or community centers. A favorite trick was to manufacture ethnic heroes billed as Italians in Italian neighborhoods or Germans in German neighborhoods. It was not unusual for stars to change ethnicities and names overnight to cater to a specific ethnic crowd (Ball 1990, 51).

This form of ethnic stereotyping was intended to overcome the boredom associated with amateur wrestling. Whatever the rationale, this playing to the audience no doubt had an impact on the values and attitudes of the audience. But what precisely did professional wrestling bring forth through the use of ethnic stereotypes? Was it truly nothing more than the juxtaposing of good and evil, the emotional lashing out at injustice, as suggested by Roland Barthes?

Unfortunately, no. Barthes's analysis is insightful and useful, especially for understanding European matches before 1960. But it does not seem sufficient for understanding the deeper passions—violence and rage—characterizing the modern American wrestling world. Professional wrestling has gone from a relatively boring participant ritual to an action-packed form of theater. While its progress as a sport may be questioned, it is clear that wrestling has adapted to the ritual needs of audiences and successfully provided spectacular shows in return for spectacular profits. The drama it has become is contagious, especially among the poor and oppressed. A case in point is Mexico. It was recently reported that in Mexico professional wrestlers are considered warriors, superheroes, celebrities, and saints (*Atlanta Journal and Atlanta Constitution* 1992). Such representations belie the more brutal, destructive side of this entertainment.

That professional wrestlers might be viewed as saints is uncanny, if we recall Barthes's observation that wrestling is symbolically a moral play. But such representations belie the more brutal, destructive side of this entertainment. Wrestling is violent; it is brutal; it is savage. Some argue that the faked aspect of the fights neutralizes the sport as brutal. Challenging those who view professional wrestling as a harmless form of lower-class entertainment are those who see the psychological and social problematics accompanying it. For instance, William C. Martin wrote in *Atlantic Monthly*, "Professional wrestling offers fans an almost unparalleled opportunity to indulge aggressive and violent impulses. . . . They want hitting and kicking and stomping and bleeding. Especially bleeding" (1972, 86). As Michael Ball has cogently argued,

> While the actual inflicting of pain and the punishing of opponents are more histrionics than fact, that does not diminish the glorification of such tactics. In such a scenario, wrestling becomes a lamination . . . of brutality. Its theatrics are not meant to diminish the viciousness and ferocity of wrestling but to enhance it while saving the wrestlers themselves from real injury. Wrestling, while containing little or no actual brutality, becomes the embodiment of brutality. (1990, 61)

Thus a ritual drama pitting good against evil or local ethnic heroes against a less favored ethnic group member is not the essence of professional wrestling. Animal savagery is the drug that has attracted so many to this sport. It remains true that justice, good, and evil are organizing themes for the ritual drama called wrestling. But the passions called forth are not a better understanding of justice, good, and evil in the world, or even one's own small part of the world. On the contrary, the taunting and teasing only serve to intensify and deepen rage and anger. The taste for blood has, so to speak, been increased by a steady diet of manufactured madness, where minute after minute men maul and maim each other. That the damage is fictional has been seen, by some, as exonerating; however, others correctly observe that the very phoniness of the violence betrays the sickness of the message. Beyond this, televised fights add something more to the celebration of ethnic chauvinism and the thirst for blood to wrestling. It has brought the manipulation of oppressive stereotypes into the purview of youth like my daughter (whose only guilt was a father whose curiosity exposed her to the scary Papa Shango).

POSTMODERN WRESTLING AND OPPRESSIVE STEREOTYPES

The growth of television and professional wrestling has been seen as symbiotic, and the expansion of the stereotyping tendencies of this entertainment is heavily implicated in this mutuality. Over time wrestling went from a participant sport to audience entertainment. The audience grew to include an anonymous television audience. These two changes—from sport to entertainment and anonymous, diversified television audience—are critical factors in the arrival of wrestling as a media-driven ritual that exploits negative stereotypes.

Wrestling promoters would likely deny any intentional negative stereotyping and argue that their characters are reflections of audience desire or just harmless fun and humor (Gresson 1995). They would certainly deny a connection between televised wrestling and an intensified exploitation of negative stereotypes. Yet, writing in the *Saturday Evening Post* nearly three decades ago, Myron Cope saw the collusive bond: "The advent of television in 1947 multiplied fans at least a thousandfold, and created such outrageous caricatures as wrestlers in long blond hair, Indian headdress, and fur capes. This mixture of showmanship and violence packed arenas as tightly in New York City as in Wichita Falls, Texas" (1966, 90).

Interestingly, wrestling promoters have deemphasized the violence, arguing that television enlarges the demography of the audience to include the middle class and other traditionally absent groups. This position has not been substantiated by the little available research (Ball 1990). What is evident, however, is the persistence at arena matches of those behaviors associated with the working and lower classes. But let's assume that a more diverse audience has become attracted to televised shows. What precisely are they being presented?

Professional wrestling began to prosper through television precisely at the point when America was entering the radical 1960s. A dominant feature of this period has been the various liberation movements: black power, women's power, kid's power, gray power, gay power, and white power. Because wrestling promoters have reproduced daily events and dramas in their wrestling matches, they have reproduced the very stereotypes that were challenged in the 1960s and 1970s liberation movements. Thus ethnic neighborhood scenarios were replaced with larger societal themes.

There are two major issues embedded in the contemporary multimedia manufacturing of "wrestlemania." First, promoters have settled on using the stuff of daily life to construct their dramas. Included here are classist, sexist, and racist themes that reproduce specific characters such as Junk Yard Dog (a black male), Miss Elizabeth (a pretty but dominated white female), Macho Man (a narcissistic, sexist white male), Country Cousins (two unkempt "hillbillies"), and the Ultimate Warrior (a muscular blond/white Indian brave). Michael Ball's characterization of Junk Yard Dog is suggestive of the stereotyping issue:

> "JYD, as he is known, wears a spiked collar with a heavy chain attached. The crowd throws him dog biscuits which he eagerly retrieves and eats. JYD is characterized as a poor black who grew up in the projects and survived through street tactics, including violence and theft. . . ."
>
> It is perhaps clear why Blacks are not heavily represented in the wrestling drama as either wrestler or audience: the basic characteriza-

tion of black wrestlers is unabashedly racist. Few blacks are likely able to disassociate themselves sufficiently from the regular negative stereotyping of blacks to enjoy the live matches. But the increased use of negative social stereotypes to stimulate the audience is not the only modification televised wrestling has witnessed.

By using television and the special effects of a high technology, the old traditional stereotypes both reach a wider potential audience and impact in a more intimate way. Additionally, on television, the audience acts as a combination backdrop and cuing device for home viewers. The audience is lighted as deeply as possible, and the lighting drops abruptly where the audience ends. This emphasizes the large audience-filled auditorium events . . . and gives the impression that the audience continues into the darkness in case of smaller . . . events. The cheers and boos of the studio audience act in the same way as canned laughter in situation comedies, cuing a similar response from home viewers. (Ball 1990, 75)

A critical outcome of this use of the television audience is the domestication of brutality. Anyone who watches televised matches cannot help seeing—and being influenced by—the large percentage of females and small children in the audience. Female attendance at professional wrestling matches is a paradox: Professional wrestling is unabashedly sexist, so why do women attend? Various answers have been offered, but none are conclusive. What is usually agreed is that professional wrestling is a "family affair." The presence of women and children as regulars at the wrestling matches affects the structure of the arena; it is not a males-only site. We might say that the "rhetorical condition" (Asante and Atwater 1976) or persuasive message of the setting itself dissuades accusations of sexism, racism, or brutality. The brutality and violence enacted on the wrestling mat reaches a televised audience buffered by a live audience of men, women, and children. This fact, moreover, clues us in to the complex character of the audience and the fact that children are learning to receive and own wrestling's stereotypes and the audience's shared savagery under the watchful eye and collusion of their parents.

THE PSYCHOLOGY OF WRESTLING

Wrestling impinges on the psyche of the developing child in specific ways. First, wrestling rehearses "horseplay." It is a ritual expression of something very familiar to most children: Children wrestle and tussle "naturally." Without the presence of adults or other "judges" to regulate this play and aggression among children, there are two or three basic scenarios that have psychological implications. First, through the bodily contact that wrestling allows, children become psychosexually aroused in the Freudian sense; that is, they may experience strong connective arousal (libido), strong disconnected feeling (aggression), or a combination of both (ambivalence). Most of us have at one time or another during childhood known these feelings. If we were stronger, we pushed on with the attack; if we were weaker, we pulled away, often getting angry at the other's overwhelming power.

In short, wrestling, even more than boxing, carries powerful emotive potential. I believe that this highly eroticized potential is critical to the child's attraction to wrestling. The developing child is at the height of her emotional vulnerability and is exposed to two simultaneous fictive constructions: One is the possibility of these strong, powerful men brutalizing each other without serious harm to anyone; the other is the "naturalness" of conflict and conflict resolution through violence. Because the child may come to wrestling by way of play, she or he may already have an experiential basis for these two constructions of professional wrestling. Attending live matches or watching televised fights becomes a context for expanding the child's understanding of this "natural" child's play or conflict. New layers of meaning are offered, as well as a validated context: "They do it on TV."

Professional wrestling, then, becomes a participant in the education of children regarding the use of their bodies on another. But children occupy different positions in society, and the need to understand and use their bodies differ accordingly. Two boys may wrestle each other without much criticism, but a boy and girl, or two boys of different classes or races may be less favorably received if they are found locked in bodily combat. Thus race and gender influence our understandings of wrestling.

Most importantly, wrestling is primarily working-class, lower-class white entertainment. There is evidence that some middle-class children watch televised wrestling matches, and there is a minority audience at live arena matches. Still, by and large, the wrestling drama is intended for and supported by lower-class whites. And discussion of kinderculture must address this specific condition.

WRESTLING, SOCIAL CONSCIOUSNESS, AND CLASS

Professional wrestling has taken on a peculiar or uncanny function for the lower class. In the years before 1950, the chief frustration of white ethnics was the "social order," and "good" and "evil" were the organizing principles. To exploit these conditions, it was sufficient to portray different ethnic groups as the good and bad guys. Today "government" is the chief frustration and "affirmative action" and "white as victim" are the organizing principles. Accordingly, the wrestling drama has routinely reconstructed its rituals to rehearse a recovery from the evils associated with stereotypes reminiscent of the radical liberation period. Characters such as the Million Dollar Man, Slick, Virgil, Junk Yard Dog, Coco Beware, Macho Man, Sergeant Slaughter, Sheri, Miss Elizabeth, and the Nasty Boys are constructed to achieve this end.

What fuels professional wrestling is the outrage generated among the audience. Like the standup comic, the professional wrestler "lives for the taunt or tease." This is so because the constructed action, "professional wrestling," is contrived for an audience that is aware, at some level, that this cannot be real (for the most part). Yet the audience experiences the action as real. This capacity to experience the unreal as real is precisely what makes the wrestlers' gestures "genuine" and the constructed stereotype "true."

The traditional appeal of wrestling to the lower-status person has been interpreted by social researchers and critics as a function of the "defective mentality" attributed to them. For example, Gregory P. Stone and Ramon A. Oldenburg argued that "lower-status persons seldom question the concrete world about them. Consequently, they are more susceptible to staging than persons on higher status levels" (Stone and Oldenburg 1967, 526).

Perhaps "concrete operations" are more evident among lower-class persons than middle-class persons. I think that the evidence on this point is mixed and best explained in terms of specific contexts or issues. There are many issues about which middle-class persons seem as conservative (i.e., gullible, rigid, and inflexible) as those identified as lower-class. The predominance of lower-class persons as wrestling fans is related less to their concreteness than to their need for certain "safety valves." Professional wrestling allows a particular group, privileged by skin color but damned because of class, to vent its frustrations. A variety of working-class whites share this need.

Have you ever seen the "little old ladies" at wrestling matches? In years prior to the 1980s, they were a familiar part of arenas. It was common for the television cameras—again, in a normalizing gesture—to focus in on one of these "small, frail creatures" flaring out at the wrestler with her purse. This sight, despite its relative infrequency, invites us to see professional wrestling as intergenerational in its appeal. And there is a level of truth to this rhetorical turn. Wrestling audiences include a wide range of age-groups: from little tots to senior citizens. Their presence together suggests the familial aspect of the sport, a quality shared with many other sports. And yet this quality differs from those other family-oriented sports because it invites a certain kind of participation: emotional outburst. In recent history this shared quality across the lifespan found expression in such post–black power concepts as "kid power" and "gray power," allusions to the empowerment needs of children and the elderly.

But what precisely are these empowerment needs? I believe that they are essentially the need for non-alienation, non-detachment from the heart of the community, the heart of—and here is the clear disjuncture—the "heart of the social order." Of course, there is no heart within social orders; this is the essential message of the early sociologists, men such as Ferdinand Toennies and Robert Redfield, who wrote cogently about the shift from the agrarian communities to the urban societies, a shift away from more intimate and "primitive" visions and missions to more rational and legalistic forms of understanding and living. Of course, it was precisely at the zenith of the industrial revolution and urbanization that the old became obsolete and the youth exploitable capital.

I believe that wrestling, always an intimate form of connection and communication, became even more pivotal for expressing certain frustrations around self and other, and the nature and quality of the relational bond and contract in force. It is here that wrestling becomes especially pertinent to unfulfilled desire bordering on angst and searching for catharsis—terms particular to the rise of modernism.

It is against this contextual backdrop that the problem of child consciousness must be understood. I return briefly to my opening story: Ariane's entrancement by the televised drama and her recoiling from my touch immediately after watching a black man seemingly hurting a white man. I shied away from constructing her understanding of the wrestling event or her reaction to me. But let me now use that event to construct my own understanding of the invitation such a spectacle offered her young mind: She saw a black man dressed differently than any of the white males in the ring; she saw him do "magic."

All this is seen by the young child, whether at an arena or on television. The difference afforded by viewing site is thus less significant than might be otherwise expected. This is so because the oppressive codes of society around race, sexuality, gender, and so forth are paralleled in the larger society. The consciousness of the young child, or even the adolescent, is greatly influenced by the given. The given social codes of oppression are among the organizing codes of the society that the child uses to make sense of her or his place in society and her or his relationship to others, especially different others. For example, the concept "white boys can't jump" is a social construction that belies experience; white males can jump, but this fact is compromised by a pervasive social message that jumping is an animal quality possessed largely by black males, as evidenced in the person of Michael Jordan. This illustration is one indicator of what we mean by consciousness—the awareness of oneself as self, the ability to look at oneself as object, to assess one's place and processes. During the years between six and twenty, the age range most associated with attending and watching wrestling matches on television, the child is especially aware of his or her body, increasing competition with the other. Wrestling is full of social codes that impinge on the operation of consciousness in the young. This is particularly true of the working-class male youth because of his special investment in the ritual dramas of wrestling. In an important sense, professional wrestling helps teach the lower-working-class family how to feel and express its feelings. If this group is nonreflective with respect to the ritual drama called professional wrestling, perhaps this is so merely because consciousness would be even more dangerous and deadly. Remember, wrestling for some is like religion, which has long been understood to have addictive qualities as, in the words of Karl Marx, "an opiate of the people." And still, despite this capacity to contain the bodily explosions of the working-class white family, professional wrestling represents the occasion to transgress the codes of "civility" as much as it encourages the rehearsing of society's oppressive codes toward women and various minorities.

THE CONTAINMENT OF CIVILITY

Civility, the soothing, constructive channeling of irrational, erratic, and sometimes destructive passions into socially mediated and sanctioned behaviors, is never a complete achievement. Sigmund Freud is credited with saying that humans are only partially socializable. By this is meant that we forever retain spaces or places within our being that may say no to the reigning social order. Thus, for example, society may dictate that people wear shoes, but some will find occasions for going barefoot and even turn it into a countercultural gesture, as during the so-called hippie era.

Civility, for the socially oppressed, the least fortunate, becomes a yoke precisely because society's strictures seem to do double duty with respect to them. They already occupy a "one down" position due to the machinations of the "cognitive elite" and then they are told by a "blind" social order to "behave," to "play by the rules." And for the most part, the masses exercise their agency within the boundaries set for them. But there are times when they, like the hero of the movie *Network,* open the window wide and shout, "We're not going to take it any more!"

This, I believe, is largely the emotional environment that professional wrestling came to occupy in the years before television. Audience participation was an opportunity for emoting. Although some saw clearly its role as perpetuating violence (Arms et al. 1957), whatever violence occurred was restricted to the world of the lower-class. Indeed, what was perhaps seen but not voiced is the convergence of mid-twentieth-century professional wrestling with the two forms that existed in the late 1800s, when both football and wrestling were under siege as brutal sports.

> The professional style was used in urban areas and was bureaucratically restricted by rules and regulations. A referee was always present to enforce the rules and often the matches lasted for many hours. By contrast, the rural style of wrestling resembled a barroom brawl. Circuses, county fairs, and individual promoters would often feature the "World's Champion," willing to wrestle any challengers. Because of the unsophisticated nature and lack of knowledge of rules of many challengers in small towns, rules were few and enforcement was lax. Wrestlers were often unequal in ability, so the matches were relatively short, bloody, and action-paced. (Ball 1990, 41)

Over time and through several transitional phases of the sport, these two styles converged. Because professional wrestling is essentially orchestrated, the "real violence" is minimal. But the emotions that are stimulated are like those of the rural wrestling of the past, and it is these emotions that were largely an excess of feeling associated with the frustrations necessary to group life. For group life demanded, under the economy of civility, the suppression and sublimation of affect that might lead to conflict and destruction. And that segment of American society permitted to address this suppression of affect is largely the working-class, lower-class white classes. Other lower-class groups—African American, Native American, and so on—share the class frustrations but were not permitted to exercise this "safety valve." Ironically, this access to a restricted (for whites only) mode of acting out, while itself repressive, serves as a kind of status symbol, evidence that even the poor white is superior to those other wretched souls.

There is also evidence that some of these people actually internalized feelings toward various wrestler archetypes, sometimes attacking them in the arena as well as on the streets (Ball 1990). By and large, however, wrestling and its impact on the imaginations and behaviors of the citizenry seemed to be a rather provincial matter. I have had reports from several teachers (students in my class on minority education) concerning the growing popularity of wrestling among working-class white males at school. They note that these youth like to try out the various wrestling holds on each other.

The arrival of television and later the pluralistic, radical 1960s effected a dramatic repackaging and remarketing of this primal play of suppressed passion. Yet the important quality remained this capacity to "live in the spectacle." As citizens, the audience relives the constructions of "fairness," "evil," and "good" through the visceral, the physiocerebral. This is important: Wrestling takes place in the audience's mind and is cathartic precisely because the audience engages in the ritual. This ability to enter the arena, to taunt and be taunted, to scream and yell unabashedly at the spectacle of injustice, vanity, and shameless hype is critical for the "civilized" management of "civility." After all, the central hypocrisy of civility is that truth and justice are essential and complete, even as we live its barbarism and destructiveness.

THE MIDDLE CLASS AS VOYEUR

The middle-class spectator also derives enhancement from the wrestling match. While more sophisticated viewers may disavow belief in the "realness" of the action, they may still vicariously join in the pleasures obtained from the spectacle. Thus the expression, "Look at what they're doing!" Glee, at the very least, is contained in this utterance by the slightly detached, deeply amused, and entertained "elite viewer." This "social distance"—through giving tacit recognition to professional wrestling similar to my own interest in the sport—is part of the oppressiveness of the middle class. To be sure, many middle-class people refuse to watch, to give "life" and license to the sport. But isn't this too a role in the structural arrangement? I am here reminded of a favorite comeback of KKK apologists when facing off with so-called white liberals: "You're just like me, you're racist too; you let me do the dirty work, say what we really feel." Perhaps this gaze from afar—in the privacy of our television rooms—is the most subtle and deadly oppressiveness of professional wrestling. What precisely do we mean when we say "look at them"? Are we not fusing both wrestler and audience, constructing them as an other without subjectivity? Are they mere peasants, mindless automatons willing to believe anything, watch anything, do anything? And if they are, what does that say about us, for don't the lower and working classes exist, in part, because we consider ourselves middle-class? And aren't their frustrations and their drugs partly constructions of those who gaze on them?

And what of our children's vulnerability to professional wrestling? Has not our quest for and formulation of civility created this vulnerability? Professional wrestling thrives partially because it serves as a corrective to the "denial of play" where play is read as an unprescribed, indeterminate possibility and explosion of energy. The rise of civility is an assault on play; this assault, moreover, is signaled in genteel situations—when two youngsters lock in combat—with the exhortation "Stop it!" The exhortation is inspired by a need for order, stability, containment. These are precisely the threatened objects of professional wrestling as unharnessed energy. To be sure, wrestling does entail discipline, order, application of will and body to a set task and timeline. But the spectacle itself, beyond the control of the professional, invites chaos.

CONCLUSION

Professional wrestling allows one segment of American society, notably the lower-class white ethnic, to derive primary entertainment and enhancement from the variously constructed rituals. In much the same way as stock car racing, fishing and hunting, and country music are available to all Americans but earmarked for working-class whites, so is professional wrestling. Through this entertainment all are invited to internalize certain oppressive stereotypes, but it is for the working-class white male to assimilate the petty biases associated with the stereotypes and construct his consciousness of self as physically violent and aggressive. This fact, moreover, clues us to the character of the audience and the profound significance that children are learning to receive and own these and related stereotypes under the watchful eye and collusion of their parents.

To understand the consciousness of the child in relation to wrestling, I believe we must understand wrestling as possessing control and containment qualities not unlike basketball for African American youth. We must see its evolution from a participant-dominated sport to rural and urban poor entertainment in much the same way as stock car racing, rodeos, and country music have become "proprietary" for this class.

Professional wrestling is a massive enterprise. With more than three major promotional organizations, thousands of wrestlers, prime time week and weekend matches, and a strong presence in the toy industry, this once small-time sport has grown to multinational stature.

Capitalism's economic elites control the drama and its operation. Fuel for the drama comes from the critical events marking everyday life. Primal passions are elicited by the dramas as they have come to be played out. These passions are unlikely to be stimulated by a more boring form of wrestling, as the history of the sport indicates (Ball 1990). There is evidence that even the promoters are unwilling to push certain buttons; for example, racial conflict is not included in the drama for the most part.

Because wrestling has become largely a family affair, it is not readily feasible for parents to critique the drama. To ask this is to miss the current status of the sport. The family that wrestles together stays together. Self-reflection is thus suicidal to family unity, solidarity, togetherness.

Parents are most essential in containing the play, especially for the very young child who is less able to distinguish play from real physical violence. Of course, the more significant danger is the possibility of misreading the kinds of things that the wrestlers can really do without severe damage to themselves; this is, after all, what is really concealed. Helping children to see what really is involved in terms of physical preparations for these stunts is one possibility. Another is introducing the child to amateur wrestling. This form of wrestling retains much of the fast-paced excitement of the professional match but employs real rules and procedures.

Ultimately, I believe, professional wrestling's containment function will be recognized and its brutality—once recognized as such—will be identified by its name and societal purpose. Until then, children and adults alike will continue to rely on it as an occasion and context for primal screaming. Likewise, there will continue to be "spillage," where young people, notably but not exclusively lower-class white males, act out their frustrations and aggressions in public school gyms, on playgrounds, and similar sites. In such a condition, the call to civility will remain a mockery, a sham.

POSTSCRIPT, 2004

A Look Back at "The Containment of Civility"

In 1997, I saw the emphasis on unbridled energy and rage coalesce around racial-ethnic-gender stereotypes—the other—as something that keeps many whites contained and many minorities protected from an additional containment—the "containment of civility." In 2003, this is perhaps no longer the case. Professional wrestling now reflects the complex racial profile and enacts a similarly complex diversity spectacle that attends the nation at large. In particular, the nation's minority population, while growing, has been fused to a shared civility where the persisting exploitation of otherness is hidden beneath the constitutive hype that is professional wrestling. Professional wrestling has become part of the global communications management matrix that sells everything and nothing.

For instance, in 1997, I noted in a footnote that NASCAR, then on the brink of going into superdrive as a national icon, had been "invaded" by world federation wrestling. By buying a racing team, professional wrestling was expanding the ways in which emotions and self-understandings were blended; wrestling's economic divestiture—worth over $1 billion—enabled a visual diversity, as wrestling grabbed for a larger audience. Earlier, wrestling had largely offered psychomoral outlets to poor whites—vehicles for the channeling of social energies. Now desires were being directly engaged as the speed, spectacle, and fantasies swirling around the speedway would bear the image of wrestling as creative force.

In 2003, this enlargement has continued, and in an intriguing manner. Desire has grabbed hold of urban hip-hop culture. Hoop dreams, a metaphor for minority desire/fantasies of scoring it big in the American mainstream, have coalesced with the special magic of professional wrestling. The growing attractiveness of professional wrestling among minorities—especially African Americans—has been so dramatic that Def Jam Recordings founder Russell Simmons and World Wrestling Entertainment chairman Vince McMahon recently announced a joint venture: wrestling stars and hip-hop artists will visit colleges and high schools across the country to help with voter registration.[1]

The idea is heady: Wrestlers are now role models for minority youth, including new immigrants. Like so many other venues in American society, professional wrestling has "colorized" its sphere of influence, often with dramatic outcomes. Consider the African Samoan wrestling superstar, The Rock. In 2001 *Ebony* magazine featured an interview with him.[2] The interview made it clear that Dwayne Douglas Johnson was a racially conscious and racially proud man, from wrestling ancestors on both sides of the family. In emphasizing The Rock's social, cultural, and financial successes, *Ebony* was naming him one of black America's own. Recalling that his popularity nearly reaches that of Michael Jordan, the article noted his multimillion dollar income and wide commercial success in movies, books, children's toys, and games. The use of The Rock to foster role modeling for minority youth was telling in the interview.

What, if anything, do the interview in *Ebony* and the hip-hop/WWF partnership say about professional wrestling at the dawn of a new millennium? Wrestling carries a different color now because of stars like The Rock, and minority audiences are swelling, partly due to him and the WWF/WCW initiatives. While rumors of white fan alienation and minority wrestler exploitation circulate, the dominant theme is successful diversity and assimilation. Thus professional wrestling has crossed both racial/ethnic and class barriers once more clearly defined among both wrestlers and fans.[3] With stars like Goldberg, for instance, those of us who were never quite certain if Abe Jacobs, wrestling in the 1950s, might be a Jew, are now readily told: "Fans of all races scream and wave signs: 'Will You Marry Me Goldberg?' 'Goldberg Rules!' 'Goldberg, Nice Jewish Boy!'"[4]

Marketing a new wrestling image and script has been understood as pertinent to these changes. Some understand the sport as a combination of athleticism and soap opera, aimed to stimulate and deflate the passions; and there are those who see the diversity as truly a social and cultural breakthrough, an important aid to the education of the youth for a diverse, if not multicultural, society. But does this diversity truly break with the traditional tension? Is the economic sufficient to overcome the built-in class, gender, and racial/ethnic tensions?

Professional wrestling, at core, is much like the mockingbird. It has an "essence," a particularity: It sings the songs of other birds. In this, we see both its uniqueness and its lack. But a society hungry for stimulation, driven by shallow yet spectacular and addictive stimulants, requires a source that can reflect back to it that which it sends off. Professional wrestling remains this for all the various changes. It remains visceral, fusing verbal and visual rhetorics of flawed human nature locked in eternal combat with itself for "the good" within.

Ultimately, the message to children has become increasingly less precise, less predictable. There is increasingly less to be grasped and held onto; maybe this is the ultimate message. But perhaps Steve Sailer, in "The Rock and Race," best summed up the contemporary condition. Describing a 2001 WWF smackdown in Los Angeles, where 16,000 fans converged to see The Rock do his thing, Sailer muses, "Yet The Rock looks neither Samoan nor black. Instead, he gives the impression of being some sort of future human, a superbly handsome specimen from a race that will someday evolve from all that is most formidable in existing humanity."[5]

I began writing this chapter back in the 1990s, wondering what my daughter, Ariane, saw when she was startled by the sight of Papa Shango "mutilating" a defenseless white male (one of the so-called pretty boys of professional wrestling). I feared a demonizing of minorities in wrestling that adversely impacted youth: recreating negative stereotypes among whites and keeping blacks away from the arena. Now, with The Rock, we need not fear the minority countenance as demonic because of traditional racial myths. Rather, we have come to a place where new, more deadly, more seductive fantasies and cultural forms are being forged—in the name of diversity.

REFERENCES

Arms, Robert L., Gordon W. Russell, and Mark L. Sandilands. "Effects on the Hostility of Spectators of Viewing Aggressive Sports." *Social Psychology Quarterly,* September 1979, 275–279.

Asante, Molefi, and Deborah Atwater. "The Rhetorical Condition as Symbolic Structure in Discourse." *Communication Quarterly,* Spring 1986, 170–177.

Ball, Michael R. *Professional Wrestling as Ritual Drama in American Popular Culture.* Lewiston, N.Y.: Mellen, 1990.

Barthes, Roland. *Mythologies.* New York: Hill & Wang, 1972.

Brean, Herbert. "Wrestling Script Gone Awry." *Life,* December 2, 1957, 165–166.

Cope, Myron. "The Rich, Full Life of a Bad Guy." *Saturday Evening Post,* February 12, 1966, 88–89.

Deegan, Mary Jo. *American Ritual Dramas: Social Rules and Cultural Meanings.* Contributions in Sociology, no. 76. New York: Greenwood, 1989.

Gresson, Aaron David. *The Recovery of Race in America.* Minneapolis: University of Minnesota Press, 1995.

Mano, K. "Heavyweight Fraud." *National Review,* June 21, 1974, 705–706.

Martin, William C. "Friday Night in the Coliseum." *Atlantic Monthly,* March 1972, 83–87.

Stone, Gregory P., and Ramon A. Oldenburg. "Wrestling." In Ralph Slovenko and James A. Knight, eds., *Motivations in Play, Games, and Sports,* 503–532. Springfield, Ill.: Thomas, 1967.

Chapter 9

HOME ALONE AND BAD TO THE BONE: THE ADVENT OF A POSTMODERN CHILDHOOD

Joe L. Kincheloe

HOME ALONE (1990) and *Home Alone 2: Lost in New York* (1992) re-volve around Kevin McAlister's (Macaulay Culkin) attempts to find his family after (1) being left behind on a family Christmas trip to Paris and (2) being separated from his family on a Christmas trip to Miami. Wildly successful, the two movies portray the trials and tribulations of Kevin's attempts to take care of himself while his parents try to rejoin him. In the process of using these plots to set up a variety of comedic stunts and sight gags, the movies inadvertently allude to a sea of trou-bles relating to children and family life in the late twentieth century. As we watch the films, an entire set of conflicts and contradictions revolv-ing around the lives of contemporary children begin to emerge. In this way *Home Alone* and *Home Alone 2* take on a social importance unimagined by producers, directors, and screenplay writers. In this chapter I use the family dynamics of the *Home Alone* movies to expose the social forces that have altered Western childhood over the past cou-ple of decades. In all three films a central but unspoken theme involves the hurt and pain that accompany children and their families in post-modern America. The *Home Alone* films are modern classics.

A GENERATION OF KIDS LEFT HOME ALONE

Child rearing is a victim of the past fifty years of cultural change. Divorce and both parents working means that fathers and mothers are around their children less each day. As parents are still at work in the afternoon when children get home from school, children are given latchkeys and expected to take care of themselves. "Home aloners" are kids who in large part raise themselves. We have witnessed a change in family structure that must be taken seriously by parents, educators, and cultural workers of all stripes. Since the early 1960s the divorce rate as well as the percentage of children living with one parent has tripled. Only one-half of today's children have parents who are married to each other. In the twenty-first century only one-third of U.S. children will have such parents. Among children under six, one in four lives in poverty. The stress that comes from the economic changes of the past twenty years has undermined the stability of the family. Family incomes have stagnated, as costs of middle-class existence (home ownership, health care, and higher education) have skyrocketed. Since the late 1960s the amount of time parents spend with their children has dropped from an average of thirty hours per week to seventeen (Lipsky and Abrams 1994; Galston 1991). Increasingly left to fend for themselves, contemporary children have turned to TV, video games, and the Internet to help pass their time alone.

Any study of contemporary children must analyze the social conditions that shape family life. Rarely do mainstream social commentators point out that the American standard of living peaked in 1973, followed by a declining economic climate that forced mothers to work. While the effects of international competition, declining productivity, and the corporate reluctance to reinvent the workplace all contributed to a depressed economy, not all recent family problems can be ascribed to the declining post-Fordist economy. The decline of the public space and the growth of cynicism have undermined the nation's ability to formulate creative solutions to family dysfunction. The 1970s and 1980s, for example, while witnessing the birth and growth of a family values movement, also represented an era that consistently privileged individual gratification over the needs of the community (Paul 1994; Coontz

1992). Such an impulse justified the privatistic retreat from public social involvement that was institutionalized in the 1990s as part of a larger right-wing celebration of self-reliance and efficient government. Unfortunately, it is often our children who must foot the cost of this perverse abrogation of democratic citizenship.

One scene in *Home Alone* highlights the decline of the public space in postmodern America. While Kevin's parents attempt to arrange a flight from Paris to their home in Chicago, the rest of the family watches *It's a Wonderful Life* dubbed into French on TV. This positioning of movie within a movie confronts viewers with the distance between the America of Jimmy Stewart's George Bailey and Macaulay Culkin's Kevin McAlister. Kevin has no community, no neighbors to call for help—he is on his own in his "private space." George Bailey had a score of neighbors to bail him out of his financial plight and help him fight the capitalists' efforts to destroy the community. Kevin is not just home alone—he is socially alone as well. But such realizations are not present in the conscious mind of the moviemakers. On the surface the McAlisters live in a desirable community and are a perfect family. Like millions of other late-twentieth-century families, they are physically together but culturally and emotionally fragmented. Plugged into their various "market segments" of entertainment media, they retreat into their "virtual isolation booths."

Like millions of other kids, Kevin feels isolated in such an existence, and isolation leads to powerlessness, hopelessness, and boredom. How could kids with everything handed to them, adults ask, become so alienated from their parents, schools, and communities? The answer to this question involves on some level the pervasive violation of childhood innocence. Popular culture via TV promised our children a *Brady Bunch* family circus, but they had to settle for alienated, isolated homes. The continuing popularity of *The Brady Bunch* testifies to the mind-set of American children. *The Brady Bunch,* with its family values and two engaged parents, seemed to provide what children found lacking in their own homes. This melancholy nostalgia for suburban family bliss indicates a yearning for a less lonely childhood. All those hours home alone have taken their toll (James 1990; Rapping 1994; Ferguson 1994).

THE UNWANTED

Although *Home Alone* and *Home Alone 2* work hard to deny it, they are about an unwanted child, as are many other films of the 1980s and early 1990s. The comedic form supposedly renders the unwanted theme harmless, in the process revealing contemporary views of parenting and the abandonment of children. In one particular scene in *Home Alone* Kevin's mother (Catherine O'Hara) pays for abandoning her son by riding home to Chicago through Midwestern snowstorms in a truck carrying a polka leader (John Candy) and his band. In one dialogue mother and band leader engage in a confessional on bad parenting and child abandonment:

> MOTHER: I'm a bad parent.
> BAND LEADER: No, you're not. You're beating yourself up. . . . You want to see bad parents. We're [band] on the road 48 to 49 weeks out of the year. We hardly see our families. Joe over there, gosh, he forgets his kids' names half the time. Ziggy over there hasn't even met his kid. Eddie, let's just hope none of them [his children] write a book about him.
> MOTHER: Have you ever gone on vacation and left your child home?
> BAND LEADER: No, but I did leave one at a funeral parlor once. Yeah, it was terrible. I was all distraught and everything. The wife and I, we left the little tike there in the funeral parlor all day, *all day*. We went back at night when we came to our senses and there he was. Apparently, he was there alone all day with the corpse. He was okay. You know, after six or seven weeks he came around and started talking again. But he's okay. They get over it. Kids are resilient like that.
> MOTHER: Maybe we shouldn't talk about it.
> BAND LEADER: You brought it up.

So comfortable are marketers with the theme of abandonment that promos on the home video of *Home Alone 2: Lost in New York* pitch a

Home Alone Christmas Album. Commodifying child abandonment, promoters urge viewers to "begin a tradition in your house." Something is happening in these movies and the promotions that surround them that is not generally understood by the larger society. By the early 1990s social neglect of children had become so commonplace that it could be presented as a comedic motif without raising too many eyebrows. There was a time when childhood accorded protected status, but now safety nets are disintegrating and child supports are crumbling. As children are left to fend for themselves, few public institutions exist to address their needs.

In *Home Alone* and *Home Alone 2* not only is Kevin left to take care of himself, but his parents and family treat him with disdain and cruelty. In one scene Kevin's uncle unjustifiably calls him a "little jerk." After understandably asking why he always gets "treated like scum," Kevin is banished to the attic, where he proclaims on behalf of his generation, "Families suck." These early experiences set up the comedic bread and butter of *Home Alone*: Kevin transfers his anger for his family to burglars Marv (Daniel Stern) and Harry (Joe Pesci) and subsequently tortures them. These two films are not the only movies of the era that address child abandonment and child revenge. In horror-thrillers *Halloween* and *Friday the 13th* the only individuals spared from violence are those who give time to and care for children. Those who neglect children ultimately pay with their lives. As neglected social rejects, children are relegated to the margins of society. It is not surprising, therefore, that in *Home Alone 2* Kevin forges an alliance with a homeless pigeon lady who lives in Central Park—they are both social castoffs. Together they learn to deal with their cultural status.

THE AMERICAN AMBIVALENCE TOWARD CHILDREN

After World War II Americans began to realize that childhood was becoming a phase of life distinctly separate from adulthood. This distinction was most evident in the youth culture beginning to take shape in the 1950s; this youth culture convinced parents that they were losing the ability to shape their children's lives. This fear has informed the aca-

demic study of youth in the last half of the twentieth century, often focusing attention on children as "the problem." Too often refusing to
question the dominant culture and values of the adult world and the
tacit assumptions of the field of childhood studies itself, mainstream
scholars have often viewed conflict between children and parents as
dysfunctional. Childhood "experts" and the mainstream education establishment have often insisted in this academic context that children
need to be instructed to follow directions. This functionalist orientation assumes that the order and stability of environments must be
maintained (Paul 1994; Lewis 1992; Griffin 1993; Polakow 1992).
This, of course, ensures that institutions such as schools become unable
to accommodate change, as they regress into a state of "equilibrium"
(i.e., rigidity).

The virtual ubiquity of parent–child alienation and conflict is
rarely perceived at the individual level of human interaction as a social
phenomenon. When such conflicting dynamics occur in almost all
parent–child relations, it is not likely that fault rests solely with individual parents and individual children. As already noted, something larger
is happening here. Individual children cannot help but judge parents
for their inconsistencies and shortcomings. On the other hand, parents
cannot help but resent being judged and strike back with equal venom
(Ventura 1994). Adults must understand the social nature of this familial phenomenon and, based on this recognition, attempt to transcend
the demand for order inscribed into their consciousness by the larger
culture. Americans don't understand their children or the dynamics of
children's culture. Kids understand that adults just don't get it, as they
listen and watch adults express and act on their misunderstandings of
the differences between generational experiences and mind-sets.
Schools are perceived by children as virtually hopeless; indeed, they are
institutionally grounded on a dismissal of these differences. Little has
changed since the 1960s, when Kenneth Keniston wrote that adult
misunderstanding of youth contributed to a conclusion reached by
many children: American mainstream culture offers us little to live for
(Lewis 1992).

Understanding this adult–child alienation, children slowly begin to
withdraw into their own culture. Culkin's Kevin has absolutely no need

for adults, as he shops (with newspaper coupons even), takes care of the house, and defends himself against robbers. This is quite typical for the films of John Hughes. Children and teenagers rule in a world where youth culture is the only one that matters. Parents in these films are notoriously absent, either at work or on vacation; their advice is antiquated, consisting generally of pompous pronouncements about subjects they obviously know nothing about. Typical of the genre is *The Breakfast Club,* which revolves around the stupidity of parents and adult authority. While it is a flagrant attempt by Hughes to commodify and exploit youth culture, the film does point out the width and depth of the chasm that separates kids and adults (Rapping 1994). Children's culture, of course, takes shape in shadows away from the adult gaze—as well it should. Consequently it behooves parents, teachers, social workers, and other cultural workers who are interested in the welfare of children to understand the social dynamics that shape children and their culture in the early years of the twenty-first century. When parents intensify their anxiety about the threat of postmodern kinderculture and strike out against it, they simply widen the chasm between themselves and their children. In this situation, the assertion of parental control becomes simply an end in itself, having little to do with the needs of children.

As adults in the 1950s and early 1960s began to understand the power of children's culture and the separations between childhood and adulthood it represented, parental and educator anxiety levels reached new highs. Adult fears that the kids were out of control expressed themselves in a variety of ways, none more interesting than in two British films of the early 1960s, *Village of the Damned* and its sequel, *Children of the Damned. Village of the Damned* is based on an invasion by an intergalactic sperm that impregnates earth women to produce a new race of mutant children who mature quickly and are capable of reading adult minds. Reflecting adult anxieties of the era concerning the growing partition between childhood and adulthood, the movie offers a "solution" to the youth problem. Adults in *Children of the Damned* reluctantly decide that they must kill their children. Understanding that child murder is suicidal in that it involves killing a part of oneself, parents sacrifice themselves in order to eradicate the iniquity their children embody. The youth rebellions of the mid- and late 1960s that followed *Children of the Damned* served to raise the emotional ante expressed in the movie's fantasized infanticide.

The adult hostility toward children is omnipresent in *Home Alone* and its sequel, but such issues are consistently hidden from overt recognition. Previous films—*The Other, The Exorcist, The Bad Seed, Firestarter, It's Alive*—recognized adult hostility but projected it onto evil children as a means of concealing it. The abundance of these evil children films points to a social tendency of parents to view their children as alien intruders. This child-based xenophobia positions children as foreigners whose presence marks the end of the family's configuration as a couple (Paul 1994). Old routines are undermined and new demands must be met, as harried adults experience the child's power as manipulator. Such familial dynamics set the scene for the postmodern child custody case, where lawyers, judges, and parents decide who takes the kids.

Commercial children's culture understands what parents and educators don't—children and adolescents are wracked by desire that demands stimulation and often gets out of hand. We see its manifestation in children and children's culture with the constant struggle to escape boredom. Of course, most adults view this childhood desire as a monstrous quality to be squashed by any means necessary even if it requires the stupidification of young people in the process. In the *Home Alone* movies Kevin constantly feels as if he has done something terribly wrong, as if he were a bad kid. In *Home Alone 2: Lost in New York* Kevin prays to the Rockefeller Square Christmas tree: "I need to see my mother, I need to tell her I'm sorry." Exactly for what he should be sorry, no one is quite sure. One can only conclude that he is sorry for being a child, for intruding on the smooth operation of the family, of being goaded by his monstrous desire.

If we equate children with monstrousness, it is not a long jump to the position that the manipulative aliens are evil. In *The Bad Seed*, a successful novel, play, and movie of the mid-1950s, Rhoda is an eight-year-old murderess endowed with a greed for material things—childhood desire run amuck. As the first work that explored this homicidal dimension of childhood, *The Bad Seed* equates youth with absolute malignancy—concealed at first in an innocent package. As Rhoda's landlady says of her: "She never gets anything dirty. She is a good child, a perfect child. She saves her money and keeps her room clean." The appearance of evil so close to goodness and innocence made the child monster that much more horrible. Children who are so evil (or at least so capable of it) in a perverted sense justify child abuse. This image of the bad child was used for comic effect in *Problem Child* (1990) and *Problem Child 2* (1991). The way adults in the *Problem Child* movie reacted to the problem child is revealing:

> SCHOOL PRINCIPAL: Being a principal's great 'cause I hate kids. I have to deal with the weenies.
>
> SCHOOL TEACHER to principal after he brings problem child to her class as a new student: O God, another one. How many kids are they going to make me teach?
>
> LAWANDA, the owner of the bank: What's this thing [referring to problem child]? This kid's a nightmare. . . . Kids are like bum legs. You don't shoot the patient, you cut off the leg.
>
> PROBLEM CHILD'S GRANDFATHER to father: You little psycho— you're an evil boy. You got to learn to respect your elders.
>
> LAWANDA: Listen, you little monster. I'm going to marry your father and send you to boarding school in Baghdad.
>
> SCHOOL PRINCIPAL: You rotten kids should be locked in cages.
>
> LAWANDA: I hate children. They ruin everything. If I had enough power, I'd wipe them off the face of the earth.

Child murderer Sharon Smith never stated it this clearly and unambiguously.

Whenever the problem child seeks to subvert the status quo, viewers are alerted to what is coming by George Thorogood's blues guitar riff from "Bad to the Bone." Such innate "badness" cannot be indulged. As with the neofolk wisdom in contemporary America that criminals cannot be rehabilitated, there is no hope for the growth and development of the problem child. *Home Alone's* Kevin, who is capable of "badness" and sadistic torture, is still struggling with parental forgiveness; the problem child is beyond all that. Parental and educational authority is concerned simply with control; the issue is naked power—there is no need for ameliorative window dressing in this realpolitik for children. In this context kindness becomes the cause of juvenile delinquency, child advocacy the response of dupes and bleeding heart fools. Movie audiences want to see the problem child punished, if not physically attacked. Child abuse lurks not far from such sentiments.

In John Carpenter's *Halloween* the camera shows the audience the point of view of an unidentified murderer who approaches a middle American suburban house occupied by two teenagers making love in an upstairs bedroom. As we watch through the murderer's eyes, he picks up a carving knife in the kitchen, observes the teenage boy leave the house, and walks back up the stairs to the bedroom where the teenage girl is now in bed alone. Looking directly into the camera, the girl expresses her annoyance with an obviously familiar character wielding the knife. At this point the hand carrying the knife stabs the girl to death, principally focusing the attack on her bare breasts. It is only after the murder that we are granted a reverse angle shot of the killer—a six-year-old boy. By 1978, when *Halloween* was made, movie commentators made little of the age of the murderer (Paul 1994). So accustomed was the American audience to children's "innate" potential for evil that moviemakers perceived no need to explain the etymology of the child's violent behavior. The end of the 1970s saw headlines such as "Killer Kids" and newspaper copy such as, "Who are our children? One day they are innocent. The next, they may try to blow your head off" (Vogel 1994, 57). No more assumptions of innocence, no surprises. A new era had emerged.

THE BLAME GAME

Clusters of issues come together as we consider the role of mothers and fathers in the family wars of the late twentieth century. The battle to ascribe blame for family dysfunction in general, and childhood pathology in particular, plays out on a variety of landscapes: politics, religion, and popular culture. The political terrain of the 1990s included the Dan Quayle–Murphy Brown showdown over single mothers as parents, while on the religious battleground right-wing Christian fundamentalists fingered feminism as the catalyst for maternal child neglect. The analysis of this blame game as expressed in popular culture offers some unique insights.

In *Home Alone* and its sequel Kevin's mother has internalized the blaming of women for the neglect (abandonment) of Kevin in particular and for family pathology in general. There is no doubt about who is to blame. Banished to the attic because he has been perceived as a nuisance, Kevin is (justifiably) hurt and angry.

> KEVIN: Everyone in this family hates me.
> MOTHER: Then maybe you should ask Santa for a new family.
> KEVIN: I don't want a new family. I don't want any family. Families
> suck.
> MOTHER: Just stay up there. I don't want to see you again for the
> rest of the night.
> KEVIN: I don't want to see you again for the rest of my whole life.
> And I don't want to see anyone else, either.
> MOTHER: I hope you don't mean that. You'd be pretty sad if you
> woke up tomorrow morning and you didn't have a family.
> KEVIN: No, I wouldn't.
> MOTHER: Then say it again. Maybe it'll happen.
> KEVIN: I hope I never see any of you again.

The mother is the provocateur, the one who plants the ideas that emerge as Kevin's wishes. Insensitive to his emotional hurt, she induces him to request a new family; she is the first to speak of not wanting to see him; she is the one who dares Kevin to tempt fate by wishing away his family (Paul 1994). In the *Home Alone* movies child care is the mother's responsibility. John Heard's father character is virtually a nonentity. He is uninterested in, condescending toward, and hostile to Kevin. He knows (along with the audience) that he is not responsible for Kevin's abandonment even though he was present during the entire episode. He has no reason to gnash his teeth or rend his garment in displays of penitence—this is the domain of the mother. And pay she does with her polka band trip in the first *Home Alone* and her frenzied night run through the streets of New York calling for her son in *Home Alone*

2. In an era when child abuse and child murder by mothers occupy national headlines, this mother's quest for forgiveness may signify a greater guilt. The blame that the right-wing male places on women for the ills of the family, however, is grotesquely perverse, implying that battalions of strong but tender men are struggling with their wives to let them take charge of child rearing—not hardly (Rapping 1994).

Feminist research and analysis of child abuse and domestic violence have subverted the happy depiction of family life as a safe haven far removed from pathologies emanating from internal power inequities. As scholarship documented how family life oppressed women and children, pro-family conservative groups responded by calling for a reassertion of patriarchal control in the home. Women, they argued, should return to child rearing. Some conservatives even maintain that women who don't adequately perform these "maternal" chores should have their children taken away and placed in orphanages. The most optimistic estimates place the number of children who would be institutionalized under this plan at over 1 million; the cost of such care would run over $36 billion (Griffin 1993; Morganthau et al. 1994). The male backlash to the assertive feminist critique has only begun with its depiction of women's political organization as the rise of a dangerous special interest group. Protectors of male power are waging an effective public relations battle. Any campaign that deflects blame for family failure from absent, often abusive fathers to mothers possesses a superior penchant for persuasion and little concern for truth.

Home Alone displays these gender dynamics in refusing to implicate the father in the abandonment. On learning that Kevin is not in Paris with the family, his mother exclaims, "What kind of mother am I?" The lack of affect on the part of the adult males of the family, Kevin's father and his uncle, is perplexing. The careful viewer can only conclude that they neither like nor care about the eight-year-old. The father's dismissiveness is never explained. All the viewer can discern is that the father and the uncle seem to be fighting for their manhood, expressing perhaps their resistance to the "breadwinner-loser" male character who forfeits his "male energy" in his domestication and subsequent acceptance of fidelity in marriage, dedication to job, and devotion to children (Lewis 1992). Such a male figure was ridiculed by beatniks as square, by

Playboy devotees as sexually timid, and by hippies as tediously straight. The search for a hip male identity along with a healthy dose of irresponsibility has undermined the family as a stable and loving environment. Doing the right thing in regard to one's family as a man means losing status among one's fellow men.

An examination of adult male behavior in families indicates that many men are desperately concerned with peer group status. For example, men on average pay pitifully inadequate child support to their former spouses, if they pay it at all. Only half of women awarded child support ever receive what they are owed, a quarter receive partial payments, and the remaining quarter get nothing at all (Galston 1991). This ambiguous role of the father in the family highlighted by the indifferent father of *Home Alone* is addressed in a more overtly oedipal manner in other movies of the last couple of decades (Paul 1994). *The Shining,* for example, retrieves a father's hostility toward his own son, which has always been repressed in Western culture, and builds an entire plot around it. Danny, the child protagonist in *The Shining,* develops the psychic power to see beyond the limits of time and space after his father (Jack Nicholson) broke Danny's arm in an alcoholic stupor. Danny's power, his shining, is expressed through his imaginary friend, Tony, who lives in Danny's mouth. Tony exists to help Danny cope with his violent, abusive father. Danny's presence and growth remind his father of his emasculation, his stultification by the family. The father's solution to his problem—an attempt to murder his wife and child with an ax—allows for none of the *Home Alone* ambiguity; the movie jumps headfirst into the maelstrom of the conflict between virile masculinity and the demands of domesticity.

As the screen image of the crazed, ax-wielding Jack Nicholson fades into a blurred image of *Jurassic Park* (1993), the continuity of the child-hating adult male remains intact. Even in this "child-friendly" Spielberg-produced dino drama, the paleontologist (Sam Neill) hates children and refuses to ride in the same car with them. In response to a prepubescent boy's sarcastic question about the power of dinosaurs, Neill evokes the image of the violent Nicholson circling and threatening the child with the ominous claw of a velociraptor. The difference between *Jurassic Park* and *The Shining,* however, involves Neill's moment of epiphany; when the children are endangered by the dinosaurs, Neill sheds his hatred and like a good father risks mutilation and death to save their lives. As in the *Home Alone* movies, the issue of the father's hatred is buried in a happy ending: the safe children celebrating with the "reformed" Neill and the happy McAlister family celebrating Christmas in a frenetic present-opening ritual. The demand for family values in the 1980s and 1990s changed the cultural landscape: Family values must triumph, adult men must be depicted as ultimately devoted to their children, the feminist portrayal of the "bad father" must not be reinforced.

AND AS IF THE AMBIGUITY WEREN'T BAD ENOUGH, SOME KIDS MATTER MORE THAN OTHERS

In class dynamics of the American childhood, poor children don't matter as much as upper-middle-class children (i.e., privileged children like the ones portrayed in the *Home Alone* movies). The frequent assertion that America is not a class society, uttered so confidently by mainstream politicians and educators, holds profound psychological and political consequences. This class silence undermines the understanding among the well-to-do that they were granted a head start, while paralyzing the less successful with a feeling of personal inferiority. On the political level, as it sustains the fiction, the belief that reifies the status quo: When the poor are convinced that their plight is self-produced, the larger society is released from any responsibility (Rubin 1994).

An overt class silence pervades *Home Alone* and its sequel. Even newspaper reviewers referred to the upper-middle-class, white, Protestant "bleached and sanitized" microcosm of the two movies (Koch 1990). The McAlisters are very wealthy, living in an enormous brick colonial in a generic Chicago suburb filled with extravagant furnishings and conveniences. Indeed, they are an obnoxious and loathsome crew; being privileged, they believe they can act any way they want. The filmmakers go out of their way to make sure viewers know that the family deserves its money—as father McAlister (John Heard) drinks from crystal in first class on the plane to Paris, he alludes to his hard work and humble origins. The message is clear—the American Dream is attainable for those willing to put in the effort. The McAlisters deserve their good fortune.

Into this restricted world of affluent WASPs Harry and Marv (two small-time robbers with an attitude) make their appearance as the only poor people and the only non-WASPs in the two movies. Harry (Joe Pesci) and Marv (Daniel Stern) are quickly positioned as "the other." They speak in lower-class accents; obviously ethnic, Pesci exaggerates his working-class Italian accent, and just so we are not confused Stern signifies his Jewishness with a curiously gratuitous "Happy Hanukkah" reference as he steals money from a toy store. They are ignorant and uneducated—Pesci refers to the fact that he never completed the sixth grade; they hold an irrational hatred of the affluent; their "crime signature" involves flooding affluent homes after each robbery (they are known as the "wet bandits"). These class- and ethnic-specific traits set Marv and Harry apart to such a degree that the audience can unambiguously enjoy their torture at Kevin's hands.

Home Alone and its sequel pull their weight in the larger social effort to erase class as a dynamic in American life. Under interrogation the movies confess their class complicity, as evidenced through the "otherization" of Marv and Harry. Compare Marv and Harry with Mr. Duncan, the toy store owner who appears in *Home Alone 2*. Imbued with the sweetness and generosity of Joseph the angel in *It's a Wonderful Life*, Duncan is the most charming character in the *Home Alone* movies. After the McAlister's reunification in *Home Alone 2*, he showers them with scores of presents. His only motivation for being in business is that he loves children and wants to see their happy faces when they open presents from his store. His loving smiles prove that capitalism cares and the status quo is just. He deserves every penny of his profits just as much as Marv and Harry deserve their torment. Such characterization gently dovetails with the dominant political impulses of the moment, marked by a callous acceptance of poverty, child poverty in particular, in the midst of plenty.

Over 12.6 million children live below the poverty line, making one out of every five American children poor. Too often unaware of such class realities, Americans and their institutions are far removed from the insidious effects of such poverty. Poor children too infrequently escape the effects of living with parents scarred by their sense of shortcoming, of having to negotiate movie and TV images of the poor and the working class as dangerous and oafish caricatures (as in *Home Alone* and its sequel), and of confronting teachers and social workers who hold lower expectations for them than their middle- and upper-middle-class peers. A key feature of the class dynamic in *Home Alone* and its sequel involves the public reaction to the McAlisters' child abandonment episodes as "good fun," as opposed to the real-life home alone cases that surfaced in the 1990s. When Kevin's parents report that he was left alone in New York to the police after they reach their vacation destination in Miami, it's no big deal. Even when they admit that abandoning the child has become "a family tradition," no one is excited—after all, the McAlisters are upper-class, well-to-do people. Almost daily, parents (especially single mothers) who leave their young children home alone for sometimes just a few hours are arrested and forced to relinquish their children to foster care. With child care often costing $200–400 a month, poor mothers are trapped in virtually impossible circumstances (Seligman, August 1, 1993). Society's refusal to address poor and single mothers' need for child care has contributed to the feminization of poverty (Polakow 1992). The first two *Home Alone* films indicate the double standard that dominates the American view of the rich and the poor and the mean-spirited class bias of some expressions of popular culture in this conservative age.

POSTMODERN CHILDHOOD

In *Home Alone* and its sequel—amid the bizarre mix of child abandonment and child–parent alienation, children caught in the crossfire of gender wars, crass class bias, and comedy—resides something profound about the role of children in contemporary American culture. The movies could have been made only in a culture experiencing a profound shift in the social role of children. For all individuals who have a stake in understanding childhood—parents, teachers, social workers, family counselors, and so on—knowledge of these changing conditions becomes a necessity. A no-growth economy has mandated that all adults in the family must work outside the home; subsequently children find themselves saddled with daily duties ranging from house cleaning, baby-sitting, and grocery shopping to cooking, laundry, and organizing carpools. With the "family values" agenda of right-wing movements threatening to eviscerate governmental support of poor and middle-class families, the economic problems of children look to get worse before they get better.

The new era of childhood, the postmodern childhood, cannot escape the influence of the postmodern condition with its electronic media saturation. Such a media omnipresence produces a hyperreality that repositions the real as something no longer simply given but artificially reproduced as real. Thus media-produced models replace the real—simulated TV kids on sit-coms replace real-life children as models of childhood. In this same media-driven postmodern condition a cultural implosion takes place, ripping apart boundaries between information and entertainment as well as images and politics. As media pushes the infinite proliferation of meaning, boundaries between childhood and adulthood fade as children and adults negotiate the same mediascape and struggle with the same impediments to meaning making. Children become "adultified" and adults become "childified" (Aronowitz and Giroux 1991; Best and Kellner 1991). Boundaries between adulthood and childhood blur to the point that a clearly defined, "traditional," innocent childhood becomes an object of nostalgia—a sure sign that it no longer exists in any unproblematic form (Lipsky and Abrams 1994; Postman 1994).

There is nothing childlike about a daily routine of child care, cooking, and shopping. In *Home Alone* and *Home Alone 2* Kevin is almost completely adultlike in meeting the demands of survival on his own. He checks into hotels, uses credit cards, orders pizzas, and grocery shops, all as a part of a day's work. He needs no adult figure; he can take complete care of himself. In the postmodern childhood being home alone is an everyday reality. Children now know what only adults used to know. Postmodern children are sexually knowledgeable and often sexually experienced; they understand (and many have experimented with) drugs and alcohol. New studies show they often experience the same pressures as single working mothers, as they strive to manage school attendance, work at home, and interpersonal family dynamics. When the cultural dynamics of hyperreality collide with post–baby boom demographics and the economic decline of the early 1970s, 1980s, and 1990s, the world changes (Lipsky and Abrams 1994). The daily life of media-produced family models such as the Cleavers from *Leave It to Beaver* is convulsed. June must get a job and Wally and Beaver must take care of the house. No longer can Beaver and his friends Larry and Whitey play on the streets of Mayfield after school. Anyway, it's dangerous—Mayfield is not as safe as it used to be.

Children under twelve belong to a generation only half the size of the baby boomers. As a result, children as a group garner less attention now than forty years ago and have a correspondingly diminished voice in the society's social and political conversation. In such a context, youth issues are not as important as they once were. Add to this a declining economy complicated by rising expectations. As American manufacturing jobs have disappeared and dead-end service jobs have proliferated, advertising continues to stimulate consumer desire. Frustration levels among children and teenagers rise as a direct result of this socioeconomic contradiction. Given the centrality of TV in the lives of this postmodern home-alone generation, the awareness of the desirability of children's consumer goods becomes a central aspect of their lived reality. Consumer desire, however, is only one aspect of the effect of TV and other electronic media on American children. TV introduces children to American culture. It doesn't take a movie critic to see how often Hollywood has drawn on the TV-taught-me-all-I-know theme. In *The Man Who Fell to Earth*, David Bowie as an alien learns all about earth culture from TV; in *Being There* Peter Sellers as idiot savant Chauncey Gardner knows nothing about the world but what he saw on TV. The movie ends with Chauncey on his way to a possible presidential candidacy—life imitates art? The robot in *Short Circuit*, the mermaid in *Splash*, the aliens in *Explorers,* and the Neanderthal in *Encino Man* all are socialized by TV (Lipsky and Abrams 1994).

What does the repeated invocation of this theme say to observers of childhood? With the evolution of TV as a medium that attempts to more or less represent reality, children have gained an adultlike (not necessarily informed) view of the world in only a few years of TV watching. Traditional notions of childhood as a time of sequential learning about the world don't work in a hyperreality saturated with sophisticated but power-driven views of reality. When a hotel porter asks Kevin in *Home Alone 2* if he knows how the TV in his hotel room works, Kevin replies, "I'm ten years old; TV's my life." The point is well taken, and as a consciousness-dominating, full-disclosure medium, TV provides everyone—sixty-year-old adults to eight-year-old children—with the same data. As postmodern children gain unrestricted knowledge about things once kept secret from nonadults, the mystique of adults as revered keepers of secrets about the world begins to disintegrate. No longer do elders know more than children about the experience of youth; often they know less, for example, about video games, computers, TV programs, and so on. Thus the authority of adulthood is undermined as kids' generational experience takes on a character of its own.

The social impact of such a phenomenon is profound on many levels. As I discuss in more detail in Chapter 5 on McDonald's in this book, a subversive kinderculture is created, in which kids through their attention to child-targeted programming and commercials know something that mom and dad don't. This corporate-directed kinderculture provides kids with a body of knowledge adults don't possess, while their access to adult themes, on TV at least, makes them conversant with marital, sexual, business-related, criminal, violent, and other traditionally restricted issues. When combined with observations of families collapsing, single mothers struggling to support their families, parents involved in the "singles" scene, and postdivorce imposition of adult chores, children's TV experience provides a full-scale immersion into grownup culture.

In the context of childhood education the postmodern experience of being a kid represents a cultural earthquake. The curriculum of the third grade is determined not only by what vocabulary and concepts are "developmentally appropriate" but by what content is judged to be commensurate with third grade experience in the lived world (Lipsky and Abrams 1994; Postman 1994). Hyperreality explodes traditional notions of curriculum development—third graders can discuss the relationship between women's self-image and the nature of their sexual behavior. While parent groups debate the value of sex education in the public schools, their children are at home watching a TV docudrama depicting a gang rape of a new inmate in a federal penitentiary. When teachers and the school culture treat children as if they know nothing of the adult world, the kids come to find school hopelessly archaic, out of touch with the times. This is why the postmodern subversive kinderculture always views school with a knowing wink and a smirk—how quaint school must look to our postmodern children.

There is nothing easy about the new childhood. Many teenagers and young adults speak of stress and fatigue originating in childhood. If a teenager has juggled the responsibilities of adulthood since the age of seven, physical and psychological manifestations of stress and fatigue in adolescence should surprise no one. Adolescent suicide did not exist as a category during the "old childhood, " but by 1980 it was second only to accidents as the leading cause of death among teenagers. By the 1990s, 400,000 young people were attempting suicide yearly and youth suicide was being described in the academic literature as an epidemic (Gaines 1990). The covenant between children and adults has been broken by parental and clerical child abuse and the pathological behavior of other caretakers. Too often children of the late twentieth and early twenty-first centuries have been shunted into inadequate child care institutions administered on the basis of cost-efficiency concerns instead of a larger commitment to the welfare of children. The tendency to segregate by age is well-established, and unless steps are taken to reverse the trend more generational alienation and antagonism will result (Gaines 1994; Polakow 1992).

In the context of this child segregation, cultural pathologies manifest themselves. Excluded from active participation in the social order, children find themselves both segregated and overregulated by institutional forms of social control. The overregulators pose as experts on child raising, child development, child morality, and early childhood education with their psychodiscourse on the rigid phases of child development and the strict parameters of normality. In the name of "proper child-rearing techniques" experts tap into a larger ideology of personnel management that adjusts individuals to the demands of an orderly society. Like all strategies of personnel management, mainstream child psychology masks its emphasis on control. Intimidated by the scientific language of the experts, parents lose faith in their own instincts and surrender control to the authority figure on Sally Jesse. Play gives way to skill development, as structure permeates all aspects of the child's life. While middle- and upper-middle-class children suffer from the hyperstructure of skill development, poor children labeled "at risk" are medicated and drilled in a misguided effort to reduce chaos and disorder in their lives. In the name of order the experience of poor children is further bureaucratized (Seiter 1993; Polakow 1992).

THE WORLDLINESS OF POSTMODERN CHILDHOOD: THE WISEASS AS PROTOTYPE

The *Home Alone* movies can be understood only in the context of the postmodern childhood. Kevin McAlister is a worldly child; light-years separate Kevin from Chip, Ernie, and Robbie Douglas on *My Three Sons* of the late 1950s and early 1960s. As a black comedy for children, *Home Alone* struck an emotional chord with movie watchers that made it one of the most popular and profitable films of all time. Kevin, as kiddie-noir hero, is a smart kid with an attitude; Macaulay Culkin's ability to portray that character turned him into an overnight celebrity—a role model for the prepubescent wiseass.

Kevin as postmodern wiseass could not tolerate children from the 1940s and 1950s with their simpleminded "the policeman is our friend" view of the world. Bizarre in their innocence, such children are viewed by postmodern kids as antimatter reflections of themselves without responsibilities or cynicism. "What would we talk about?" Kevin might ask of a meeting with such kids. Unless Kevin had watched old movies or lived near a separatist group such as the Amish, he would have never seen such unworldly children. Almost every child depicted on TV in the contemporary era—Alex Keaton on *Family Ties*, Michele in *Full House*, Lisa and Bart Simpson on *The Simpsons*, Malcolm from *Malcolm in the Middle*, Cartman from *South Park*—is worldly and wise. Bart Simpson and Cartman may be underachievers, but only in school—a place that is boring, confining, and based on a childhood that no longer exists. Bart and Cartman are not childish; the school is. The Culkin-style smart-ass child (e.g., Bart and Cartman) is the symbol for contemporary childhood. Imagine their reaction to a "Yes, Virginia, there is a Santa Claus" adult monologue: "Right, dude, now eat me."

The wiseass is the hero of the subversive kinderculture. The appeal of *Home Alone* and its sequel is connected to this insurgent response to middle-class propriety with its assumption of child helplessness and its worship of achievement. Child and adult are pitted against each other with the child as the sympathetic character. In these two films no one could feel much sympathy for Kevin's parents with their lack of empathy for Kevin's position in the family and their lack of attention to his needs. Kevin's behavior is an act of righteous resistance to this unjust status quo. Like his kindred spirits, Bart Simpson, Cartman, and Malcolm, Kevin thrives on disorder—a chaos that undermines the social order constructed around bourgeois stability. As Cartman might put it, order "sucks," disorder is "cool." The subversive kinderculture of the postmodern childhood thrives on this disorder.

One of the subtexts running through both *Home Alone* movies involves the humorous juxtapositioning of comments of family members concerning poor, helpless little Kevin with the visual depiction of Kevin happy and in control of the disorder of his solitude. The appeal of the film revolves around Kevin's ability to tell his parents: "Even in the middle of all this exciting chaos, I don't need you." The self-sufficient boy hero of the postmodern era—what a movie-marketing bonanza. He shows no remorse on learning that his parents have left him home alone: (with eyebrows raised Kevin speaks to the audience) "I made my family disappear." Compare this postmodern reaction to parent–child separation to Dorothy's in *The Wizard of Oz*—Judy Garland's raison d'être is getting back home to Kansas. Kevin is self-actualized, living out the childhood fantasy of life without parental encumberment. Since he "can't trust anybody in this family," Kevin decides he would rather vacation alone than with "such a group of creeps." As a bellman scoops ice cream for him in his posh New York hotel room, it is obvious that Kevin's intuitions are correct. "This is a vacation," he sighs.

CONFRONTING THE INTENSITY OF YOUTH
IN A POSTMODERN CHILDHOOD

As parties interested in the status of contemporary childhood, we ask, what does the popularity of the *Home Alone* movies tell us about the inner lives of children and their attempt to understand their relationship with the adult world? For a generation of home-aloners, Culkin's Kevin is a character with whom they can identify, as he negotiates the cultural obstacles they also confront. He offers them a sense of hope, a feeling that there is something heroic in their daily struggle. Once again, the corporate marketers are one step ahead of the rest of us, as they recognize the changing nature of childhood and colonize the psychological ramifications such changes produce. In retrospect it seems so easy: to canonize a child who is left home alone for Christmas is to flatter every postmodern child in the audience. Kevin's predicament validates a generation's lived experience, transforming them from unwanted children into preteen ninja warriors. If nothing else, *Home Alone* is a rite of passage story about a boy home alone, endangered, besieged who emerges victorious and transformed (Koch 1990). "I'm no wimp," he proclaims as he marches off to battle, "I'm the man of the house." Ironically, as a postscript, the real-life character of Macaulay Culkin has become a replicated Kevin, with parental separation, parental litigation, and a troubled youth and young adulthood.

The *Home Alone* films have ushered in a plethora of smartass, parent-eschewing, bored, self-sufficient media icons. In a postmodern era where children have already seen everything, have watched the media sell laundry detergent by exploiting a mother's love for her children, it is no surprise that contemporary kids experience difficulty with emotional investment. As a result the interpersonal affect of postmodern children tends to be minimal—everything is kept at a distance and treated ironically (Grossberg 1994). Kevin offers such children something in which to invest and a sense that their desire for real experience is not pathological. This childhood and adolescent desire for intense sensation is typically viewed by the adult world as dangerous and misguided. Indeed, the very purpose of certain forms of traditional schooling and child rearing has been to tame such feelings. This visceral energy of the young—so central to Kevin in *Home Alone* and so enticing to young moviegoers—lays the foundation for a progressive postmodern child rearing and childhood education. Too often adults who are "in charge" of children forget the nature and power of this visceral energy/life force of young people. In their adult amnesia they fail to connect with the force and, as a result, relinquish the possibility of guiding it or being replenished by it. They have often blamed rock music, hip-hop, MTV videos, video games, communists, or Satanists for creating the energy, forgetting that historically mediated forms of it have expressed themselves from ancient hunter-gatherer societies to modern and postmodern ones (Ventura 1994; Rodriguez 1994).

Suppressing this energy in the postmodern North American culture at the beginning of the twentieth-first century undermines our civic, psychological, and intellectual growth. The very qualities adults fear most in children—their passion, visceral energy, and life force—can be used as the basis for a postmodern childhood education. In a sense the genie is out of the bottle and is not going back in. As the communication revolution has opened adult esoterica to children, we find there is no turning back. The endless debates over movie and record ratings are futile exercises; the question now revolves around how we provide children the emotional and intellectual supports that help them balance the interaction between their visceral energy and their newfound insights. Just as traditional forms of teaching and childhood curricular arrangements are passé given the "new times," forms of discipline and control strategies are obsolete. Can kids who hold Kevin's knowledge of the world in general and the anxieties and tribulations of adulthood in particular be domesticated and controlled (not to mention the question of should they be) in the same ways as children of a different era of childhood were? Custodial schooling is no longer adequate for children; indeed, it was never adequate for children no matter what the era.

Education for domestication assumes that the information a child encounters can be regulated and sequentially ordered (Polakow 1992; Gaines 1990). Much schooling and child rearing is still based on such an archaic assumption, resulting in strategies that negate children's exploration, invention, and play. Indeed, the purpose of many of these strategies is to prevent the integration of acquired information from a variety of sources into the cognitive and emotional structures of an evolving personhood—growth itself. Thus child rearing insufficiently prepares children for adulthood or even postmodern childhood, as it ignores the world that surrounds children and shapes their lives. The lessons to be excavated from this quick analysis of the *Home Alone* movies are sobering in their urgency. The state of the contemporary family and the inability of the public conversation about it to transcend the most trivial forms of platitudes to the value of family in our "national character" is distressing. An effort to examine the nature of kinderculture and the forces that shape it simply does not exist in the surreal image-based politics of the present era. The ambivalent adult relationship with children is a suppressed feature of the cultural landscape, rarely, if ever, addressed in even the professional schooling of child welfare professionals, child psychologists, or elementary educators. These silences must end.

REFERENCES

Aronowitz, S., and H. Giroux. 1991. *Post-Modern Education: Politics, Culture, and Social Criticism.* Minneapolis: University of Minnesota Press.

Best, S., and D. Kellner. 1991. *Postmodern Theory: Critical Interrogations.* New York: Guilford.

Coontz, S. 1992. *The Way We Never Were: American Families and the Nostalgia Trap.* New York: Basic.

Ferguson, S. 1994. "The Comfort of Being Sad." *Utne Reader,* July-August, 60–61.

Gaines, D. 1994. "Border Crossing in the USA." In A. Ross and T. Rose, eds., *Microphone Fiends: Youth Music, Youth Culture,* 227–234. New York: Routledge.

———. 1990. *Teenage Wasteland: Suburbia's Dead End Kids.* New York: Harper Perennial.

Galston, W. 1991. "Home Alone: What Our Policymakers Should Know About Our Children." *New Republic,* December 2, 40–44.

Griffin, C. 1993. *Representations of Youth: The Study of Youth and Adolescence in Britain and America.* Cambridge, Mass.: Polity.

Grossberg, L. 1994. "Is Anybody Listening? Does Anybody Care? On the State of Rock." In A. Ross and T. Rose, eds., *Microphone Fiends: Youth Music, Youth Culture,* 41–58. New York: Routledge.

James, C. 1990. "Scrooge Pens the Screenplay." *New York Times,* December 23.

Koch, J. 1990. "Home Alone Hits Home with a Powerful, Disturbing Pop-Culture Potion." *Boston Globe,* December 27.

Lewis, J. 1992. *The Road to Romance and Ruin: Teen Films and Youth Culture.* New York: Routledge.

Lipsky, D., and A. Abrams. 1994. *Late Bloomers, Coming of Age in Today's America: The Right Place at the Wrong Time.* New York: Times Books.

Morganthau, T., et al. 1994. "The Orphanage." *Newsweek,* December 12, 28–32.

Paul, W. 1994. *Laughing Screaming: Modern Hollywood Horror and Comedy.* New York: Columbia University Press.

Polakow, V. 1992. *The Erosion of Childhood.* Chicago: University of Chicago Press.

Postman, N. 1994. *The Disappearance of Childhood.* New York: Vintage.

Rapping, E. 1994. *Media-Tions: Forays into the Culture and Gender Wars.* Boston: South End.

Rodriguez, L. 1994. "Rekindling the Warrior." *Utne Reader,* July-August, 58–59.

Rubin, L. 1994. *Families on the Faultline: America's Working Class Speaks About the Family, the Economy, Race, and Ethnicity.* New York: Harper Collins.

Seiter, E. 1993. *Sold Separately: Parents and Children in Consumer Culture.* New Brunswick, N.J.: Rutgers University Press.

Seligman, K. 1993. "Poor Kids Often Home Alone." *San Francisco Examiner,* August 1.

Ventura, M. 1994. "The Age of Endarkenment." *Utne Reader,* July-August, 63–66.

Chapter 10

POWER PLAYS:
VIDEO GAMES' BAD RAP

Stephanie Urso Spina

VIDEO GAMES, with annual sales over $10 billion in the United States and an estimated $20–$30 billion worldwide, are a powerful force in the entertainment and economic sector as well as the cultural landscape. As technology becomes more sophisticated, video games continue to evolve from the simple shooting gallery format of early models to include increasingly realistic graphics and, in the more controversial games, depictions of ever more grotesque violence. Given the pervasiveness of video games and the popularity of many games that feature virtual bloodbaths, the games have been scapegoated by politicians and other cultural commentators, especially since they are a significant component of youth culture. Foremost among the criticisms leveled at video games is that they are addictive and violent and lead to antisocial, aggressive behavior. On what basis are these claims made and how justified are they? While the sensational content of many video games is inherently alarming to adults, judgments about their actual effects on kids must await a more considered analysis of the precise nature of the games' appeal and of the role they play in kids' lives.

Adults tend to regard young people as economically dependent, low-status, incompetent creatures who must be sheltered and disciplined to conform to adult expectations. The young are either deficient (e.g., lacking shame, experience, knowledge, manners, and tact; deficiencies disguised and romanticized as "childhood innocence") or they are creatures of sinful excess "in need of civilizing restraint and rehabilitation" (views grounded in Calvinist notions of original sin and innate evil or Freudian notions of children's "polymorphous perversity" [Goldstein 1998, 84]). Either way, the child fails to measure up to adult standards. Anxious about the loss of their authority (Wartofsky 1983), adults have increasingly infantilized younger generations, even while envying their adamantly exuberant, energetic, inquisitive, audacious nature. This has led to the simultaneous demonization and romanticization of youth and their culture. It is not surprising then, given the fact that adult society is awestruck by technology, that the fascination and facility of youth with complex technologies and sophisticated media have led to further alienation between young people and adults. When youth are seen as other and at risk, they become objects of blame and pathology (Spina 2000a,b), including, by extension, the elements of their culture: their clothes, hairstyles, music, and video games. This dark view perpetuates a vicious cycle that even encompasses research. Empirical studies, for example, often use children and teenagers to examine the effects of technological media but rarely use media to explore how the unique cognitive, social, and personality development of children and youth influence and are influenced by their participation in media-related activities.

Media and other cultural forces and institutions exert a great influence on how adolescents think about themselves and their world. Contrary to popular adult opinion, video games are not at best alienating and a waste of time or at worst a catalyst for violent behavior. In this chapter I argue that the opposite is the case: Video games, especially violent ones, serve important social and psychological functions and may even avert violent behavior.

This is not to say that video games are completely blameless. There simply has not been enough reliable and valid research conducted on the many different genres and aspects of gaming to support any general claim about them. Social science research on the games is almost exclusively focused on content or on chronicling the effects of game violence. For instance, studies enumerate acts of violence

(Provenzo 1991, 1992) or count the numbers of male versus female characters or calculate the racial composition of a game's cast (Deitz 1998; Douglas, Dragiewicz, Manzano, and McMullin 2002); or they use the length of time involved with gaming to focus on negative effects of not spending that time on other activities. Inconsistencies in research findings may result from a too narrow approach rooted in ignorance about video games' complexity and diversity and from a failure by researchers to recognize that the hours spent in media-related activities indicate their importance in the lives of youth beyond mere entertainment or recreation.

I have tentatively concluded that video gaming does more good for more players than harm. As the parent of an avid video gamer, I know this can be a difficult realization to come to terms with. I began researching the role of video games in the lives of youth more than eight years ago in part because I was concerned about their dominance and influence in the lives of my son and other young gamers. I confess I am still concerned with many of the images and messages I see in games like the controversial, ultraviolent, and (although I admit it reluctantly) equally enthralling Grand Theft Auto series, in which players beat up old men, kill prostitutes after having sex with them, and decapitate police officers, among other atrocities.

Nevertheless, my studies, as well as my assessment of the current research, do not support my earlier, negative hypotheses or my fears (Spina 1997–1998, 1998, 2001). We all feel fear, rage, greed, and the thirst for power and control, although we are taught to deny it. We have learned to disapprove of natural feelings of aggression in much the same way that Victorians disapproved of sexuality, and we send that message to our children.

Attempts to protect children (and ourselves) from stigmatized feelings and media images that evoke those feelings are counterproductive. We end up "protecting" children from self-empowerment (which may be the point for those unwilling to relinquish control to the next generation). By experiencing these inescapable, natural feelings through fantasy play, children can learn to master their rage. The world can be a frightening place to the young and small. Pretending to have superhuman powers, to be invincible and in control, helps children conquer their feelings of powerlessness (Jones and Ponton 2003) and gives them tools to face their fears and master their rage. Identifying with a rebellious, even destructive, character helps children learn to deal with a contemporary culture that cultivates fear. We think of rage as a bad thing—a negative emotion to avoid at all costs. But rage can also be mobilizing. It can give us the courage to overcome our fears and face life's challenges: to do what we thought we could not do. Through immersion in violent video games and imaginary combat, players engage the rage, lust, and greed they've been encouraged to suppress and reintegrate these emotions into a more well-rounded, healthier, and more resilient self.

MORAL PANIC

The controversies surrounding video games are reminiscent of earlier generations of social science research on media violence. In the 1920s and 1930s, comic books, movies, and radio broadcasts were the answers to questions similar to those being asked today about television, video games, and the Internet. Where do children learn violent behavior? What is the cause of social violence? Who or what can we blame for disturbing events we cannot explain without implicating ourselves?

Video games, like movies, comics, and radio before them, have drawn frequent criticism from parents, professionals, and organized groups. Most of this criticism concerns the overwhelming violence in some games and the "addictive nature" of most games. Critics with this mind-set fail to consider two related phenomena: (1) violent crime, particularly among the young, decreased dramatically during the last decade while video games have steadily increased in popularity, depictions of violence, and use; and (2) children and teenagers are not just passive consumers of popular culture; they appropriate and integrate its symbols and forms for their own purposes. Video gaming does not just take place between an individual and a machine. Perhaps more important than playing the games, frequently with one or more friends, is the social function games serve away from the console or monitor. Video games provide a common bond, a shared interest with its own insider lingo, a vehicle for building relationships and gaining and displaying skills, and a tool for mediating conscious and unconscious thoughts and feelings (Spina 2001).

Although the focus of research and anti-video game violence campaigns is on adolescents, the Federal Trade Commission (2000) recently reported that 90 percent of video games are purchased by adults over eighteen for their own use and that the average American video game player is twenty-nine. Nonetheless, video games continue to be singled out as a particularly dangerous influence on youth. If these games are really teaching kids to become trained killers, then the question is, Why aren't there more violent acts? Conversely, if they are not a bad influence on children, why is there such a sense of moral panic?

Cohen (1980) used the term "moral panic" to characterize the reactions of the media, the public, and agents of social control to youth disturbances. The term "moral" implies that the perceived threat is a threat to the social order itself. The response is likely to be a demand for greater social regulation or control and a demand for a return to traditional values. Not coincidentally, moral panics occur before definitive research can be performed and evidence uncovered on what truly does or doesn't cause "deviant behavior" in youth.

According to Cohen (1980, 9), the key elements or stages in a moral panic are (1) identification of a condition, episode, person, or group of persons as a threat to societal values and interests; (2) representation of the threat in a stereotypical form by the mass media; and (3) a rapid buildup of public concern fueled by expressions of moral outrage by religious and community leaders, politicians, and other self-righteous folks along with diagnoses and solutions from socially approved experts. Ultimately the panic recedes (often superseded by a new moral panic) or it results in social changes.

Video games were first identified as a threat to society shortly after December 1, 1997, the day Michael Carneal, age fourteen, shot eight students at a school in Paducah, Kentucky. The press noted that he liked to play point-and-shoot video games. The following year, two school shootings, also presumably caused by video games, followed in Jonesboro, Arkansas, and Springfield, Oregon. When two Colorado teens killed thirteen students and then themselves in April 1999, once again leaving friends, relatives, and the rest of the country struggling to make sense out of seemingly senseless acts, "experts" were called on to impart meaning to the tragedy. Many of these psychologists, social workers, psychiatrists, and other professionals blamed the usual scapegoats: elements of teenage culture such as the black trench coats worn by the Littleton murderers, the music, television shows, and movies they watched, but especially the video games they played (Anderson and Dill 2000). Rather than face the real socioeconomic and ideological issues that contribute to our country's proclivity for violence (Spina 2000a), attention was diverted, with strong support from the gun lobby (Klein and Chancer 2000), to media violence. We are still in the midst of the moral panic this created, despite evidence that only a minority of boys involved in those and similar violent acts were fans of violent video games (Borum 2000).

REFINING OUR UNDERSTANDING OF VIOLENCE

Violence can be physical, psychological, institutional, and symbolic (Bourdieu 1977; Freire and Macedo 2000). Each of these interrelated forms of violence can have serious consequences. However, life-threatening physical acts of violence are qualitatively different from other forms of violence (Spina 2002). If we define violence as intentionally injuring or killing another person, can we label any media truly violent? Semantics aside, simulated aggression is not the same as real acts of violence. Does the audience at a production of *Macbeth* or *Chicago* leap onto the stage to stop a murder? Video game players, like movie- and theatergoers or readers engrossed in a good novel, willingly suspend disbelief and become immersed in the blend of aesthetic, narrative, visual, verbal, and ideological conventions that create an alternate "reality" of experience that we feel is—but know is not—real, much the same way video gamers know the violence in a game is not real (Spina 2000). It is a "place" that can be entered and left at will, whether by leaving the theater, closing the book, or ending the game. This is not the case in real life.

The incidence of violent crime in foreign countries is considerably lower than in the United States. In 1999, over 26 million video games were sold in Great Britain. Yet crime in Britain, which has consistently had one of the lowest rates in the world, declined an additional 33 percent between 1995 and 2000, with the largest ever decrease occurring after 1999 (Insalaco 2001). The media in Japan is more graphically brutal than that in America, and video games are even more popular with both men and women. Yet a teenager in America is over 32 percent more likely to commit a homicide than his Japanese counterpart. In 1996 the murder conviction rate for Japanese teenage males (ages fourteen to seventeen) was 0.6 per 100,000; in the United States, it was 19.6 per 100,000 (United Nations 2000). The facts are not consistent with claims that the increasing availability and violence in video games are producing more violence. This suggests that the cause of violent crime lies elsewhere. By focusing on the effects of video game violence on violent behavior, more vital risk factors—such as poverty—remain unaddressed. Without an underlying national ethos that supports, if not promotes, various forms of violence, would video games be seen as contributing to crime statistics?

WHAT THE RESEARCH DOES AND DOESN'T TELL US

Repeated attempts by researchers, in both experimental studies and field studies, to find evidence of increased aggression and other undesirable consequences of playing violent video games have produced no conclusive evidence. Current research simply does not support the major public concern that violent video games lead to real-life violence. Video games, once condemned publicly by former Surgeon General C. Everett Koop for causing aberrations in childhood behavior and having "no redeeming qualities at all"(Mayfield 1982), have been all but cleared of those charges by Koop's successors, who admit with apparent reluctance that "the overall effect size for both randomized and correlational studies [is] small for physical aggression and moderate for aggressive thinking" and conclude that violence in any media is not a major long-term factor in violent behavior (Office of the Surgeon General 2001, 92).

Regardless of the type of research, only a few studies provide evidence that supports a causal relationship between violent video games and behavior, and even then the effects are moderate at best (Provenzo 1991; Anderson and Bushman 2001). Other studies find evidence against such an effect, and others show no effects (Durkin and Barber 2002; van Schie and Wiegman 1997; Griffiths 1999). The only constant in this body of work is its inconsistency. Despite the ubiquity of video games, there has not been a great deal of research about them and much of what there is suffers from methodological problems. Of the twenty-two published research reports Anderson and Bushman (2001) included in their meta-analysis, only nine studies focused on aggressive behavior. Yet, even with such a small and problematic body of work, they conclude that exposure to violent video games has a negative effect on a variety of measures, including an increase in aggressive behavior, and that they are therefore a threat to public health. To further complicate the issue, some correlational studies find a correlation between the amount of time spent playing (violent) video games and aggressive behavior but provide no evidence that the games are the cause of aggression (Colwell and Payne 2000; Roe and Muijs 1998). None consider that there are at least several plausible alternatives that can also account for the effects found, from direct exposure to violence to personality traits (Freedman 2001). There are people who play video games without becoming violent, and violent people who do not play video games. Thus the existence of the correlation between playing violent games and aggressive behavior tells us nothing about whether violent video games cause aggression.

Experimental studies of video games and aggression have also produced weak and inconsistent results. Four such studies claimed to find at least some support for the hypothesis that violent video game content can increase aggression, but these studies also suffer from conceptual and methodological problems (Cooper and Mackie 1986; Irwin and Gross 1995; Schutte, Malouff, Post-Gorden, and Rodasta 1988; Silvern and Williamson 1987). Not only do definitions of aggression vary, but studies of violent video games do not always distinguish aggressive play from aggressive behavior, which can lead to faulty conclusions. Aggressive play lacks the determining feature of aggression: the intent to injure another person. Another faulty assumption here is that thinking about violence leads to behavioral violence, when it can also mean that one feels badly about and wants to avoid violence. One study (Cooper and Mackie 1986) that distinguished between aggressive play and aggressive behavior (although the constructs were questionable; see below) found that violent video games affected violent play but not violent behavior. Another experimental study (Funk, Buchman, and Myers 2000) found no relationship between playing violent or nonviolent video games and aggression or empathy, but it did find that children's preexisting aggression scores predicted their total aggression measure. Another meta-analysis of video game research (Sherry 2001) found that playing time was actually a negative predictor of effect size. That is, the more one played video games, the weaker the relation to aggressive behavior. In most studies, time spent playing a game is a mere five to fifteen minutes (Calvert and Tan 1994; Funk, Buchman, and Myers 2000) and the games used are not equivalent in terms of one or more key components such as type and degree of violence, genre, complexity, technological quality, and interest. Regardless of their outcomes, all of these studies have validity problems stemming from the fact that they measure simulated aggression and not "real aggression," and none of these studies can rule out the possibility that key game-related variables such as excitement, difficulty, frustration, or enjoyment created the observed increase in "aggression."

I enclosed the word "aggression" in quotes because the measures used are often analogies for aggression, and sometimes pretty poor ones at that. One study equated a child's choice to play with an "aggressive" over a "nonaggressive" toy with being aggressive (Cooper and Mackie 1986). Playing with an aggressive toy is hardly the same as being aggressive. Moreover, even if playing one aggressive game increases the likelihood that children will choose to play another aggressive game, this does not tell us anything about effects on actual aggression. A similarly puzzling surrogate for aggression was Anderson and Dill's (2000) use of the intensity and duration of a loud noise made by pushing a button. I cannot fathom how one can equate something children might even find fun to real aggression. Other equally questionable dependent variables that served as measures of aggression have included hitting a Bobo doll (Schutte, Malouff, Post-Gordon, and Rodasta 1988), coding how much violence appeared in children's interpretations of ambiguous stories (Kirsh 1998), and withholding a monetary reward from another student for making errors (Winkel, Novak, and Hopson 1987).

Another problem with much of the video game research is that laboratory studies cannot, by definition, capture the experience of playing games at home. Play is a voluntary, self-directed activity. At home, the surroundings are familiar and comfortable. In the lab, the child is in a strange environment, and often the game and the duration of play are determined by the researcher, not the child. In most studies, the time spent playing a game is nowhere near long enough to approximate the average two to four hours per session children and adolescents are likely to play on their own, and too short to experience the suspension of reality that players identify as one of the major attractions of gaming (Spina 1997–1998) or to attain the state of "flow" described by Csikszentmihalyi (1990). As Cumberbatch notes,

> The real puzzle is that anyone looking at the research evidence in this field could draw any conclusions . . . let alone argue with such confidence and even passion that it demonstrates the harm of violence on television, in film and in video games. While tests of statistical significance are a vital tool of the social sciences, they seem to have been more often used in this field as instruments of torture on the data until it confesses something which could justify a publication in a scientific journal. If one conclusion is possible, it is that the jury is not still out. It's never been in. Media violence has been subjected to lynch mob mentality with almost any evidence used to prove guilt. (2001, 15–16)

It is puzzling that the research on video games rarely looks at issues that players consider important. Children and adolescents are the subjects of many cultural and educational debates. Yet their voices are often absent or ignored. At best, they are sometimes invited to observe or occasionally participate in relevant discussions, but their views are seldom taken seriously. This is most unfortunate, since we have much to learn from them. We need to learn to listen to what youth are telling us—to their real messages. Young people bring their entertainment choices and experiences to bear on their intense concerns with issues of identity, belonging, and independence. Nearly all of their public behavior—their style of dress, the music they listen to, the slang they speak, and the games they play—has a social purpose. We need to look at game players as members of social groups, not at isolated individuals forced to play a video game for a few minutes as part of an experiment. This was the theoretical and methodological starting point of a research program I have been building on since 1995.

LOOKING FOR ANSWERS

In my study, I have found that the participants overwhelmingly (96 percent) preferred role-playing games (RPGs). In RPGs, as in many areas of life, players do not know the rules in advance: They must figure out what the characters and objects mean and how they act and interact. Winning depends on more than the perceptual and physical coordination to push the right buttons with the right speed at the right time. Thus the findings may not be applicable to other game genres or populations.

Each participant claimed to be good at his favorite game, indicating that the participants consider themselves competent at these skills. Competency is important because it is necessary for the individual to see himself as having agency in "a particular game or cultural system" (Holland 1992, 81). This results in "emotional involvement and identification" (Holland 1992, 82), allowing one to develop a concept of self one wants to either realize or avoid (Dreyfus, in Holland 1992). (In many video games, one literally has multiple lives and can assume multiple identities.) Similarly, role-playing offers opportunities to experiment and practice a variety of behaviors and relationships.

POLYMORPHOUS PLAY

Each participant in the study mentioned the experiential "reality" of playing games as a critically important feature of gaming. During a game, each player would speak in the first person, as the character he had chosen to assume. According to the boys, the choice is determined by the character's abilities and suitability for advancing the game without regard to sex, ethnicity, or even species. Yet, particularly for male adolescent players, the sexuality of the games is an important element. The *New York Times Sunday Magazine* Styles page (July 11, 1998) featured a character from the game Final Fantasy VII, Tifa Lockheart, as the pinup of the cyber generation. Her animated competitor, *Tomb Raider*'s Lara Croft, receives steamy letters from males of all postpubescent ages.

The teenage boys in this study had no reservations about adopting female roles in the games. Similarly, a variety of races, ethnicities, and species are equally assumable identities. Although I question the exaggerated physiques of both male and female characters and the negative representations and treatment of women and marginalized ethnic and racial groups in some games, I applaud the blurring of those divisions and the positive possibilities suggested by games where players readily "become" a character based on the relationship between that character's attributes and matched with the skills needed in the game regardless of race, sex, or even species (Spina 2001).

Some games feature characters with a blend of racial features that defy categorization so that race becomes ambiguous and irrelevant. In fact, racial ambiguity is a hallmark of Anime-style games. Other games also feature characters that are androgynous and allow players to break with the constraints of gender identification. For example, to win Sega Saturn's *NiGHTS into Dreams*, the player must become both the male and the female protagonists and they must join forces as the androgynous character NiGHTS for the final level. Transcending gender gives the player (as NiGHTS) the freedom and ability to fly. The penalty for failure in this virtual world is to be trapped on the ground and as a single gender.

This is more than a cathartic or orgasmic "brave new world" experience of power and sensuality. While these elements contribute to the experience, they remain ephemeral. Although there are differences in each game and character, the iconography and fantasy center on power play of frequently mythic proportions.

SLAYING MONSTERS

Part of the pleasure of gaming is related to identification with the grotesque violence and corporeal destruction in the games that symbolically transgress conventional standards of behavior. Yet even the youngest participants in my study emphasized the following:

> It's not real.
> It's fun.
> It helps me unwind after a hard day at school.
> It gets the anger out.
> Nobody gets hurt and I feel better after I play.

As in animated cartoons—where Roger Rabbit, Yosemite Sam, or Wile E. Coyote are graphically beaten, flattened by an anvil or steamroller, or sent flying over incredible distances by a single right hook, and then suddenly return to life virtually unharmed—the exaggerated violence of video games serves as a symbolic transgression of conventional standards of behavior (and sometimes the laws of physics). It is becoming, change, and renewal. It is death and resurrection.

Video game themes follow the basic narrative patterns of literary plots that rely on action, adventure, and mystery. Like many of the original versions of fairy tales and the epics of literature such as *Beowulf* and the *Odyssey*, narratives in video games are often constructed around stories of life and death or good and evil and feature a bestiary of mythical monsters and magical creatures, exaggerated or ambiguous sexuality, and, not coincidentally, a great deal of violence. Such deeply embedded symbols make visible some of the invisible forces of life and society (Gerbner 1973) and provide dramatic ground for the complex negotiations of meaning and the resolution of inter- and intrapersonal conflicts.

Video games provide access to a world where it is possible to practice negotiating unknown rules (or taking risks). It is also a domain devoid of the consequences that taking similar risks in the real world might engender. Creating opportunities for symbolic risk taking, whether in video games, drama, or similar activities, appears to have considerable value. While symbolic risk taking does not involve real-world consequences, the perception of risk may be as psychologically salient as actual risk. Perception has been found to be as important or more important than more objective measures in other psychological processes such as the emotional and physical benefits of social support (Minkler 1990). For example, according to Bandura and his colleagues, persistence in activities that are subjectively threatening but relatively safe enhance self-efficacy through experiences of mastery, which leads to higher self-esteem. They found no difference between performance that originated in active mastery or in vicarious experience alone (Bandura 1990; Bandura and Cervone 1986; Bandura and Schunk 1981; Bandura 1977). Lightfoot's (1997) work with adolescents indicates that fantasizing risk may contribute to identity development in much the same way experiencing risk does. If this is the case, participation in symbolic risk taking may reduce actual risk taking and violent behaviors.

Adults assume that violence is the main reason video games are attractive to youth, but the popularity of the games does not necessarily imply that the violence itself is enjoyable. People are highly selective in the violence they seek or tolerate. Violent images are only appealing when the viewer feels relatively safe. The context and circumstances are crucial to experiencing violent imagery as entertaining. Zillman, Bryant, and Sipolsky (1989) have argued that violence may increase enjoyment because it heightens perceptions of suspense and drama. For violence to be entertaining, it must have a moral story in which good triumphs over evil, and it must carry indications of its unreality—music, sound effects, a fantasy story line, cartoonlike or otherwise obviously "not-real" characters, settings, or situations (McCauley 1998; Zillmann 1998; Spina 1997–1998). Lacking indications of their unreality, bloody images lose their appeal (McCauley 1998; Holmes and Pellegrini 1999).

Even when those conditions are met, players report that they like the games in spite of—rather than because of—the violence, or that they see the violence mainly as an inconvenience: a part of the game to get through. (The most popular video game of all time, *Myst*, is a nonviolent game [Miller 1999].)

> LUIS: Well, yeah, it's fun shooting, the sound effects and visuals are cool . . . but if that's the whole game it can get boring when that's all there is and just make it take longer to get to the next level. . . . Yeah, so I guess it's okay, y'know, but not my favorite part of the game. . . . My thing I like the best is like figuring out how to beat the game. If I gotta kill too many guys it kinda takes away from the fun of more fun (pause) more different like parts of the game.

Although they are part of the social fabric of our culture, video games can paradoxically provide a means of escape from the pressures of this culture. For example, while the participants demonstrated and verbalized resistance to traditional roles of male identity and dominant codes of authority, they simultaneously identified with them in on-screen games of power, knowledge, and control.

The strength and appeal of video games lie in their ability to breach boundaries and play with contradictions. The games provide not only a means of escape and a forum for symbolic risk taking, but also an opportunity for identification with the expectations of society. These three themes (escape, identification, and risk taking) are evident in answers to questions about why the participants found the games so compelling and exciting.

> MATT: Because it makes me feel strong and powerful. It lets you do things that you couldn't do in real life and I can, like, get out all my anger from like school and stuff.
>
> JASON: With all of the realism, you feel like you're in the game. You always want to know what's going to happen next so you keep playing. I have to stay very focused when I play or I could miss a key point I need to win the game. That concentration is

something I enjoy. It makes all my troubles and bad feelings disappear.

Luis: The game has a first-person perspective so you see it through the eyes of your character. The characters talk so it feels like you're really part of the scene but you don't really kill or get killed. It's almost like sort of a virtual reality. You're in the game, not in your living room.

Scott: I love the fast pace and the players. I love hockey and when I play this game I feel like I'm out there on the ice and it's like a real game with the pros and I'm one of them! Anything can happen. You never know how it will turn out.

Travis: When I play this game, I feel like I'm in another world and I'm in charge. I become the character I've chosen.

In video game worlds there is little moral complexity or ambiguity. Bloodied bodies disappear like the spilled milk of yesterday's childhood—but with fewer consequences. Participation in such games may be seen as a ritual and vicarious encounter with power and authority that bridges the familiar role of "child" with some aspects of the adult male role that boys are expected to take on.

This was also evident in the enthusiastic answers to a question nine of the boys in the original study named as their "favorite" or "the most important question" in the interview. Since the boys experienced such a strong sense of fusion with characters that already existed in the games, it was supposed that asking them to create a new, personalized character would provide a better vehicle for identification and self-representation than the commercial versions. (When listening to the tapes, you can hear the enthusiasm in their answers. Unfortunately, the printed word cannot convey the sense of excitement as strongly.) The question was: Suppose you could be a new character in the game. Who or what would you be? Why?

Responses to this question varied more than almost any other. While there were similarities (eleven of the twelve boys created a character who was stated to be the "best"), there were also, as would be expected in symbolic self-representation, many individual differences. While space precludes in-depth analysis of each response, some overall themes can be illustrated with the following excerpts. For example, there was a tendency to make the characters more dimensional, more "real," more "human" than they were in the games. (In fact, video games have begun to do just that. Characters are becoming less stylized and more realistic in both appearance and attributes. The film versions of *Tomb Raider* even use actors instead of animation.) Their responses echo Gerbner's claim that "characters come to life in the symbolic world of mass culture to perform functions of genuine social import" (1973, 475).

STEVE: My character would be a fighter who had superstrength and superweapons. He would not have a definite shape but be shaped like a big blob of goo. I'd call him "Supergoo" and he would change colors according to what mood he was in.

INTERVIEWER: Why?

STEVE: Because it would be cool and everyone would know how he felt from what shape he was in and from his color so like, um, if he was in a bad mood they'd know to stay out of his way and if he was purple say they'd know he was sad and needed to be cheered up. . . . He'd be the best guy in the game but he'd, like, be, you know, more real than the other characters.

INTERVIEWER: What do you mean by "more real?"

STEVE: He'd, like, have more feelings and things. Like, not always be the same every time . . .

EVAN: I would be a humanoid iguana. Because iguanas are cold-blooded, he would be able to absorb the heat energy from projectiles and it would fill up his life force. That way he wouldn't be able to be hurt. His tail would be a powerful weapon and he'd have wings and be able to fly . . . and do a lot of other things.

INTERVIEWER: Why an iguana, Evan? How is what you described "humanoid"?

EVAN: I know a lot about iguanas and I have one for a pet. . . . He'd be humanoid because he'd, like, be able to walk upright like a human and stuff. Even though humans aren't cold-blooded he'd be, like, more like a combination of human and reptile. He'd have these superpowers as a fighter and stuff but he'd be able to think more like a human than a reptile. (pause) Oh, yeah—And he'd wear clothes. (grins) . . . and use a bathroom so I don't have to clean up his shit . . .

While all of the responses described characters who were the strongest, bravest, and most powerful, these were not usually the most important attributes:

SHIV: My character would look like a gargoyle and have powers like a wizard. He'd have infinite lives and be skilled in weaponry but mostly would use his magic and deductive powers to save people and make friends. He would have wings and claws and flippers and be able to fly and dig and swim . . .

Even when power was the most important trait of a new character, there was a moral purpose for the use of power:

JOE: I'd be a new superhero in a game where the goal would be to save the world.

INTERVIEWER: Tell me more. What would the superhero's name be? What would he save the world from?

JOE: I'd call him Ejo. E-J-O. That's Joe all mixed up. (grins) He'd save the world from everything like, um, attacks from space and comets and things. (pause)

INTERVIEWER: And once the world was saved—then what?

JOE: You play the game again. (laughs) No, really, then I guess I, er, he'd set up a new government and be president of the world so he could keep saving it again and again and there would be no earthquakes or wars or homeless people anymore.

In constructing these identities, the participants borrowed selectively from a variety of sources. Most came from video games and other forms of popular culture. Others (like Evan's transformed pet iguana) reflect individual life histories. Whatever their source, the self-representations "refer not just to the visible features of the physical body but include psychological qualities, the spiritual essences that people either experience in themselves or wish to attain" (Csikszentmihalyi 1993). These individual "essences" are, however, embedded in the social context. Provenzo (1991) writes about how video games support isolation and argues strongly for the lack of community fostered by video games where the individual is out for himself. I have not found this to be the case. While the game itself may emphasize the self-as-player as an autonomous being, the culture around game playing involves an intricate social network with skills, "codes," and experience serving as the basis for considerable communication and learning among the group of boys studied. Much of the knowledge constructed in gaming culture is acquired through participation in an interpretive community. Symbols and characters from the games are used not only to distinguish self from other, but also to identify self with other. Book covers decorated with drawings of game characters by a player or a prominently displayed game magazine invite relationship among those with similar interests. Half of the boys frequently drew characters or scenes from their favorite game. Another quarter sometimes did. These usually adorned schoolbook covers and notebook margins and were intricately detailed. When asked what purpose these drawings served, replies centered on issues of self-representation and social mediation:

JASON: It makes it more my book, you know, like I, and I can tell all the textbooks apart easier and find the right book faster. And when I get bored in class I can work on the drawing.

MING: It lets other kids know what I think is cool.

DAN: It gives me a way to make friends. Like if another kid recognizes the picture then he knows we like the same games and stuff so maybe we'll talk about it and even hang out together to play games.

Similarly, discovery of a new code (codes allow players to take short cuts or gain strategic advantages in a game) provides a reason for a flurry of telephone exchanges among friends. Game strategy is a common topic in school cafeterias and other gathering places. Sharing of information about video systems and games invites and cements relationships. Every boy knew his best friend's favorite game, what level the friend had reached in the game, and why the friend preferred that particular game. Eleven of the twelve boys named as best friends were also participants in the study, so it was possible to verify the accuracy of this information.

In pairs or small groups, the boys watching an individual play are engaged in active strategy learning. Players are carefully observed and often asked what they are doing and why. Sometimes players explain their strategy as they go along by using a metanarrative. For example, while playing with a friend new to a particular game, Luis carried on a monologue for his friend's instruction without pausing for a second in his concentrated play:

> The first thing you wanna do is to stop all enemies from entering the room because you can't afford to lose hit points by fighting with them . . . (He explains as he prevents one character's entrance with a few rapid moves of his fingers on the control panel) You can defeat them without losing hit points but you want to save them for later in the game because you don't know what to expect later on. (He now positions his character to search a vase) Second, you have to search anywhere and everywhere that might hold an important item and all items are important. (He finds a small mirror in the vase) In this game, everything you find is important and has a use, even if it doesn't seem like it . . . (He moves into another room) You repeat this process for each room but as you go on you can't always prevent attacks by the enemies. Like the mirror. (He continues to play, searching for items and fending off enemies while he talks) For a long time I couldn't figure it out and then I found a book about the Golden Fleece (in the course of playing the game) and it said to polish your shield so it shines like mirrors, and I remembered the story of Medusa from school, so I positioned the mirror to reflect the monster's image back at it and it worked so now I know how to use the mirrors and I don't have to look for the clue in the book anymore. (pause) Some items I still haven't found clues for and some I figured out on my own . . .

While this speech serves an apparently instructional purpose (i.e., by making explicit the hidden rules of the game, the more experienced player is teaching his novice friend how to negotiate them), it also reveals some other less obvious levels of meaning. During subsequent questioning, Luis said it felt good to be able to teach the game to his friend; it felt good to be better at it and "to be able to figure out how to beat the game without being told . . ." He felt "important," or what one might call empowered. Gerbner (1973, 476) defines cultural power as "the ability to *define the rules of the game* of life that most members of a society will take for granted" (italics added).

Video games provide access to a world where it is possible to practice negotiating unknown rules (or taking risks) without fear of the consequences that taking similar risks in the real world might engender. They often feature adversarial relationships that need to be shifted for growth to occur. Echoing what Luis said in the previous excerpt about not fighting enemies in the beginning because you might lose points you'll need later, Jason explained, "Sometimes, instead of struggling to beat the guy, you have to let him win so you can get to the next stage. You have to maybe sacrifice some ground now to beat the game later."

Although Luis and Jason have learned a lesson appreciated by chess players and other strategists such as military generals and business executives, chances are that most adults would not appreciate the boys' intense involvement in video games. The adults (and girls) in these boys' lives overwhelmingly did not relate to video game culture. While some parents were indifferent, most parents and teachers were critical of the games and the boys' involvement with them. Only Scott said a parent expressed any interest in a game (his father, a hockey fan, played the video version sometimes). Although three boys said they were sure some girls played video games and maybe even liked the same ones they did, none of the boys personally knew any girls who did so.

Perhaps this makes the games more attractive to the boys by differentiating them from the older generation and opposite sex and aligning them with peers at a time when such identification is critical to cultivating significant social distinctions as well as loyalties (Erikson 1968). As Shaw points out, people, and especially youth, favor "symbolic markers" they feel "belong" to the subculture that supports and sustains their identity, permitting "individuals to distinguish the evaluative standards of their group from those of other status groups and simultaneously, to express and reinforce solidarity and loyalty with local moral communities" (Shaw 1994, 91). Another factor that may contribute to the popularity of video games in male culture is that games provide a situation in which it is acceptable for them to feel a wide range of emotions—not only fear, power, and aggression but also wonder, competency, empathy, and connection.

UNEVEN PLAYING FIELD

The experiences associated with video gaming appear to have considerable value for young people. However, it is critically important to emphasize the unevenness of the playing field: the "technological divide" among children of different backgrounds. Access to computers and video game consoles is either nonexistent or restricted for those with low incomes who live in poorer school districts. A 2001 report by the National Center for Educational Statistics found that schools with high numbers of poor students—those where at least 75 percent of students are eligible for free or reduced-price lunches—and with high numbers of minority children are less likely to have access to technology than schools whose students are better-off and white. In 2000, only 40 percent of families earning $30,000 or less per year had a computer in their homes compared to 80 percent of those earning $30,000–$75,000 per year and 90 percent of families with annual incomes above $75,000 (Annenberg Public Policy Center 2000).

There is also a vast gender gap in gaming culture. Estimates vary, but it is probably safe to say that at least twice as many boys as girls play video games, and boys spend at least 75 percent more time playing the games than girls do. This puts girls at a disadvantage in several ways, many of which also hold for low-income and other marginalized groups. Female students continue to compose a minority of computer science majors in the United States and composed just 16 percent of the high school Advanced Placement computer science test takers in 1995 and 1996 (American Association of University Women 1999).

Because the interactivity of video games, whether played on a console or computer, is an important part of the experience, gaming cannot be compared to watching television, movies, or videos, or listening to music. Although more universally available, these are more passive entertainments. The lower working class and poor often do not have the opportunities, for example, to try on new roles without long-term risk, to practice cognitive strategies, to relieve internalized pressures safely. Girls may have the access, but they need to be encouraged to take advantage of it. Making technology available to those who would not have access to it otherwise may even the playing field in multiple ways.

Indeed, experience in video gaming is one predictor of success in computer science courses in college (Wilson 2002). Video games provide a popular introduction to digital technology at an early age, fostering computer literacy and often an interest in pursuing technology-related fields (Subrahmanyam and Greenfield 1998; Cassell and Jenkins 1998). Gaming improves computer literacy by enhancing players' abilities to attend to multiple images simultaneously and to understand images in a three-dimensional space (Subrahmanyam and Greenfield 1996).

GAMES AND EDUCATION

Students today inhabit a physical, social, economic, political, and technological world different in important ways from that experienced by their parents and teachers. However, adults tend to address the kinderculture of children and youth from their own generational perspectives. Teachers, parents, and others engaged in education belong to a generation that grew up with television and film, which provided media experiences that differ from those of today's generation. This becomes a problem when adults represent their own perspectives as an implicit norm in culture, politics, and education (Fromme 2000). This implies that the newer forms of media are something to be distrusted. In addition, it seems that the majority of the older generation exemplify the "Protestant ethic" emphasis on rationality, practical work, and self-control. Parents and teachers, for example, want children to use computers, but only for educational (i.e., writing, learning software) purposes or more serious activities that may lead to a career in, say, computer programming, not for playing games.

But during the next decade, video game players will likely run classrooms and Congress. They will be teachers, construction workers, doctors, secretaries, firefighters, letter carriers, lawyers, and parents. Douglas Lowenstein (2002), president of the American computer games industry group, Interactive Digital Software Association (IDSA), recently pointed out in his address to its annual trade forum that "within 20 years, the person sitting in the White House will be a once and future video gamer."

Yet we continue to run our schools and teach as if nothing had changed in the past hundred years, let alone in the past generation. The current conservative political climate in this county is looking to the past for ways to improve schooling instead of looking to the future—to the changing nature of the kinds of knowledge that are required in the workplace and the home. There is a critical need to reform schooling, but in radically different ways than have been suggested. The increased emphasis on covering standard curricula, imposing standardized testing, dividing learning into isolated subject areas segmented into rigid time periods, and similar practices will have only deleterious effects. Our resistance to significant structural changes, our unwillingness to address broader issues of economic and social justice, and our vocationalization of the teaching profession constrain our vision and limit, if not doom, our future.

We systematically and systemically ignore ways to reconceptualize and reinvigorate education to better prepare our children and future generations for a world where vast quantities of information, available at the touch of a fingertip, has to be managed rather than memorized, a world where a different set of cognitive skills—critical thinking, problem solving, creativity—and technological fluency are needed. And then we wonder why students lack interest in schools that do not teach those things.

As Stanley Aronowitz argues, "The best preparation for the work of the future might be to cultivate knowledge of the broadest possible kind, to make learning a way of life that in the first place is pleasurable and then rigorously critical" (2000, 161).

CONCLUSION

Video games serve young people as social, cognitive, and psychological tools, as signs of individual and social identity, as meaning-full experience. They compose a unique culture whose potential for transformative possibilities may be more far-reaching and unexpected than we realize. There is great promise here. Given the absence of convincing research evidence indicating that violent video games are harmful, and given the seductive aesthetics of their carefully choreographed, hypnotically hypervisual representations of unspeakable horrors, it seems premature to celebrate and encourage their excesses. There is something to be said for upholding basic humanistic values, and I would encourage game designers and corporations to imagine and develop new games that marshal all the creative and technological sophistication currently mesmerizing kids while engaging the self-expressive and even altruistic impulses voiced by some of the boys whose interviews are quoted in this chapter. Shiv wanted a character who could use his special powers "to save people and make friends." Joe imagined a game about "saving the world" and even rescuing the homeless. If these kids can envision the pleasure of such fantasies, shouldn't the video game industry be listening?

REFERENCES

American Association of University Women. 1999. *Gender Gaps: Where Schools Still Fail Our Children.* New York: AAUW.

Anderson, C. A., and B. J. Bushman. 2001. "Effects of Violent Video Games on Aggressive Behavior, Aggressive Cognition, Aggressive Affect, Physiological Arousal, and Prosocial Behavior: A Meta-Analytic Review of the Scientific Literature." *Psychological Science* 12: 353–359.

Anderson, C. A., and K. Dill. 2000. "Video Games and Aggressive Thoughts, Feelings, and Behavior in the Laboratory and Life." *Journal of Personality and Social Psychology* 78: 772–790.

Annenberg Public Policy Center. 2000. *Media in the Home 2000.* Edited by E. H. Woodard and N. Gradina. Philadelphia: University of Pennsylvania Press.

Ariès, P. 1962. *Centuries of Childhood: A Social History of Family Life.* New York: Vintage.

Aronowitz, S. 2000. *The Knowledge Factory: Dismantling the Corporate University and Creating True Higher Learning.* Boston: Beacon.

Bandura, A. 1990. "Perceived Self-Efficacy in the Exercise of Control Over AIDS Infection." *Evaluation and Program Planning* 13, no. 1: 9–17.

———. 1977. "Self-efficacy: Toward a Unifying Theory of Behavioral Change." *Psychological Review* 84, no. 2: 191–215.

Bandura, A., and D. Cervone. 1986. "Differential Engagement of Self-Reactive Influences in Cognitive Motivation." *Organizational Behavior and Human Decision Processes* 38, no. 1: 92–113.

Bandura, A., and D. H. Schunk. 1981. "Cultivating Competence, Self-Efficacy, and Intrinsic Interest Through Proximal Self-Motivation." *Journal of Personality and Social Psychology* 413: 586–598.

Borum, R. 2000. "Assessing Violence Risk Among Youth." *Journal of Clinical Psychology* 5610: 1263–1288.

Bourdieu, P. 1977. *Outline of a Theory of Practice.* New York: Cambridge University Press.

Bowman, R. F. 1982. "A Pac-Man Theory of Motivation: Tactical Implications for Classroom Instruction." *Educational Technology* 229: 14–17.

Calvert, S. L., and S. Tan. 1994. "Impact of Virtual Reality on Young Adults' Physiological Arousal and Aggressive Thoughts: Interaction Versus Observation." *Journal of Applied Developmental Psychology* 151: 125–139. Special Issue: Effects of Interactive Entertainment Technologies on Development.

Cassell, J., and H. Jenkins. 1998. "Chess for Girls? Feminism and Computer Games." In J. Cassell and H. Jenkins, eds., *From Barbie to Mortal Kombat: Gender and Computer Games,* 2–45. Cambridge: MIT Press.

Cohen, S. 1980. *Folk Devils and Moral Panics: The Creation of the Mods and the Rockers.* New York: St. Martin's.

Colwell, J., and J. Payne. 2000. "Negative Correlates of Computer Game Play in Adolescents." *British Journal of Psychology* 91: 295–310.

Cooper, J., and D. Mackie. 1986. "Video Games and Aggression in Children." *Journal of Applied Social Psychology* 168: 726–744.

Csikszentmihalyi, M. 1993. *The Evolving Self: A Psychology for the Third Millennium.* New York: HarperCollins.

_____. 1990. *Flow: The Psychology of Optimal Experience.* New York: Harper Perennial.

Cumberbatch, G. 2001. *Video Violence: Villain or Victim?* Video Standards Council, U.K. www.videostandards.org.uk/video_violence.htm. Accessed December 4, 2003.

Deitz, T. L. 1998. "An Examination of Violence and Gender Role Portrayals in Video Games: Implications for Gender Socialization and Aggressive Behavior." *Sex Roles* 38: 425–442.

Douglas, C. A., M. Dragiewicz, A. Manzano, and V. McMullin. 2002. "United States: In Video Games, Black Women Are Victims, Latinas Don't Exist." *Off Our Backs* 433, no. 4: 6.

Durkin, K. 1999. *Computer Games and Australians Today.* Australian Government Office of Film and Literature Classification.

Durkin, K., and B. Barber. 2002. "Not So Doomed: Computer Game Play and Positive Adolescent Development." *Applied Developmental Psychology* 23: 373–392.

Erikson, E. 1968. *Identity: Youth and Crisis.* New York: Norton.

Federal Trade Commission. 2000. *Marketing Violent Entertainment to Children: A Review of Self-Regulation and Industry Practices in the Motion Picture, Music Recording, and Gaming Industries.* www.ftc.gov/opa/2000/09/youthviol.htm.

Freedman, J. 2001. "Media Violence and Aggression: A Review of the Research." Manuscript, University of Toronto.

Freire, P., and D. Macedo. 2000. "Scientism and the Ideological Construction of Violence, Poverty, and Racism." In S. U. Spina, ed., *Smoke and Mirrors: The Hidden Context of Violence in Schools and Society,* 163–176. Boulder: Rowman & Littlefield.

Fromme, J. 2001. "The Impact of New Media: The Distrust of Adults and the Media Practices of Children." In M. K. W. Schweer, ed., *The Impact of Media: Trust and Social Responsibility,* 157–181. Opladen: Leskie & Budrich, 2001.

Funk, J. B., D. D. Buchman, and D. Myers. 2000. "Playing Violent Video and Computer Games and Adolescent Self-concept." Paper presented at the 108th Annual Convention of the American Psychological Association (APA).

Gee, J. P. 2003. *What Video Games Have to Teach Us About Learning and Literacy.* New York: Macmillan.

Gerbner, G. 1973. "Teacher Image in Mass Culture: Symbolic Functions of the Hidden Curriculum." In D. R. Olson, ed., *Media and Symbols: The Forms of Expression, Communication, and Education.* Chicago: University of Chicago Press.

Goldstein, J. 1998. "Immortal Kombat: The Attractions of Video Games with Violent Themes." In J. Goldstein, ed., *Why We Watch: The Attractions of Violent Entertainment,* 53–68. New York: Oxford University Press.

Griffiths, M. 1999. "Violent Video Games and Aggression: A Review of the Literature." *Aggression and Violent Behavior* 4: 203–212.

Grodal, T. 2000. "Video Games and the Pleasures of Control." In D. Zillmann and P. Vorderer, eds., *Media Entertainment: The Psychology of Its Appeal,* 197–214. Mahwah, N.J.: Erlbaum.

Holland, D. C. 1992. "How Cultural Systems Become Desire: A Case Study of American Romance." In R. G. Andrade and C. Strauss, eds., *Human Motives and Cultural Models,* 61–89. New York: Cambridge University Press.

Holmes, R. M., and A. D. Pellegrini. 1999. "Children's Social Behavior During Video Game Play with Aggressive and Non-Aggressive Themes." Paper presented at International Toy Research conference, Halmstad, Sweden.

Insalaco, R., ed. 2001. *National Statistics Digest.* United Kingdom: Office for National Statistics.

Interactive Digital Software Association. 2002. *Ten Facts About the Computer and Video Game Industry: What You May Not Know Could Surprise You.* www.idsa.com/IDSA_ Top_Ten.pdf.

Irwin, A. R., and A. M. Gross. 1995. "Cognitive Tempo, Violent Video Games, and Aggressive Behavior in Young Boys." *Journal of Family Violence* 10: 337–350.

Jones, G., and L. Ponton. 2003. *Killing Monsters: Why Children Need Fantasy, Super Heroes, and Make-Believe Violence.* New York: Basic.

Kirsh, S. J. 1998. "Seeing the World Through Mortal Kombat-Colored Glasses: Violent Video Games and the Development of a Short-Term Hostile Attribution Bias." *Childhood* 5: 177–184.

Klein, J., and L. Chancer. 2000. "Masculinity Matters: The Omission of Gender from Highly Profiled School Violence Cases." In S. U. Spina, ed., *Smoke and Mirrors: The Hidden Context of Violence in Schools and Society.* Boulder: Rowman & Littlefield.

Lightfoot, C. 1997. *The Culture of Adolescent Risk Taking.* New York: Guilford.

Malone, T. W. 1980. *What Makes Things Fun to Learn? A Study of Intrinsically Motivating Computer Games.* Palo Alto, Calif.: Xerox Palo Alto Research Center Report.

Mayfield, M. 1982. "Video Games Only Fit for Old." *USA Today,* November 10, 191.

McCauley, R. C. 1998. "When Violence Is Not Attractive." In J. Goldstein, ed., *Why We Watch: The Attractions of Violent Entertainment,* 144–162. New York: Oxford.

Menduno, M. 2001. "January Adventures in Mind Control." *Wired* 90, no. 1.

Miller, Stephen C. 1999. "Most-Violent Video Games Are Not Biggest Sellers." *New York Times,* July 29, 193.

Minkler, M. 1990. "People Need People: Social Support and Health." In R. E. Ornstein and C. Swencionis, eds., *The Healing Brain: A Scientific Reader,* 85–99. New York: Guilford.

Myers, David. 1991. "Computer Game Semiotics." *Play and Culture* 4: 334-346.

Office of the Surgeon General. 2001. *Youth Violence: A Report of the Surgeon General.* Washington, D.C.: U.S. Department of Health and Human Services.

Provenzo, E. F., Jr. 1992. "The Video Generation." *American School Board Journal* 1793: 29–32.

_____. 1991. *Video Kids: Making Sense of Nintendo.* Cambridge: Harvard University Press.

Roe, K., and D. Muijs. 1998. "Children and Computer Games: A Profile of the Heavy User." *European Journal of Communication* 13: 181–200.

Schutte, N. S., J. M. Malouff, J. C. Post-Gorden, and A. L. Rodasta. 1988. "Effects of Playing Videogames on Children's Aggressive and Other Behaviors." *Journal of Applied Social Psychology* 185: 454–460.

Shaw, T. A. 1994. "The Semiotic Mediation of Identity." *Ethos: Journal of the Society for Psychological Anthropology* 22, no. 1: 83–119.

Sherry, J. 2001. "The Effects of Violent Video Games on Aggression." *Human Communication Research* 27: 409–431.

Silvern, S., and P. A. Williamson. 1987. "The Effects of Game Play on Young Children's Aggression, Fantasy, and Prosocial Behavior." *Journal of Applied Psychology* 84: 453–462.

Sorensen Holmes, B., and C. Jessen. 2000. "It Isn't Real: Children, Computer Games, Violence, and Reality." In C. van Feilitzen and U. Carlsson, eds., *Children in the New Media Landscape.* Goteborg, Sweden: UNESCO International Clearinghouse on Children and Violence.

Spina, S. U. 2001. "Taking a Walk on the Wild Side: The Carnivalesque Culture of Video Gaming." *Journal of Curriculum Theorizing* 17, no. 1: 73–84.

_____. 2000a. "Violence in Schools: Expanding the Dialogue." In *Smoke and Mirrors: The Hidden Context of Violence in Schools and Society,* 1–39. Boulder: Rowman & Littlefield.

_____. 2000b. "The Psychology of Violence and the Violence of Psychology." In *Smoke and Mirrors: The Hidden Context of Violence in Schools and Society.* Boulder: Rowman & Littlefield.

_____. 1998. "Carnival and Carnage: The Semiotics of Video Game Culture." Multimedia presentation at the annual meeting of the Semiotic Society of America, Toronto, Canada, October.

_____. 1997–1998. "Wired for Growth: A New Perspective on Video Games and Their Implications for Child and Youth Care Workers." *Journal of Child and Youth Care Work* 12–13: 22–45.

———. 1996. "The Genesis of the Sega Generation: The Semiotics of Video Game Culture and the Construction of Self." Paper presented at the Harvard Graduate School of Education Research Forum, Cambridge, Mass., March.

Subrahmanyam, K., and P. M. Greenfield. 1998. "Computer Games for Girls: What Makes Them Play?" In J. Cassell and H. Jenkins, eds., *From Barbie to Mortal Kombat: Gender and Computer Games,* 46–71. Cambridge: Harvard University Press.

———. 1996. "Effect of Video Game Practice on Spatial Skills in Girls and Boys." In P. M. Greenfield and R. R. Cocking, eds., *Interacting with Video,* 95–114. Norwood, N.J.: Ablex.

United Nations. 2000. *The State of Crime and Criminal Justice Worldwide: Report of the Secretary General to the United Nations Congress.* Vienna, Austria, April.

Van Schie, E. G. M., and O. Wiegman. 1997. "Children and Video Games: Leisure Activities, Aggression, Social Integration, and School Performance." *Journal of Applied Social Psychology* 27: 1175–1194.

Wartofsky, M. 1983. "The Child's Construction of the World and the World's Construction of the Child: From Historical Epistemology to Historical Psychology." In F. S. Kessen and A. W. Sigel, eds., *The Child and Other Cultural Inventions,* 188–215. New York: Praeger.

Wilson, B. C. 2002. "A Study of Factors Promoting Success in Computer Science Including Gender Differences." *Computer Science Education* 12: 141–164.

Winkel, M., D. M. Novak, and H. Hopson. 1987. "Personality Factors, Participant Gender, and the Effects of Aggressive Video Games on Aggression in Adolescents." *Journal of Research on Personality* 21: 211–223.

Zillmann, D. 1998. "The Psychology of the Attraction of Violent Entertainment." In J. Goldstein, ed., *Why We Watch: The Attractions of Violent Entertainment,* 179–210. New York: Oxford University Press.

Zillman, D., J. Bryant, and B. Sipolsky. 1989. "Enjoyment from Sports Spectatorship." In J. H. Goldstein, ed., *Sports, Games, and Play.* Hillsdale, N.J.: Erlbaum.

Chapter 11

HIP-HOP AND CRITICAL PEDAGOGY: FROM TUPAC TO MASTER P AND BEYOND

Greg Dimitriadis

The first edition of *Kinderculture* (1997) forwarded several groundbreaking ideas about the role and importance of popular culture and education. Perhaps most importantly, the editors and contributors argued for the fundamentally important role of the popular culture industry in "educating" youth. Popular culture, the authors collectively maintained, has become a key site of "cultural pedagogy," a key site where curricular "power is organized and deployed" (Steinberg and Kincheloe 1997, 4). They go further: "The organizations that create this cultural curriculum are not educational agencies but rather commercial concerns that operate not for the social good but for individual gain" (4). The charge was severe, the implications far-reaching. Because popular culture has become an increasingly important pedagogical site, the volume maintained, the need for critical, liberatory education has become more pressing. Traditional educative institutions have largely lost claim to exclusive hold on young people's lives. We are, it seems, in the middle of several key tensions and paradoxes, which have acquired greater urgency since the first edition of *Kinderculture* was published.

No cultural movement marks these various tensions as clearly as hip-hop. This musical genre may be the preeminent cultural movement of our time, a statement of the complexities facing this generation of youth and young adults. Nearly a quarter of a century after the release of the first hip-hop single, "Rapper's Delight," the music is still at the epicenter of popular controversy and critique. Over the past twenty-five years, hip-hop has reinvented itself again and again, pushing its own creative parameters in important, unpredictable ways.

Hip-hop emerged in the late 1970s and early 1980s in areas of New York City blighted by deindustrialization (Rose 1994). The collective, party-oriented ethic of this moment spoke to the intense needs and desires of youth, the impulse to carve out space in increasingly hostile social and cultural terrain. In years hence, the music has morphed and grown into a complex medium, reflecting a wide range of creative and substantive interests and impulses. The aggressive "gangsterism" of 50 Cent, the entrepreneurialism of Jay-Z, the pro-sex feminism of Foxy Brown, the pro-black sentiments of Mos Def, the ironic self-deprecation of Eminem, and the reflective poetics of Common sit side by side. Hip-hop has again and again defied the impulse to contain and control it.

I argue in this chapter that taking up the challenges of hip-hop means giving up our certainty and control over our understandings of young people and youth and entering into more thoughtful kinds of relationships with more and more unpredictable constituencies. Hip-hop has collectively challenged those of us in education to wrestle with the specificity of our moment, in ways that force us beyond our ready-made pedagogical theories and models. Drawing together textual and ethnographic approaches, I highlight the history and importance of hip-hop music and culture, particularly that of Tupac Shakur and Master P. I intend to go beyond nostalgia for the civil rights movement to take seriously the ways that contemporary popular artists are self-reflexively theorizing what it means to live in what Mark Neal calls a "post-soul" moment. This work, I conclude, provides us with models for rethinking our roles as pedagogues and intellects, a necessary gesture at this historical conjuncture.

TUPAC AND THE TRANSITION FROM SOUL TO POSTSOUL

No artist reflects the contradictions and paradoxes of hip-hop as well as rapper Tupac Shakur. Tupac began his career in hip-hop in 1990 when he joined the rap group Digital Underground as a dancer and rapper. He released several albums over the next few years (e.g., *2Pacalypse Now,* 1990) and starred in several films (e.g., *Juice,* 1992). Perhaps his best-known song, "Dear Mama," a tender ode to his mother, was released in 1995 on the album *Me Against the World.* At the time, Tupac was incarcerated for sexual assault. He went on to have numerous scuffles with the law. He was shot and almost died in 1995, an incident for which he blamed fellow rapper Notorious BIG (or Biggie Smalls). The high-profile feud between the two escalated when Tupac signed onto the record label Death Row Records, which cultivated an outlaw image. The conflict became known as the War of the Coasts—the West Coast (represented by Tupac Shakur and others on Death Row Records) versus the East (represented by Notorious BIG and others on Bad Boy Records). Sadly, the conflict ended in death for both. Tupac was shot and killed in 1996 in Las Vegas. Six months later, BIG was shot and killed in Los Angeles. Both homicides remain unsolved, but there has been speculation the murders were linked (see Nick Broomfield's 2002 film *Biggie and Tupac*).

In many respects, Tupac's life was an allegory for the transition from a civil rights to a "postsoul" ethic. Tupac's mother was a Black Panther, one of the so-called New York 21 arrested for a series of suspected bombings. Under intense government pressure and surveillance, her ideals were increasingly challenged and she eventually became addicted to crack cocaine. Tupac was at the center of these tensions from a very young age, the idealistic impulses of the civil rights and pro-black movement side by side with more immediate and individualistic kinds of compelling physical gratifications that emerged in the movement's wake. In fact, he "claimed" two fathers, one a Black Panther, the other a local gangster.

As Mike Dyson (2002) made so clear in his brilliant book, *Holler If You Hear Me: Searching for Tupac Shakur,* Tupac had to figure his own way through these tensions and complexities, surrounded as he was by activists as well as gangsters. From a young age, Tupac was deeply interested and invested in the arts both in school (he attended Baltimore School for the Arts) and out (his early interest in hip-hop). Dropping out of school, he never stopped pushing his intellectual boundaries and limits. In a moving, provocative chapter, Dyson looks at Tupac's collection of books, highlighting the eclectic nature of his reading interests from Richard Wright to Frederick Nietzsche to JD Salinger to Maya Angelou to Gabriel Marquez to Henry Miller (94). Largely on his own, Tupac wrestled with complex ideas outside of traditional school settings. Dyson writes, "Tupac's voracious reading continued throughout his career, a habit that allowed him to fill his raps with acute observations about the world around him. . . . Tupac's profound literary rebutted the belief that hip-hop is an intellectual wasteland. . . . Tupac helped to combat anti-intellectualism in rap, a force, to be sure, that pervades the entire culture" (99-100).

Tupac's music reflects the paradoxes and conflicts he faced as a youth and ranges from tender odes to his mother (e.g., "Dear Mama") to brutal invectives to his rivals (e.g., "Hit Em Up"). He looked toward a broad black power agenda, just as he detailed his own intense conflicts with other black artists. These conflicts and paradoxes marked his high-profile career. He publicly presented himself as an "unfinished project," always struggling to make sense out of a broader social context while dealing with the pressing immediacies of the moment. He could not fall back on notions of monolithic black community, just as he could not ignore the historical durability of those narratives.

In many respects, Tupac signals a transition from the relative certainties of narratives of racial uplift to more uncertain contemporary terrains. Tupac's life reflects the landscape academics now face, which challenges our own certainties. His work forces us—intellectuals, pedagogues, and concerned adults alike—to decenter our ready-made intellectual and political paradigms. To understand Tupac, we cannot only look to the discourses that pervade academic life. As Tupac's own mother, Afeni Shakur, so eloquently said:

I've heard enough of [our youth] to know that we ought to be holding them up and sharing with them what we know instead of standing on top of them telling them what they're not doing right. They're doing a lot right and some things wrong. We continue to fail these brilliant, very talented, very creative and courageous young people because they're not saying what our message was. But for Christ's sake . . . we're about to enter the 21st century. Something should be different. And they may be right about some things. (Kitwana 2002, 3)

In giving up her own sense of certainty about racial politics, Afeni Shakur provides a model for what it means to reposition oneself as an intellectual. For me, this repositioning was effected through four years of ethnographic work I did in the urban Midwest, analyzing the relationship a group of young black adolescents and teens had with hip-hop. Working out of a community center, I held weekly focus groups and also functioned as a volunteer and staff member. In the book that resulted, *Performing Identity/Performing Culture: Hip-hop as Text, Pedagogy, and Lived Practice* (2001), I looked at how young people constructed notions of tradition, history, and self through talk about hip-hop. In the follow-up book, *Friendship, Cliques, and Gangs: Young Black Men Coming of Age in Urban America* (2003), I looked closely at the lives of two teens over a six-year period, as well as my evolving relationship with each. I discussed what it meant to decenter my own agenda on popular culture in time.

I found that Tupac provided many of these young people with a certain kind of "equipment for living" (to evoke Kenneth Burke), discursive strategies for confronting and coping with specific day-to-day concerns. For example, a youth who had a history of personal and familial confrontations with the police drew on Tupac to talk about these experiences: "Like when he's [Tupac's] talkin' about the police harassin' him all the time? . . . Every time the police see me, they got something to say to me, about my daddy, and my brothers . . . tellin' me I sell dope and all this." This young person's feelings toward the police and the life stance he had to take gelled together into a kind of philosophy of invulnerability and a kind of grim resignation to death. Drawing on the work of Tupac, he noted:

To live in fear is not to live at all. . . . You can't run from every damn thing all the time. . . . You might as well not even live. . . . It's like you dead anyway, you keep thinking motherfuckers gonna kill you. . . . I ain't trying to say make yourself die. . . . [But] don't worry when it comes to you 'cause it's gonna happen anyway. . . . We live to die. You know what I'm saying? That's one thing we know for sure. Like, like you say you're gonna go to college when you get older? You might not make it to older. Like you say. . . . I finna go down to the gas station and get some squares [cigarettes]? I might not make it to the gas station. . . . But I know I'ma die. I know I'ma die. We live to die. . . . Don't fear no man but God. . . . Just like Pac [Tupac] said.

This research gave me greater focus on young people's relationship to and with black popular culture, helping me expand my extant textual and historical work in important ways. I would come to see the role of rap in offering these young people (especially the young men) hyperreal, superinvulnerable figures, ones which helped to mitigate against a brutal and unforgiving social context. Clearly, Tupac was a mythic figure to this young man, one who allowed him to face the contingency of life with a steely resolve toward death. His relationship with Tupac speaks to the specificity of concerns and needs of the "postsoul" generation.

POST CIVIL RIGHTS AND "SOUL"

In his controversial book, *The New H.N.I.C. (Head Nigga in Charge): The Death of Civil Rights and the Reign of Hip-hop,* author Todd Boyd argues that we live in a post–civil rights moment, that the complexities and contradictions of hip-hop music and culture have supplanted the transcendent claims of earlier generations. Above all else, Boyd stresses the dangers of nostalgia. Elsewhere, Cameron McCarthy and I have linked nostalgia to a broader set of "resentment" discourses, all of which try to contain the complexities of our contemporary moment (Dimitriadis and McCarthy 2001). These include the certainties of race and nation that were critical to the civil rights movement of the 1960s. Yet, as Boyd so powerfully implores us,

> We cannot live in the past forever. Civil rights had its day; now it's time to move out of the way. Civil rights was a struggle, and it remains an ongoing struggle for all disenfranchised people of color to pursue their civil rights. But many in the civil rights era have for too long gloated in a sanctimonious fashion, assuming that their day would never come to an end. This arrogant posture did little to inspire a new generation but went a long way toward alienating them. The posture of civil rights was such that it made future generations uncomfortable having to wear such restraints as they attempted to represent themselves. (2002, 152)

Boyd argues throughout his book that hip-hop music and culture "attempt to navigate the world in a very different way." Boyd's comments clearly dovetail with Afeni Shakur's need not to lodge critiques from previous generations but perhaps listen and learn as well.

Boyd points to the stress on material survival and wealth that marks this generation's needs, concerns, and desires. We see a desire to survive and access the resources of capitalism, while retaining a strong notion of blackness. We see these concerns instantiated in the critiques of black men who have attained some degree of wealth. Boyd documents the intense public criticism from older blacks as well as whites that many rap artists and record label owners face, many of whom are accused of "selling out" when they make some money. He cites Master P, Snoop Dogg, and Puff Daddy, among others. In part, such changes reflect an ambivalence about African Americans entering mainstream American life. Boyd notes, "What in an earlier generation might have been called 'showing off' has now grown into an integral part of self-expression in hip-hop circles. The idea of the 'come up' represents social mobility in spite of overwhelming obstacles and the politics of this move are deeply embedded in hip-hop's master narrative. The expression of this upward mobility by these lower class individuals, flossin' on one's cars, homes, clothes, money, and lifestyle, have become commonplace" (77).

Boyd is not uncritical of these tendencies. But he stresses that their whole-cloth condemnation is often about earlier and nostalgic notions of blackness. He writes, "Change in status, be it financial, cultural, or political, is not always the worst thing in the world, nor should it be. Actually, it represents progression. Change is at the heart of creativity, and that should be embraced while one maintains a solid understanding of the history that precedes it" (101). According to Boyd, charges of "selling out" sometimes impede the organic creativity and unpredictable social impacts of rap music. Such charges work mostly to maintain center/periphery or, better yet, mainstream/underground dichotomies that no longer strictly hold.

Others have wrestled with the specificity of this moment and this generation in similarly powerful ways. For example, Mark Anthony Neal's *Soul Babies: Black Popular Culture and the Post-Soul Aesthetic* describes what he calls a "postsoul" moment, the moment when the transcendent certainties of the civil rights and black power movements have largely been elided. According to Neal, "soul" was the most powerful expression of modernity for African Americans of previous generations (3). For the next generation of African Americans, however, these claims to certainty have been called into question. This new generation "came to maturity in the age of Reganomics and experienced the change from urban industrialization to deindustrialism, from segregation to desegregation, from essential notions of blackness to metanarratives on blackness, without any nostalgic allegiance to the past (back in the days of Harlem, or the thirteenth-century motherland, for that matter), but firmly in grasp of the existential concerns of this brave new world" (3).

For this next generation, hip-hop music and culture has emerged as the defining cultural statement. The music and culture are filled with complex, often contradictory narratives. According to Neal, they need to be met with an expansive set of explanatory criteria: "We cannot simply reject these narratives on a moral basis that is itself the product of a profoundly different world; we must at least critically engage them with the same energy and passion that many of these artists themselves inject into their creative efforts" (11). Neal spends a great deal of his book attempting to unravel the work of hip-hop artists and their cultural surround.

In the book's final chapter, Neal discusses how hip-hop music and culture provides the cultural soundtrack to his own life and the lives of his students. He discusses as well the ways both try to unravel some of its complexities and contradictions. For example, many of his students have middle-class aspirations that are cross cut by some strident and at times impossible ideals about "keeping it real" and "being black." He writes,

> The radical transformation of hip-hop over time, especially its cross-ing over into the market of white youth, has complicated its ability to proclaim black identity. It has come to symbolize the utter ambivalence of the black situation; on the one hand, serving up versions of a richly "black" identity, on the other showing an eagerness to join the American dream. (189)

He continues, "the challenge to 'keep it real' and 'still get paid' may seem crass to older generations, but it is the dominant ethos of Generation Hip-hop" (194). Navigating these waters is quite complicated, the desire to "succeed in the mainstream and survive in the margins" (194). Neal, like Boyd, shows a willingness to take on the specificity of this generation, without falling into the trap of nostalgia.

Our moment seemingly necessitates moving beyond the kinds of liberation narratives often associated with modernist movements. These narratives often rely on stable notions of identity and clear notions of ideology critique. We need to give up our ideological certainties in order to meet young people "where they're at" today. More and more, we need to "work the hyphen" between these different roles, responsibilities, and positions (Dimitriadis 2003).

MASTER P AND MATERIAL IMPERATIVES OF THE POSTSOUL GENERATION

An artist who emerged in the wake of the Tupac–Notorious BIG conflict, Master P, acknowledged as much on his 1997 album *Da Last Don*, released months after BIG's murder. He said that Biggie and Tupac "took the kiss of death" so he could be the "Last Don." P was part of an emerging group of southern rap artists who seemed to look beyond and transcend the East versus West controversy that ended so tragically. His work marks many contemporary existential anxieties around racial identities, offering educators a key lens for grappling with the realities of race today.

Master P's biography, like Tupac's, is part of his public claim to authority and authenticity. Part of Master P's mythos is his former life as a drug dealer in Louisiana, his brother's violent death, and his effort to "get out of the drug game" and go legitimate with music, specifically his label No Limit Records. The label's symbol and moniker is a tank (known as "*the* tank"), and artists all wear diamond-studded tank medallions, which they frequently refer to on CDs and in films. All this is part of the group, familial ethic, which P stresses on all No Limit recordings. He has deployed Mafia-like imagery on his label's releases, including *Da Last Don* (1997), *Made Man* (1999), and *Goodfellas* (2000).

Master P's story was documented in rough autobiographical fashion in his straight-to-video film *I'm Bout It* (1997), filmed on location in the Calliope projects, New Orleans, where he grew up. The film features other members of P's No Limit family, including his brothers Silk and C-Murder, as well as Mystical, Mia X, and Fiend. The film opens with Master P and his crew sitting around a table covered with money, guns, and drugs. As the scene unfolds, group members put their fists together and say in unison, "true," a sign of solidarity and unity. Master P then rises, taking center stage, and informs the group about a stolen "kilo" of cocaine, saying "this shit is crazy . . . think motherfuckers are your friends" before confronting and shooting a suspect. The complexities of trust and betrayal play out in the notion that one's crew is one's family, cross-cut by the idea that one can only trust oneself in the end. *I'm Bout It* details these concerns throughout P's efforts to leave the drug game and invest in the music business, his confrontations with crooked cops, multiple betrayals by his "crew," and his sense of personal triumph and invulnerability.

Similar anxieties and themes play out in *I Got the Hook Up* (1998), P's follow-up effort emphasizing material survival. This film stars Master P and AJ Johnson as "Blue" and "Black," friends who run an open-air pawn shop/flea market in the South. The duo get hold of some cell phones and conspire to steal air time. Though they make a great deal of money, the phones prove faulty and both, along with various and sundry others, wind up on the run from some local thugs. *I Got the Hook Up* is about "making a dollar out of fifteen cents," the everyday hustle often necessitated by life in the ghetto. P evokes the day-to-day concerns that propel the lives of many young people, the reality of having to scheme to survive, the necessity of having friends and family to look out for you at all times. In such a world, racial affiliation is a function of moment-to-moment and day-to-day survival.

These films, like Master P's work more broadly, are part of a broad structure of feeling among young people today, who have similar desires for (and anxieties about) trust, friendship, and survival. Hence we see fierce notions of individual autonomy—one can only rely on oneself—juxtaposed and cross-cut by the necessity of local allegiances, the social networks that often make life in poor and dangerous communities livable. These twin imperatives are embodied in gang life and imagery, in the fiercely individual and independent gang member whose sense of personal respect and autonomy is paradoxically linked to his or her crew. This image reached its apex in mid-1990s rap, as noted in the public image projected by Tupac Shakur and Biggie Smalls as well as the conflict that ensued between these men and their record labels, Death Row and Bad Boy.

In many ways, such images have taken center stage in rap today. They are the "myths" that help define this particular social and cultural moment for contemporary youth. Artists like Master P foreground complex personal biographies that young people articulate with and against often fatalistic narratives that register unique tensions around trust and betrayal, vulnerability and invulnerability. On a telling track, "Would You Hesitate," from the soundtrack to *I Got the Hook Up,* Master P's brother C-Murder spells out some of these anxieties, simultaneously affirming and questioning the loyalty of label mates, including Kane and Abel, Fiend, Mac, and Big Ed. The intense anxiety is described of having to place yourself over the group as well as the uncertainty of doing so. Ultimately you cannot trust anyone, a theme evidenced by the constant anxiety of C-Murder who asks, plaintively, "Would you die for me?" "Would you kill for me?" and "Would you hesitate?" throughout. These are existential demands, demands that inform much of the fatalism and anxiety that pervade the popular imagination today, demands necessitated by the stark material reality many young people face.

We thus see a complex set of tensions registering in contemporary black film and music today, as fundamental questions of distrust versus trust and autonomy versus collectivity proliferate. Racial identity is not determined in the popular cultural forms, but is radically contingent and depends on moment-to-moment and day-to-day survival. These narratives are crucial for disenfranchised youth today, who have watched these spectacles unfold and draw on them in their own intensely fraught lives. These resources, these stories and myths, are the ones that young people gravitate toward while making sense out of their lives, in the unfortunate absence of other models and in the face of day-to-day struggle. These resources exceed the explanatory frameworks offered in traditional approaches to multiculturalism and take us to the terrain of everyday struggle, a terrain that does not privilege nostalgia and transcendence, but the very real and the very immediate. This work signals a set of concerns that cannot be explained away in a civil rights–era discourse of racial uplift, of "good" and "bad" role models.

A telling set of interactions around Master P emerged in my ethnographic study of young people and hip-hop mentioned earlier, highlighting some of the complexities around generation and generational identity (Dimitriadis 2001, 2003). Master P was a big favorite early in 1998, particularly after the deaths of Tupac and Biggie. P was not a "studio rapper," according to these youth, "wasn't fake." Clearly Master P embodied many of the dualities of the so-called hip-hop generation. In a key example, he talked about his wealth but also kept in touch with his roots. This was a precarious balance. In one focus group discussion I recall, a young person commented, "I hate rappers who talk about how all they got this and they got that." Such rappers align themselves too closely and uncritically with the mainstream. I asked if Master P talked about his wealth, this kind of conspicuous consumption. The youth responded, "He in between, he talk about both. He talk about how much money he had, and . . ." Struggling for the correct phrase, another youth finished his thought—"where he came from." Master P, it seems, occupies the kind of "in-between" space Neal evokes above.

Older community members didn't see the same balance being struck. During another focus group discussion with older teens, the education director, Bill, walked in. While Bill was supportive of young people and valued the work I was doing, he distrusted some of the tendencies in hip-hop. When he walked in, we had been talking about the history of rap and hip-hop. As an older staff member, he might have something to say. One teen said that we were talking about how "things were easier in the '80s." Bill responded:

> It was easier back in the '80s than it is now. . . . I done heard too much "murder murder" [a popular song]. That's what I think. Think teenagers done lost it. . . . They feel comfortable picking up a gun. It don't prove nothing. . . . In the '80s people had fun. I don't think people have fun these days. I think people out to see how macho they can be. How many women they can call "bitches" and "hoes" and all that. It's all about dissing somebody. Soon as somebody hit you, you ready to do something. . . . I mean they was starting in the later '80s, but early '80s [it wasn't like that]. And all because of, what's this stuff called? Rap music.

After his rhetorical question, Bill continued, "Snoop Dogg, Ice Cube, Tupac, I was never really into that," to which another teen responded, "That was old school." Bill then said, "That's old school? So what's new school? Master P? He 'bout it bout it' huh? . . . I don't know, fellas. I heard he's a millionaire. He got a lot of money. Isn't he putting some money back in his neighborhood?" Another youth said immediately that he did. Bill didn't seem convinced.

We can see some important distinctions between older and younger people around Master P. Clearly, younger people had a strong investment in P. He was "real" to these youth, and his life was evidence of this on multiple levels, wrapped up in his efforts at day-to-day survival. For Bill, a staff member in his fifties, the issue was whether or not P "gave back" to his community. In the end, rap music has provided youth super-invulnerable figures, resources for survival for dealing with a profoundly hostile social, cultural, and material reality. The conflict between Tupac and Biggie, as well as the rise of Master P, evidences much of this in ways that often escape the purview of older people.

Indeed, these young people explicitly compared Master P to Tupac. One youth said of Tupac, "He was a true mug, right there. He got shot in the balls, shot in the chest," to which another responded, "I think he got shot in the head too." Another said, "Master P gonna end up dying. He gonna be the next one to go," to which another responded "'cause he right after Tupac." The first youth continued, "What he say in his songs? . . . 'Keep an eye on your enemies.' . . . He already been shot in the back." Both Master P and Tupac talked about dying in their songs, these youth said, and in the wake of Tupac's death they combed P's songs for similar references.

Master P and Tupac both offered new models for "blackness," for what it means to engage with the American dream on fraught and dangerous terrain. Both embody the gangster archetype, standing inside and outside of the American mainstream at the same time. On the title track to his popular album *Da Last Don*, Master P evokes much of this ambivalence from the very first line, addressing "America" and its seeming hypocrisy: "Good Day America this is Mr. No Limit!" He continues, "You always point the finger at the bad guy / But what if the bad guy points the finger at you? / Fuck the politicians the media and the government / The fucking world was built on corruption." P then says he "made millions from raps," but is still tied to his "No Limit niggas," "strapped thug niggas [who] bust caps" or fire guns. It is here that he ties himself most explicitly to Tupac Shakur and his legacy—Tupac "took the kiss of death" so he could be the "Last Don."

This thread continues in rap. In 2003, as Master P's career declined slightly, a "new school" arose. In particular, the work of 50 Cent picks up on many of these themes. Material struggle, for example, is evidenced by 50 Cent's album title, *Get Rich or Die Trying* (2003), while songs like "Many Men (Wish Death Upon Me)" highlight the dangerous terrain he walks—a theme he does not shy away from in discussions of his life. 50 Cent has pointed out again and again how he survived an attempt on his life and has hinted of retaliation. He himself elaborates on his near-fatal shooting, "Sneaky motherfucker, man . . . He [the gunman] did it right. He just didn't finish. He like Allen Iverson shakin' a nigga, go to the basket and miss. . . . You don't actually feel each one hit you. . . . The adrenaline is pumping. You movin' and tryin' to get out of the way" (quoted in Toure 2003). He raps about the shooting in the song "Many Men," hinting at the retaliation he has also denied, "In the Bible it says, 'what goes around, comes around' / Almost shot me, three weeks later he got shot down / Now it's clear that I'm here for a real reason / 'Cause he got hit like I got hit, but he ain't fucking breathing."

The comparisons to Tupac were perhaps inevitable. Popular rapper Eminem notes, "One of the things that excited me about Tupac . . . was even if he was rhymin' the simplest words in the world, you felt like he meant it and it came from his heart. That's the thing with 50. That same aura. That's been missing since we lost Pac and Biggie. The authenticity, the realness behind it" (quoted in Toure 2003). On the 50 Cent song "Patiently Waiting," guest star Eminem raps about the deaths of Tupac and Biggie, "It's like a fight to the top, just to see who'll die for the spot / You put your life in this / Nothing like surviving a shot." The sense of existential angst and danger has remained a constant theme in the music, underscored by a profound ambivalence around the "American dream" and "crossing over." Reworking many of the generational distinctions discussed throughout, notions of racial uplift are inscribed on and through the bodies of performers themselves.

POPULAR CULTURE, PEDAGOGY, AND NEW ROLES FOR THE INTELLECTUAL

In this chapter I have tried to access the specificity of the "hip-hop generation" and its needs and concerns. These texts articulate much of the specificity of this moment, what Boyd has called a "post–civil rights" and Neal has called a "postsoul" moment. I have highlighted some efforts to stand "side by side" with hip-hop and not "above" it. This work can go some way in helping us rethink the nature of intellectual work today, but we need to rethink the ways we position ourselves as cultural studies of education scholars and activists. We need to understand and engage with this generation in ways that look past our own modernist notions of emancipation and liberation.

I join a growing group of scholars who are attempting to articulate a kind of specific politics from "the ground up" in hip-hop. For example, according to Bakari Kitwana (2002), young people who came of age in the 1980s and 1990s "share a specific set of values and attitudes." He continues, "At the core are our thoughts about family, relationships, child rearing, career, racial identity, race relations, and politics. Collectively, these views make up a complex worldview that has not been concretely defined" (Kitwana 2002, 4). The specific concerns of this generation are not so clearly linked to an overarching political movement like the civil rights movement, but they are no less pressing. In particular, he discusses the continuing rise of stark economic disparities, police brutality, gangs and drugs, new generation gaps within black communities, exploding racial tensions, and the continued deferment of the American dream (37–44). "The older generation can't entirely identify with the mode of oppression facing our generation. Oppression for us is not simply a line in the sand with white supremacists blocking access—us over here and them over there" (41).

For Kitwana, this emerging worldview with its specific needs, concerns, and desires first emerged in rap in the mid- to late 1980s in the "sociopolitical critiques of artists like NWA, KRS-One, Poor Righteous Teachers, Queen Latifah, and others" (Kitwana 2002, 4–5). Since then, hip-hop music and culture has emerged as a uniquely relevant landscape for this generation sorting out these issues and concerns, as evidenced by figures such as Tupac, Biggie, Master P, and 50 Cent. To echo Neal (2002), "We cannot simply reject these narratives on a moral basis that is itself the product of a profoundly different world; we must at least critically engage them with the same energy and passion that many of these artists themselves inject into their creative efforts" (11). We must face them head on, I argue, without recourse to nostalgia. At stake is a new, truly relevant critical pedagogy for urban youth.

REFERENCES

Boyd, T. 2002. *The New H.N.I.C. (Head Nigga in Charge): The Death of Civil Rights and the Reign of Hip-Hop.* New York: NYU Press.

Burke, K. 1941. *The Philosophy of Literary Form: Studies in Symbolic Action.* Berkeley: University of California Press.

Dimitriadis, G. 2003. *Friendship, Cliques, and Gangs: Young Black Men Coming of Age in Urban America.* New York: Teachers College Press.

_____. 2001. *Performing Identity/Performing Culture: Hip-hop as Text, Pedagogy, and Lived Practice.* New York: Peter Lang.

Dimitriadis, G., and C. McCarthy. 2001. *Reading and Teaching the Postcolonial: From Baldwin to Basquiat and Beyond.* New York: Teachers College Press.

Dyson, M. 2002. *Holler If You Hear Me: Searching for Tupac Shakur.* New York: Basic.

Kitwana, B. 2002. *The Hip-Hop Generation: Young Blacks and the Crisis in African American Culture.* New York: Basic.

Neal, M. 2002. *Soul Babies: Black Popular Culture and the Post-Soul Aesthetic.* New York: Routledge.

Rose, T. 1994. *Black Noise.* Hanover: Wesleyan University Press.

Steinberg, S., and J. Kincheloe, eds. 1997. *Kinderculture: The Corporate Construction of Childhood.* Boulder: Westview.

Toure. 2003. "The Life of a Hunted Man." *Rolling Stone,* April 3.

ABOUT THE CONTRIBUTORS AND EDITORS

CONTRIBUTORS

CARL BYBEE is the director of the Oregon Media Literacy Project and an associate professor of communication studies in the School of Journalism and Communication at the University of Oregon. His current research focus is on helping youth find a new vocabulary for becoming engaged, democratic citizens drawing on the connections between news, entertainment, media literacy, and new models of active democracy.

GREG DIMITRIADIS is assistant professor at SUNY Buffalo. He is the author of *Performing Identity/Performing Culture: Hip-Hop as Text, Pedagogy, and Lived Practice* and *Friendship, Cliques, and Gangs: Young Black Men Coming of Age in Urban America.*

HENRY A. GIROUX is the Global TV Network chair in communications at McMaster University. His latest books are *Take Back Higher Education: Race, Youth, and the Crisis of Democracy in the Post–Civil Rights Era* (coauthored with Susan Searls Giroux) and *The Terror of Neoliberalism: Authoritarianism and the Eclipse of Democracy.*

AARON GRESSON is professor of education and human development at Penn State University. He holds doctorates in counseling psychology and educational administration. Some of his most recent books are *The*

Recovery of Race in America; Measured Lies: The Bell Curve Examined (edited with Joe Kincheloe and Shirley Steinberg); and *America's Atonement: Racial Pain, Recovery Rhetoric, and the Pedagogy of Healing.*

DOUGLAS KELLNER is George Kneller chair in the philosophy of education at UCLA and is author of many books on social theory, politics, history, and culture. His most recent books include a study of the 2000 U.S. presidential election, *Grand Theft 2000: Media Spectacle and the Theft of an Election; The Postmodern Adventure: Science, Technology, and Cultural Studies at the Third Millennium* (coauthored with Steve Best); *Media Spectacle*; and *September 11, Terror War, and the Dangers of the Bush Legacy.*

RUTHANN MAYES-ELMA recently completed her doctorate in education at Miami of Ohio University. She is presently teaching fifth grade in Cincinnati. Her areas of research include gender studies and urban education. Her first book, *Not Empowering: The Women of Harry Potter*, will be published in 2005.

STEPHANIE URSO SPINA is an assistant professor in the Department of Foundations and Social Advocacy at SUNY Cortland School of Education. An interdisciplinary scholar, she is an internationally published author, a professional artist, and a consultant on issues related to education, violence, and the arts. Her current research focuses on inner-city students' use of the arts to mediate traumatic experiences of violence.

JOHN A. WEAVER is associate professor of curriculum studies at Georgia Southern University. He is the author of *Popular Culture: A Primer* and the editor (with Toby Daspit) of *Popular Culture and Critical Pedagogy* and *Science Fiction Curriculum: Cyborg Teachers and Youth Culture(s).* He is currently working on issues surrounding the posthuman condition and digital aesthetics.

EDITORS

JOE L. KINCHELOE is professor of education at the CUNY Graduate Center Urban Education Ph.D. Program and at Brooklyn College, where he has served as the Belle Zeller Chair of Public Policy and Administration. His areas of research involve urban education, research bricolage, critical pedagogy, cultural studies, school standards, and their relation to social justice. The author of over thirty books and hundreds of articles, his latest books include *The Sign of the Burger: McDonald's and the Culture of Power; Multiple Intelligences Reconsidered;* and *Rigour and Complexity in Educational Research: Conceptualizing the Bricolage.* Kincheloe is also the lead singer and keyboard player for Tony and the Hegemones. Along with Shirley Steinberg, he is the guardian of three uncontrollable standard poodles.

SHIRLEY R. STEINBERG is an associate professor of education and the program chair of graduate literacy at Brooklyn College. Growing up in Los Angeles, studying in Canada, and finally settling in New Jersey and New York, she claims she can only live and work amid urban chaos. Her areas of research include youth literature, popular culture, queer theory, improvisational social theater, cultural studies, and critical pedagogy. She is the author and editor of many books and articles, including *Multi/Intercultural Conversations: A Reader* and *19 Urban Questions: Teaching in the City.* Steinberg is the founding and senior editor of *Taboo: The Journal of Culture and Education.* Steinberg and Kincheloe are the parents of Ian and Christine, Meghann and Ryan, Chaim and Bronwyn; and the grandparents of Maci Loree and Luna Miri.

NOTES

CHAPTER 2

1. I say "possible" exception of preschool programming because there is evidence that Nickelodeon offers programming for preschoolers that challenges the unethical, amoral stance embedded in the child as innocent and child as consumer construction of young people. I will try to draw these aspects of Nick Jr. out later in this chapter.

2. David Buckingham and his contributors in *Small Screens* offer a critique of Nickelodeon UK. I want to make a distinction here between Nickelodeon UK and Nickelodeon, since the introduction of the former to British children raises important issues such as cultural imperialism and the well-founded concern over the Americanization of world culture. I do not want to contest or erase these concerns Buckingham and others have raised, but for my purposes I will only deal with Nickelodeon as it appears in the United States.

3. The most entertaining parody of consumerism is not a commercial but *The Amanda Show*'s hilarious farce called *Moody's Point*. This show pokes fun at the teen show *Dawson's Creek* specifically but at all teen dramas in general. All the characters are the opposite of what one finds on shows like *Dawson's Creek*, everything they try results in some kind of failure, the adults in their lives are supposed to be role models but are condescending and unsupportive, and the issues young people deal with are nonsensical. *Moody's Point* serves as an important reminder to young people that television dramas may be entertaining, but real life is often mundane and harsh.

CHAPTER 3

1. *Scholastic News: Senior Edition*, September 1, 2003.

2. Shirley Steinberg and Joe Kincheloe, eds., *Kinderculture: The Corporate Construction of Childhood*, 2d ed. (Boulder: Westview, 2004).

3. Steinberg and Kincheloe, eds., *Kinderculture*.

4. Ashcroft memo.

5. White House press release, "President Introduces History and Civic Education Initiatives," September 17, 2002, www.whitehouse.gov/news/releases/2002/09/print/20020917–1.html.

6. Robert Lenzer and Matthew Miller, "Buying Justice," *Forbes Magazine*, July 21, 2003, www.forbes.com/free_forbes/2003/0721/064.html. Accessed January 1, 2004.

7. Cynthia Gibson, "From Inspiration to Participation: A Review of Perspectives on Youth Civic Engagement" (paper presented at the Grantmaker Forum on Community and National Service, November 2001), www.gfcns.org/pubs/Moving%20Youth%20report%20REV3.pdf.

8. Scott Keeter, Cliff Zukin, Molly Andolina, and Krista Jenkins, *The Civic and Political Health of the Nation: A Generational Portrait* (Center for Information and Research on Civic Learning and Engagement, September 9, 2002), civicyouth.org/research/products/youth_index.htm.

9. *A Generational Look at the Public: Politics and Policy* (Kaiser Family Foundation, October 2002), www.kff.org/content/2002/3273/Generational_Look_Toplines3.pdf.

10. Cynthia Gibson and Peter Levine, *The Civic Mission of School* (Carnegie Foundation and the Center for Information and Research on Civic Learning and Engagement, February 2003), www.civicmissionofschools.org.

11. Albert Shanker Institute, *Education for Democracy* (September 9, 2003), www.ashankerinst.org/Downloads/EfD-release.html.

12. National Commission on Civic Renewal, *A Nation of Spectators: How Civic Disengagement Weakens America and What We Can Do About It* (College Park: University of Maryland Press, 1998).

13. Charles Quigley, "What Needs to Be Done to Ensure a Proper Civic Education?" (paper presented at the First Annual Congressional Conference on Civic Education, Washington, D.C., September 2003), www.civiced.org/pdfs/Sept21Pres.pdf?PHPSESSID=dcb2b52e0c5e783c08c67913333525c0.

14. Ezra Suleiman, *Dismantling Democratic States* (Princeton: Princeton University Press, 2003).

15. Douglas Kellner, *Grand Theft 2000: Media Spectacle and a Stolen Election* (Lanham, Md.: Rowman & Littlefield, 2001).

16. Bob Herbert, "Stalking the Giant Chicken Coop," *New York Times*, December 8, 2003.

17. Sylvia Hewlett and Cornel West, *The War Against Parents* (New York: Houghton Mifflin, 1998).

18. Henry Giroux, *The Abandoned Generation* (New York: Palgrave Macmillan, 2003).

19. Suleiman, *Dismantling Democratic States.*

20. Gibson and Levine, *Civic Mission of School,* p. 6.

21. Sheilah Mann, "Political Scientists Examine Civics Standards: An Introduction," *PS: Political Science and Politics: Essays on Civic Education* (September 1997), www.apsanet.org/CENnet/PS/mann.cfm.

22. Richard Merelman, "Symbols as Substance in National Civics Standards," in Mann, ed., *PS: Political Science,* www.apsanet.org/CENnet/PS/merelman.cfm.

23. National Governors Association and the National Association of Budget Offices, *The Fiscal Survey of States,* December 2003, www.nga.org/cda/files/FSS1203.pdf. Accessed December 11, 2003.

24. Alex Molnar, "No Student Left Unsold" (paper presented to the Commercialism in Education Research Unit, Arizona State University, October 2003), www.asu.edu/educ/epsl/CERU/CERU_Annual_Report.htm. Accessed December 11, 2003.

25. Robert McChesney, *Rich Media, Poor Democracy* (Urbana: University of Illinois Press, 1999); Benjamin Compaine and Douglas Gomery, *Who Owns the Media: Competition and Concentration in the Mass Media Industry* (Mahwah, N.J.: Erlbaum, 2000); Ben Bagdikian, *The Media Monopoly* (Boston: Beacon, 2000); Douglas Kellner, *Television and the Crisis of Democracy* (Boulder: Westview, 1990).

26. Kellner, *Television and the Crisis of Democracy.*

27. James Steyer, *The Other Parent: The Inside Story of the Media's Effects on Our Children* (New York: Atria, 2002).

28. Steyer, *Other Parent,* 139.

29. Jay Rosen, *Getting the Connections Right: Public Journalism and the Troubles in the Press* (New York: Twentieth Century Fund, 1995).

30. Committee of Concerned Journalists, "Statement of Concern," www.journalism.org/resources/guidelines/principles/concern.asp. Accessed November 12, 2003.

31. Times Mirror Center for People and the Press, *The Age of Indifference: A Study of Young Americans and How They View the News* (Washington, D.C.: Times Mirror Center, 1990).

32. Pew Research Center, *TV News Viewership Declines: Falloff Greater for Young Adults and Computer Users* (Washington, D.C.: Pew Research Center for the People and the Press, 1996); Pew Research Center, *Fewer Favor Media Scrutiny of Political Leaders: Press Is Unfair, Inaccurate, and Pushy* (Washington, D.C.: Pew Research Center for the People and the Press, 1997); Michael Olander, "Media Use Among Young People," in *The Civic and Political Health of the Nation: A Generational Portrait* (Center for Information and Research on Civic Learning and Engage-

ment, September 2002), www.civicyouth.org/research/products/fact_sheets.htm. Accessed on November 14, 2003.

33. *Children Now, Tuned in or Tuned Out? America's Children Speak Out on the News Media* (1994), www.childrennow.org/media/mc94/news.html. Accessed November 14, 2003.

34. Cable in the Classroom Web site, www.ciconline.com/AboutCIC/TheOrganization/mission.htm.

35. Kevin R., "Deep Impact: Students Get Hit Hard by the Oklahoma State Budget Crisis," www.channelone.com/news/exchange/news/2003/04/04/se_budgets/index.html.

36. Dina El Nabli, "First Ladies to Fight Poverty," World News, *Time for Kids*, September 27, 2002, www.timeforkids.com/TFK/news/story/0,6260,355697, 00.html. Accessed December 18, 2003.

37. "Extra: News for Students," *NewsHour with Jim Lehrer*, Public Broadcasting System, www.pbs.org/newshour/extra (accessed December 19, 2003); "*Frontline*'s Teacher Center," *Frontline*, Public Broadcasting System, www.pbs.org/wgbh/pages/frontline/teach (accessed December 19, 2003); and "For Educators," *Now with Bill Moyers*, Public Broadcasting System, www.pbs.org/now/classroom/index.html. Accessed December 19, 2003.

38. "Public Schools, Inc.," *Frontline*, Public Broadcasting System, aired July 3, 2003, www.pbs.org/wgbh/pages/frontline/shows/edison. Accessed December 26, 2003.

39. "Corporate Governance," *Now with Bill Moyers*, www.pbs.org/now/printable/classroom_business_print.html. Accessed December 19, 2003.

40. Milton Friedman, celebrating Laurence Jarvik's neoliberal attack on PBS. Quoted in *PBS: Behind the Screen* (Rocklin, Calif.: Forum, 1997).

41. Walter Cronkite, "Walter Cronkite on the Media," MediaChannel.org, February 3, 2000, www.mediachannel.org/originals/cronkite.shtml. Accessed January 6, 2004.

42. Bill Moyers, keynote address to the National Conference on Media Reform, Madison, Wis., 2003, www.commondreams.org/views03/1112–10.htm. Accessed December 11, 2003.

CHAPTER 6

1. The power of the Disney Company as an economic and political empire can be seen in the record of its profits and its ever expanding corporate cultural reach. For instance, it was reported in *Los Angeles Business* that "Disney earned $400 million, or 19 cents per share, in third quarter 2003 on $6.18 billion in revenue." See

"Disney Profits Up 10%," *Los Angeles Business,* www.bizjournals.com/losangeles/stories/2003/07/28/daily46.html?t=printable.

2. Cited in Tom Vanderbilt, "Mickey Goes to Town(s)," *The Nation,* August 28–September 4, 1995, 197.

3. Vanderbilt, "Mickey Goes to Town(s)," 199.

4. Eric Smoodin, "How to Read Walt Disney," in *Disney Discourse: Producing the Magic Kingdom* (New York: Routledge, 1994), 18.

5. Jon Wiener, "Tall Tales and True," *The Nation,* January 31, 1994, 134.

6. The term "marketplace of culture" comes from Richard de Cordova, "The Mickey in Macy's Window: Childhood Consumerism and Disney Animation," in Eric Smoodin, ed., *Disney Discourse: Producing the Magic Kingdom* (New York: Routledge, 1994), 209.

7. Laura M. Holson, "Leaving Board, a Disney Heir Assails Eisner," *New York Times,* December 1, 2003, A17.

8. Susan Jefford develops this reading of *Beauty and the Beast* in Susan Jefford, *Hard Bodies: Hollywood Masculinity in the Reagan Era* (New Brunswick: Rutgers University Press, 1994), 150.

9. Cited in June Casagrande, "The Disney Agenda," *Creative Loafing,* March 17–23, 1994, 6–7.

10. On its release in 1946, *Song of the South* was condemned by the NAACP for its racist representations.

11. These racist episodes are highlighted in Jon Wiener, "Tall Tales and True," *The Nation,* January 31, 1994, 133–135.

12. Yousef Salem, cited in Richard Scheinin, "Angry Over 'Aladdin,'" *Washington Post,* January 10, 1993, G5.

13. Howard Green, a Disney spokesperson, dismissed the charges of racism as irrelevant, claiming that such criticisms were coming from a small minority and that "most people were happy with [the film]" (*Washington Post,* January 10, 1993).

14. See Susan Miller and Greg Rode, who do a rhetorical analysis of *The Jungle Book* and *Song of the South* in their chapter, "The Movie You See, The Movie You Don't: How Disney Do's That Old Time Derision," in Elizabeth Bell, Lynda Haas, and Laura Sells, eds., *From Mouse to Mermaid* (Bloomington: Indiana University Press, 1996).

15. Smoodin, "How to Read Walt Disney," 4–5.

16. Such work is already beginning to appear. For example, see the special issue of *South Atlantic Quarterly,* Winter 1993, edited by Susan Willis, which takes the world according to Disney as its theme. Also see Smoodin, *Disney's Discourse*; Bell, Haas, and Sells, *From Mouse to Mermaid.*

17. For an example of such an analysis, see Stanley Aronowitz, *Roll Over Beethoven* (Middletown, Conn.: Wesleyan University Press, 1993); Henry A. Giroux, *Disturbing Pleasures: Learning Popular Culture* (New York: Routledge, 1994).

18. Inderpal Grewal and Caren Kaplan, "Introduction: Transnational Feminist Practices and Questions of Postmodernity," in Inderpal Grewal and Caren Kaplan, eds., *Scattered Hegemonies* (Minneapolis: University of Minnesota Press, 1994).

CHAPTER 8

1. Robert Gutsche Jr., "Wrestlers, Rappers Urge Voting," *Newsday,* September 23, 2003, A47.

2. Zondra Hughes, "The Rock Talks About Race, Wrestling, and Women," *Ebony*, July 2001.

3. Lori Wiechman, "Today's Wrestling All Creeds and Colors," Associated Press, August 18, 1998.

4. Wiechman, "Today's Wrestling."

5. Steve Sailer, "The Rock, Race, and Wrestling," August 23, 2001, www.iSteve.com.

INDEX